Child and family assessment in social work practice

Child and family assessment in social work practice

Sally Holland

SAGE Publications
London • Thousand Oaks • New Delhi

First Published 2004

SAGE Publications Ltd
1 Oliver's Yard
55 City Road
London EC1Y 1SP

SAGE Publications Inc
2455 Teller Road
Thousand Oaks, California 91320

SAGE Publications India Pvt Ltd
B-42, Panchsheel Enclave
Post Box 4109
New Delhi - 100 017

Library of Congress Control Number available

A catalogue record for this book is available
from the British Library

ISBN 0-7619-4901-1
ISBN 0-7619 4902-X (pbk)

Typeset by C&M Digitals (P) Ltd., Chennai, India
Printed and bound in Great Britain by Athenaeum Press, Gateshead

Contents

Acknowledgements

I would like to thank the social workers and managers who took part in the Coastal Cities research, and the families who gave permission for their assessments to be included in the study. I have a number of colleagues who have helped with this book. Ian Butler, who supervised the Coastal Cities research, and colleagues in the school who have provided advice and support: Jonathan Scourfield, Paul Atkinson, Mick Bloor, Dolores Davey, Sara Delamont, Mark Drakeford, Jonathan Evans, Andy Pithouse, Alyson Rees, Mark Rivett and Ian Shaw. Help and advice from beyond Cardiff has come from many sources, including Audrey Mullender and Derek Clifford. MA/DipSW and PQ students and various local practitioners have provided helpful critical feedback for my thinking on assessment.

I wish also to thank Joan, Bryn and my parents for practical and emotional support and, especially, Jonathan, Annie and Gareth.

All names in case examples used in this book are pseudonyms and identifying features have been excluded or altered.

Three of the chapters are partly based on previously published work. I wish to thank the following publishers for permission to draw on the following journal articles:

Blackwell Publishing for Holland, S. (1999) 'Discourses of decision-making in child protection: conducting comprehensive assessments in Britain', *International Journal of Social Welfare*, 8 (4): 276–86.

Oxford University Press/The British Association of Social Workers for Holland, S. (2000) 'The assessment relationship: interactions between social workers and parents in child protection assessments', *British Journal of Social Work*, 30 (2): 149–64.

Sage Publications Ltd. for Holland, S. (2001) 'Representing children in child protection assessments', *Childhood*, 8 (3): 322–39.

1   Introduction

The major issue for child protection work, is the process of assessment ... Casework decisions in this area are extremely complicated: firstly, because we do not have the technical knowledge to predict how a child's circumstances will develop following different placement decisions, and secondly, because there is little clarity in our society about the implicit cultural and moral values involved in these decisions. (Gough, 1993: 197–8).

One of the most controversial and complex areas of social work is the assessment of a child and their family when there are concerns about the child's welfare. Areas of decision-making can include any of the following: the provision of supportive and preventative services, the likelihood of future harm, whether a child should be removed from home, if it is safe to return a child home, or if a permanent alternative placement is necessary. The discussion in this book is relevant to all levels of assessment in child welfare, although the particular focus is on in-depth assessment work where there are complex problems. This might include families with multiple and continuing support needs or following incidents of abuse or neglect. Such assessments are also used to aid decision-making about permanent placements for children. Practitioners conducting assessments of this kind may also be reporting their assessment conclusions to civil or family courts, case conferences or other key decision-making arenas.

This book has a number of central aims. First, I aim to provide a thorough discussion of child and family assessment, introducing readers to the scope of the literature on the topic, including research findings and theory. I aim to provide the opportunity for child welfare practitioners and students to critically reflect on the range of ways that assessment may be understood, and on their own assessment practice. Findings from a case study of assessment practice – the Coastal Cities Research Study – are presented, providing data on how social workers in one geographical area carry out in-depth assessments of children and their families. Separate chapters discuss in detail some of the key themes that are central to assessment with children and their families, such as involving children and relationships with parents. Last, I aim to provide a coherent vision of assessment practice that is thorough, fair to all participants and recognises the complexities of the assessment process. This latter point requires attention to values and to theoretical matters and it is these that are considered next.

Constructing Assessment

Attempted solutions to dilemmas over the correct approach to assessment have varied over the last century and on a national and local basis. One of the key concerns has been the tension between searching for assessments of measurable scientific validity and those that reflect the individually situated nature of each family's circumstances and concerns. The first approach aims to produce assessment results that are objective, accurate and consistent, whoever is the assessor. The second approach places more emphasis on professional judgements based on an in-depth understanding.

Here, for the sake of clarity, emphasis has been placed on the differences between the two positions. In everyday policy and practice, both the writers of guidance and assessors themselves may draw from both traditions. For example, in the US, where there has been a tendency to aim for more accurate and objective assessments of risk to children, there is the facility in most assessment formats to over-ride findings if particular individual circumstances prevail (Gambrill and Shlonsky, 2000). In practice, practitioners in the US have been seen still to use much individual clinical judgement, even when using calculative tools (English and Pecora, 1994). In England and Wales a largely qualitative approach to assessment has been conceived in the *Framework for the Assessment of Children in Need and their Families*[1] (Department of Health, 2000a). However, the guidance also encourages practitioners to use checklists and ratings scales as part of an assessment. The ways in which some social workers attempt to work with some of these tensions inherent in the nature of assessment practice are seen in Chapter 3 of this book.

The approach of this book is informed by both 'scientific' and 'reflective' approaches to assessment. For example, in Chapter 9 it is suggested that practitioners approach the analysis of assessment findings in a rigorous manner, using classic analytic techniques from qualitative social scientific research traditions. Throughout the book, readers are also encouraged to reflect on the complex and contested nature of much of the information they will be working with during assessment work.

This latter understanding of assessment practice is informed by social constructionism, and this is the main theoretical underpinning of the book. Constructionism may be located within wider movements in academia; part of the post-Second World War loss of confidence in perceiving science as a march towards progress and understanding. Constructionism can be seen as part of a critical tradition in academia that includes feminism, Marxism and postmodernism (Taylor and White, 2000). Its main concern is with how knowledge and understanding is historically and culturally determined. Through our everyday interactions we build shared structures of understanding and these often become institutionalised and become, to us, an objective, external reality (Payne, 1999).

Examples of social constructions that are directly relevant to this book include constructions of childhood and child abuse. Aries (1962) and Pollock (1983) have demonstrated that our understandings of what it means to be a child have changed dramatically over the centuries. Changing and conflicting constructions of childhood can be identified in contemporary society, with debates about children who commit crimes, the place of working children and ages of consent and marriage. Parton (1985, 1991, 1996a, 1996b) has written extensively about the developing constructions of child abuse in the UK, demonstrating the practical and moral nature of much of our decision-making in this area (Parton et al., 1997). A social constructionist analysis of social problems can explore how claims about problems are made and maintained by various groups and in whose interests they serve. 'Moral panics' about perceived threats to sections of society are examples of speedy and extreme constructions of social problems (Payne, 1999).

Parton and O'Byrne (2000: 24–6) summarise some of the main components of social constructionism:

1 It problematises the view that we can straightforwardly observe the real nature of the world around us.
2 It understands social constructions as historically and culturally specific.
3 It pays attention to social processes and daily interactions, as this is how our knowledge of the world is formed.
4 It challenges the view that people and their environment have a discoverable real nature that can be uncovered.

Adopting this stance for assessment work has profound implications for how we understand our task. It has both positive aspects and potential drawbacks. First, it potentially broadens our understandings of some processes (such as our responses to bereavement) from being psychologically or biologically determined to being socially defined and maintained (Payne, 1999). Second, it liberates practitioners from the view that they must discover the 'truth' during an assessment and come to *the* correct solution. Instead we must listen hard to each participant's account and value it as just that, an account, rather than assuming that our task is to judge its truth. This requires that assessors must remove themselves from the stance of 'expert' on other people's lives and instead position themselves as listeners and facilitators (Parton and O'Byrne, 2000). Positive interventions such as those proposed by solution-focused and strength-based models can follow from taking such a stance. Third, maintaining an awareness that much of our knowledge is culturally constructed also brings about the potential for anti-oppressive practice by critically examining our own social constructions and attempting to form an understanding of others'. We can also reflect on the power relations in society that maintain the claims of some groups to have privileged access to the truth. Payne notes that:

> … we need theories which allow for the negotiation of assumptions and conceptions of the world and the purposes which we seek to undertake. (1999: 56)

There are potential drawbacks to applying social constructionism to the assessment of children and their families. Adopting a pure constructionist approach can be seen as adopting a viewpoint that there is no external, material reality. This, of course, is not a stance that practitioners dealing with experiences of child injury, neglect, poverty, domestic violence and poor housing could easily adopt. Instead, it is suggested that it is our classifications of these material realities, our experiences of them, our interests in them and the claims we make about them that are constructed (Taylor and White, 2000). A logical application of social constructionism would also imply that all constructions of the world are equally valid. Therefore, a child abuser's view that their actions were justifiable might be equally valid to that of the child who wishes the abuse to stop. Child welfare practitioners must act, not simply reflect, and must make judgements that will sometimes value one construction of the world over another. We have both a legal and moral imperative to do this. However, by drawing from the ideas inherent in social constructionism, we may understand that we will never be making an entirely objective decision, but one that is moral, practical and political. In many family situations it will be possible for a range of accounts to sit alongside each other, or for the practitioner to work alongside the family members to find a construction of their situation that will be hopeful and helpful (White, 1997; Parton and O'Byrne, 2000).

The Coastal Cities Study

Much of the discussion in this book is informed by qualitative research that I conducted between 1997 and 2001 into how social workers carry out in-depth assessments of children where there are expressed concerns about their welfare. The research was carried out in two neighbouring cities in the UK, both located on the coast. In the larger city I examined assessments carried out by state social workers (City Social Services). These social workers carried large and varied caseloads, weighted towards child protection and children looked after by the local authority, and their assessments were part of this work. In the smaller city, I looked at the work of practitioners based in a specialist referred family centre that conducted in-depth assessments referred by the local authority (Hillside Family Centre). It was owned and managed by a large national voluntary organisation. In both sites, all social workers were qualified and had post-qualifying experience of between 2 and 16 years.

The research was conducted in three stages. In the first stage, 16 assessments were examined in depth. This stage included several in-depth interviews with each social worker at different periods of the assessment process, the observation of assessment sessions that had been previously video-taped, the reading of case records and observation of staff members in their team room. The second stage followed the initial analysis of the first 16 cases. The case files of four further cases were examined to check the validity of the initial analysis and this analysis was also critiqued by a focus group of social workers from the family centre. The third stage of the Coastal Studies research involved semi-structured interviews with ten social workers from the same two agencies in 2001, to explore with them the changes and continuities in their assessment practice since the introduction of the Department of Health/National Assembly for Wales Assessment Framework earlier that year. The 20 assessments in stages one and two involved 35 children aged from six months to 12 years and one assessment involved an unborn child. Of these cases, 15 had been referred for assessments by the family court and the other five by multi-disciplinary child protection case conferences. The cases included alleged physical abuse, sexual abuse, neglect and

Munchausen's Syndrome by Proxy. The families undergoing assessment involved heterosexual couples, lone mothers and fathers and the maltreated children and their siblings. Whenever data from the Coastal Cities study are included, I have used pseudonyms and occasionally changed some identifying features in order to protect the anonymity of the participants. A fuller explanation of the research methods is located elsewhere (Holland, 1999).

Research into Practice

The inclusion of data from this research study, and from the findings of others who have researched assessment practice, affects the tone and purpose of this book. The words and actions of the Coastal Cities social workers are not included in order that either the reader or myself may pass judgement on how well or how badly a group of practitioners have carried out assessment practice. Instead, and in the tradition of others who have carried out ethnographic research into social work (for example Pithouse, 1998) and other occupations as diverse as accountancy (Coffey, 1993), medicine (Bloor, 1978b; Berg, 1992) and car manufacturing (Collinson, 1988), the intention is less directive. Following Bloor's (1997) argument, it is by providing some detailed description of how others have conducted assessment work that I hope readers may be able to reflect on their own practice, by recognising, comparing or contrasting their work with that carried out by the Coastal Cities workers. Therefore, the inclusion of the research findings is intended not only to illustrate the discussion but also to aid critical reflection. However, I am aware that readers will also want help in applying some of the research findings for action. There are suggestions for practice and exercises throughout the book, and the third section of the book provides an intentional change of tone, becoming more of a practical guide than the previous two sections.

Whilst I am currently involved in social work practice through research and teaching qualifying and post-qualifying students of child and family social work, my interest in this topic originates in my own practice experience. Upon qualifying, I worked in a busy city centre children's social work team. I carried a large and varied caseload of which ongoing assessment work was a staple part. I occasionally carried out more intensive assessments, such as those discussed in this book, usually for court hearings. I then moved on to work in a voluntary sector family centre, similar to the Family Centre in the Coastal Cities study, although not the same centre. There, I was part of a team for whom the core of our work was to carry out in-depth assessments of families referred by the local authority. Although the families referred often presented severe challenges concerning the abuse or neglect of their children, the work of the centre had a constructive tone. Even where assessments recommended that children be removed from their parents, or should not be returned home, relations between staff and family members frequently stayed positive. This was aided by very low caseloads, therefore each family was given time to express their views and be listened to. There was also a team ethos of respect for all who attended for assessment. It was from this background that I began to research and write about assessment practice. I therefore believe, from first-hand experience, that it is possible to carry out assessments of families, even where concerns are severe, in a positive and participatory manner. I acknowledge that this is aided by solid resources and low caseloads and that, as is discussed in Chapter 2, many practitioners in the Western world are struggling with rising and complex workloads. However, I would also argue that most of the suggestions for practice derived from research in this book are achievable in most social welfare settings as they are concerned particularly with a participatory ethos and adopting a critical and analytical approach.

Book Outline

There are, of course, many ways in which a book of this nature could be organised and a multitude of subjects that could be included. I have therefore had to make hard decisions about what to include and exclude from the book. Other books on assessment have helpfully concentrated on theoretical approaches (Milner and O'Byrne, 1998) or particular difficulties faced by families being assessed (Cleaver et al., 1999). This book aims to concentrate on issues of principle and process of assessment with children and families. This means that there are no whole chapters on working with, for example, disabled children, assessing families from ethnic minority groups or on difficulties such as mental health problems. This does not mean that such issues are not vital, they are, but including substantial material on these issues would have made the book too large and changed its nature. Wherever possible, issues of diversity are addressed, and some discussion is included of specific problems faced by many families such as domestic violence and caring for a disabled child. Specialist texts are cited where appropriate. It is hoped that the discussion in this book will be useful for the assessment of all families, whatever their circumstances. Exercises are included at the end of the book. These are designed to aid readers to reflect on aspects of the chapters' contents and to apply their learning to practice. The exercises might be done individually or as part of a class for qualifying or post-qualifying social workers.

This book is divided into three parts. Part I is an exploration of different approaches to assessment work. Part II is about the people in child and family assessments: the children, their parents and the relationship between the assessors and the assessed. Part III provides guidance and reflection on the process of an assessment, focusing particularly on planning, analysis and reporting. The following outline of the chapters should help the reader to understand the rationale for this book.

- **Chapter 2** outlines the policy and practice context of child and family assessment. Several approaches to assessment are outlined and current assessment practice in the US and England and Wales is discussed. Various international themes affecting assessment practice with children and families are introduced.

- **Chapter 3** further explores the nature of assessment and some of the different ways in which assessment work may be understood. Social workers' explanations of how they understand their own assessment practice and how they manage some of the contradictions inherent in their task are looked at.
- **Chapter 4** discusses the twin concepts of time and change in assessment work. Many families' lives change rapidly during and after assessments and it can be difficult to produce assessment conclusions that can work with change. The chapter explores assessment timing, length and the 'shelf-life' of recommendations.
- **Chapter 5** explores the relationship between the assessor and the assessed. The importance of the quality of engagement between families and practitioners and its impact on the outcome of the assessment is noted.
- **Chapter 6** concentrates on the role of children in assessments. The potential for children to become 'silenced voices' in assessments (of which they are main subjects) is discussed. Potential ways to meaningfully include children's perspectives in assessments are explored.
- **Chapter 7** examines parenting, a key aspect in in-depth assessment work. Both parenting of children and parental lifestyles are explored in this chapter. The complexity of deciding whether parenting standards are adequate is a well-worn dilemma in social work. Practitioners' approaches to this task are discussed, as are attitudes to parental relationships.
- **Chapter 8** is about the design of an in-depth assessment. It includes discussion of co-working, inter-disciplinary assessment and the use of a range of assessment methods. A comparison between assessment design and research design is made and it is noted that, whilst practitioners have much to offer research in terms of communication methods and attention to ethics, so can assessment practice gain from methodological approaches developed in social research.
- **Chapter 9** continues the theme of comparing in-depth assessment work to social research processes. Here, the process of analysing and reporting is discussed and a method proposed that aims to produce conclusions that are complex, fair and useful.
- **Chapter 10** concludes the book. A set of principles is proposed for working towards assessments for children and their families based on the research findings and discussion in the previous nine chapters.

Note

1 Due to the rather unwieldy nature of this title, it will be referred to as the Assessment Framework for the remainder of the book.

PART I

2   Assessment in Child Care Social Work

Chapter summary

This chapter provides a general overview of assessment in child and family social work, placing it within a practice and policy context. The contents explore research into assessment practice, and the use of research findings to construct assessment schedules and guidance. Various approaches to assessment are identified, including diagnostic, predictive, broad social and bureaucratic. International issues affecting the assessment of children's welfare are briefly surveyed, with more detailed consideration of assessment trends in the US and England and Wales. The chapter concludes with a discussion of risk and risk management in the context of current social trends.

Research into Social Work Assessment

Social work research into assessment practice may broadly be divided into two main areas: that which examines the relationships between inputs (for example factors influencing) and outputs (decisions); and that which examines the *process* of assessment (Cuzzi et al., 1993). In the former field, there has been much research into factors used by social workers in decision-making. Often the aim of this research is to aid prediction and accuracy and to attempt to reduce the influence of workers' individual idiosyncrasies and practice wisdom. Methods used to determine decision-making factors include surveys (Fernandez, 1996; Banach, 1998), the examination of files (Dalgleish and Drew, 1989), the training of social workers to record the key factors in a decision for research purposes (A. Rosen et al., 1995), use of case vignettes (H. Rosen, 1981; Craft and Bettin, 1991) and experiments (Koren-Karie and Sagi, 1992; McCurdy, 1995).

Studies that pick out factors most commonly used for decision-making in order to provide pro-forma and checklists for decision-making may be falling into the trap of simply reproducing and further institutionalising current working practices (Wald and Woolverton, 1990). In other words, they represent accumulated practice wisdom (Jones, 1993). They do serve, however, to 'give a quasi-scientific gloss to the activity of risk assessment' (Wattam, 1996: 239). An alternative approach that has been used to develop actuarial assessment instruments looks at the progress of families through the child welfare system and tracks outcomes such as incidents of re-abuse. This leads to the identification of factors empirically linked to risk (or at least risk defined and identified by child protection systems) and instruments with stronger claims to validity than those that reproduce practice wisdom (Gambrill and Shlonsky, 2000). Findings from quantitative research into decision-making factors in social work assessment have been used to help produce formal tools for risk assessment by child protection services, particularly in the US.

A second area of research into social work assessment has examined the *process* of assessment in more detail. This has generally, but not always, involved qualitative research. Such research has examined areas such as tacit knowledge and organisational culture, as well as more formal aspects of the assessment process. Some of the research studies commissioned by the British Department of Health in the early 1990s (Department of Health, 1995a) looked at decision processes from a variety of angles, such as parental perspectives (Cleaver and Freeman, 1995), partnership with parents (Thoburn et al., 1995) and the impact of case conference decisions (Farmer and Owen, 1995). Studies of the process of social work assessment and decision-making may also be looking for *factors* that affect decision-making, but these will tend to be of a *process* nature and do not tend to be linked to quantitative material such as case or worker characteristics (for example, Waterhouse and Carnie, 1992). Research that has examined in detail some of the decision-making processes in social work include those by Handelman (1983), Gilgun (1988), Wattam (1992), Thorpe (1994), Dingwall et al. (1995), Egelund (1996), Fernandez (1996), White (1998b), Pithouse (1998) and Scott (1998), whose work between them incorporates empirical data from Britain, Canada, Denmark and Australia. Studies such as these provide insights into the informal, subtle and tacit aspects of the decision-making process in child care social work. They also provide detailed descriptions of practice that may allow practitioners to recognise, compare and reflect on their own work (Bloor, 1997). They rarely provide information about outcomes or prevalence. It can be seen that both quantitative and qualitative approaches to researching assessment have the potential to provide valuable and often complementary information about the state of assessment work in child welfare settings.

Research into assessment systems has often been applied retrospectively, after new guidance or legislation has been applied. For example, in England and Wales there was little research into the system of comprehensive assessment introduced in 1988, with much criticism of it theoretical or based on practice experience (see, for example, critiques by McBeath and Webb 1990 and O'Hagan and Dillenburger, 1995). Many assessment systems in the US were introduced without research into their effectiveness (Doueck et al., 1992). Recently there have been more systematic attempts to evaluate new systems. In England and Wales, the Assessment Framework, which will be discussed in detail later in this chapter, has been researched at the pilot stage (Thomas and Cleaver, 2002) and will be adapted according to the findings. Similarly, in New Zealand, Barber and Delfabbro (2000) report the piloting and research into a standardised parenting assessment instrument being considered for use by the governmental Children, Young People and their Families Services.

Approaches to Assessment

Assessing children and their families in the welfare arena has been carried out using a range of different approaches over the last few decades. A range of approaches are identified here: diagnostic, predictive, the broad social assessment and bureaucratic assessment. These are not discrete categories and there is a considerable amount of overlap between the categories, but the division of assessment approaches into these categories aids this brief recounting of the story of the development of assessment in child welfare. The story related is mainly that of England and Wales. International themes in assessment and specific developments in the US are reviewed later in this chapter. Some of the approaches to assessment can be viewed in relation to theories of decision-making and these are briefly introduced next.

Decision-making models

The various approaches to social work assessment in childcare can be linked to broader theories of decision-making models. In his groundbreaking case study of the Cuban missile crisis, Allison (1971) exposes the implicit model underpinning many analyses of decision-making across several disciplines. He labels this the *rational decision-making model*. This model is similar to the traditional *cost–benefits model*, which is particularly rooted in the discipline of economics (Hall, 1982). Here, it is assumed that individuals (or groups working in the same way) rationally examine all possible choices towards achieving a goal. Desired objectives will be maximised and costs minimised (Allison, 1971). However, this model assumes that decision-makers act rationally, have perfect information available for analysis and that the parameters remain fixed. The impact of factors such as values, social context and political goals are not included in such an analysis. The weakness of applying such a model to social work assessment is readily apparent. It cannot be assumed that social workers (or any other social actors) always act rationally. In assessing human relationships and actions, it is not possible to know when all available information has been gathered. It cannot be assumed that no move towards a decision is made whilst information is still being gathered (Bloor, 1978b), nor that the situation being assessed is static.

Allison (1971) suggests two further models to aid analyses of decisions. An *organisational process model* emphasises the variety of factors coming into play when decisions are made in the context of organisations. These include the role of routine and organisational procedures, the control of information, personal risk-avoidance by participants and differing definitions of the problem. Allison also outlines a *government politics model* that examines decision-making in government and bureaucracies, emphasising the role of bargaining by participants who are anxious to protect parochial interests. Both of these models, but perhaps particularly the organisational process model, are highly relevant. Several studies, including the Coastal Cities research, suggest the influence of professional, organisational and broader cultural factors on social workers conducting assessments (Sheppard, 1990; Campion, 1995; Pithouse, 1998; Scott, 1998).

Assessment as diagnosis

Social work assessment leading to a diagnosis of the problem at hand was written about in detail early this century (Richmond, 1917) and, as a theme in assessment, can be seen as particularly influential until about the 1970s. Within social work in both the UK and the US psychodynamic theories were increasingly influential in the post-Second World War period (Lindsey, 1994). Social casework informed by psychodynamic theory emphasised diagnosing the problem and treating it through therapy and/or welfare (Mayer and Timms, 1970; Gordon, 1988). Childcare concerns were seen as rooted in the whole family, although with particular focus on the mother (Gordon, 1988), and work was carried out with families to treat the diagnosed problem. Two influential social work authors, Perlman (1957) and Hollis (1964), emphasised the need for a careful diagnosis of the client's problem followed by a plan of intervention or treatment.

Social casework tended to have a broad focus of family problems, and this trend continued into the 1970s. However, from the early 1960s concerns about the physical abuse of children (referred to in this decade as 'battering') began to become more prominent, having been a central welfare concern from the late nineteenth century until about the 1930s (Gordon, 1988). During the 1960s, concerns about child battering were mainly raised by the medical profession. Paediatricians and radiologists became involved in the diagnosis of child abuse (Corby, 1996). Dr C. Henry Kempe and colleagues' influential American paper concerning the use of X-rays to aid diagnosis of Battered Child Syndrome (1962) was followed up in Britain the next year by an article in the *British Medical Journal* outlining the Battered Baby Syndrome (Griffiths and Moynihan, 1963). Concerns about child abuse remained predominantly in the medical field in the UK until later in the 1960s. The medical antecedents meant that child harm, and its assessment, tended to be approached by child welfare agencies such as the NSPCC along an individualistic, medical model rather than, for example, an approach which emphasised prevention through increased universal welfare services. As Hendrick (1994) notes, child abuse was seen as a syndrome, or disease, with underlying causes, which required diagnosis and treatment. An individual and diagnostic approach has remained an important influence on social work assessment in more recent decades, but in the UK and the US in particular, a more bureaucratic approach with an emphasis on risk *management* has tended to emerge. In continental Europe, despite many national variations, it has been argued that there has been a continued emphasis on family diagnosis and treatment of child abuse (Hetherington et al., 1997; Pringle, 1998).

Assessment by prediction

The predominance of an individualistic and medical model of diagnosis, treatment and targeted services in cases of child harm highlighted a need for empirical evidence which would guide practitioners in assessing cases of non-accidental injury (which, by the late 1970s, was becoming more commonly known as 'child abuse') and even to predict and therefore prevent child abuse before it could occur.

Research in the UK and the US has, particularly since the 1970s, attempted to find empirical factors associated with child abuse. Factors common to families where children had been harmed were identified and compiled into lists of 'risk factors'. However, many of the studies that led to the identification of risk factors were carried out without a clear operational definition of maltreatment, and some of the parents studied had only been *suspected* of abusing their children (Dingwall, 1989). Factors such as the unhappy childhood experiences of the parents and their poor health were identified. It was not clear whether these factors were identified by the assessors or the parents themselves, nor how the prevalence of these compared with other parents from similar socio-economic backgrounds. Later case/control studies attempted to rectify this problem, but definitional problems remained. 'Abusive' parents constituted those referred for abuse, yet the very factors then found to be significantly identified with this group may have led to their identification and referral in the first place: their youth, their babies being in special care and concerns about them being expressed by a midwife (Dingwall, 1989).

The identification of key risk factors to aid the prediction and assessment of child abuse is understandably an attractive goal for policymakers and practitioners. It promises an element of control and rationality in an arena which is complex, unpredictable and may have severe, even fatal results. The Inquiry report into the death of four-year-old Jasmine Beckford in 1985 (London Borough of Brent, 1985) provides an example of this. The inquiry panel was particularly critical of the front-line workers' failure to recognise the symptoms and indicators of abuse in the health and development of Jasmine and her sister, and in the history and behaviour of her parents. The Inquiry report recommended that:

> Research designed to refine the techniques for predicting accurately those children who will continue to be at risk is urgently required. (London Borough of Brent, 1985: 289)

Unfortunately, accurate prediction has proved elusive (Corby, 1993; Gambrill and Shlonsky, 2000). Dingwall identifies the 'statistical fallacy' of such lists of risk factors being used to identify and predict child abuse in individual cases (1989: 45). Whilst cohort studies, such as that reported by Browne and Saqi (1988), have positively predicted the majority of child abuse cases subsequently identified by the child abuse management system, they have also falsely predicted large numbers of parents who have not been identified as causing any harm to their children (Simmonds, 1991; Murphy-Berman, 1994). In addition, some children were harmed whose parents were not predicted to be abusers.

Since the early 1990s, progress has been made with the research base of factors used in some assessment instruments, and actuarial instruments have good overall predictive results compared to other methods. However, there is still a large margin of error when using predictive instruments with *individuals*. This is due to the wide variations in people's individual circumstances, the deficit basis of many instruments (they do not measure strengths) and the levels of individual judgement still required to rate aspects such as levels of societal support (Gambrill and Shlonsky, 2000). When instruments are used to assess individuals, they are generally aimed at assessing the likelihood of *re*-abuse, yet many of the factors in assessment instruments are derived from retrospective research into common factors linking initial incidents of abuse (Wald and Woolverton, 1990). In acknowledging the lack of accuracy when applied to individual circumstances, instrument designers are faced with deciding whether to aim for high sensitivity or specificity. Increased sensitivity leads to more children at high risk being identified, but also more children identified as high risk who do not suffer re-abuse (false positives). Higher specificity correctly identified more children who are not at risk, but also will identify more children as not at risk who go on to suffer re-abuse. Sensitivity and specificity have an inverse relationship with one another (Gambrill and Shlonsky, 2000).

The broad social assessment

Two themes associated with social work assessment over the last few decades have so far been identified: assessment as diagnosis and assessment by prediction. A third theme is that of a broad social assessment. The identification of the importance of a comprehensive social assessment in families where child abuse has occurred, or is thought to be at risk of occurring, was emphasised particularly in the 1980s in the UK. Such an assessment would include examining broader elements of a child's life, rather than areas relating solely to actual or potential abusive incidents. This has been overlapped by the trend towards the legalisation and bureaucratisation of social work as described below.

The need for the thorough assessment of families where there are child protection concerns was an issue that was regularly highlighted in the child abuse inquiry reports of the 1970s and 1980s (Hallett, 1989a). Many of the inquiry panels concluded that social workers had not collected together the information which would have led to a comprehensive overview of a particular family. In particular there was a lack of co-ordination of information from the different agencies involved with a family. Partial assessments were completed with each new situation, rather than a general overview being taken which took into account a family's history (Reder et al., 1993). It was noted that no framework existed to guide social workers in the areas they should cover when assessing a family situation (Reder et al., 1993). In the inquiry following the events in Cleveland (Department of Health and Social Security, 1988), social workers were criticised for only assessing the child and not the parents (Corby, 1993). In contrast, in several of the inquiries following child deaths, social workers were found to have lost sight of the child's need for protection following an over-concentration on the needs and demands of the parents (London Borough of Brent, 1985; London Borough of Lambeth, 1987; Howe, 1992). The inquiry into the death of Tyra Henry found that no comprehensive attempt was made to piece together the information held about the parents and that cultural stereotyping was a central problem (London Borough of Lambeth, 1987).

A summary of nine research reports on children in local authority care was published (Department of Health and Social Security, 1985), which again raised concerns about the basis of social workers' decision-making, suggesting that it was based more on ideology and values rather than on knowledge. Assessments were criticised for being too narrow and problem-focused rather than broadly assessing the situation a child is living in. One of the research studies, which examined social worker decision-making when children are on the brink of being admitted to substitute care, found that there was little difference between those admitted to care and those not admitted except, paradoxically, that those admitted appeared to be less at risk of child abuse at the hands of their care-givers than those not admitted (Packman and Randall, 1989).

Despite new arrangements for comprehensive assessment in cases of child abuse being introduced in the late 1980s (Department of Health, 1988), assessments were still found to be narrow in focus in the mid-1990s. A series of research reports (Department of Health, 1995a) found an overly narrow focus on child protection issues and recommended that the broader needs of the child in his or her family situation and environment be assessed, both in child protection and general welfare cases. The Assessment Framework (Department of Health, 2000a) was designed to meet the need for a broad social assessment and could also be seen to be responding to earlier calls, such as those by the Jasmine Beckford inquiry, to base assessment work on empirical knowledge. It might also be seen to fit with the final approach to assessment to be discussed here, that is, the bureaucratic approach.

Bureaucratic trends in assessment

> ... assessment schedules and checklists structure the encounter between professional and service user. They lead the professional to explore aspects of the person's experience which have been deemed relevant by their own profession, by legislation or by policy makers. (Taylor and White, 2000: 144)

As already indicated, one response in UK social work to the inquiry reports of the 1970s and 1980s was the move towards broader social assessments of children and their families. A further, and related, development was the increased bureaucratisation of procedures, including those of assessment (Parton, 1991; Howe, 1992; Lloyd and Taylor, 1995). In this context, bureaucratisation refers to the work of practitioners becoming increasingly regulated through clearly defined procedures, in an attempt to manage practice that has been seen as too idiosyncratic. Howe (1992) suggests that this arose from a change of view from abusive parents as potentially treatable, to abusive parents as potentially dangerous. Social workers were now required to collate information about the family situation in a systematic way and to identify 'high risk' and dangerousness in families (Parton, 1996b).

Bureaucracy in social work assessment may be linked to increasingly prescribed assessment procedures. The perceived need to manage the actions of social workers and assist them in identifying and managing potentially dangerous parents has led to the introduction of many more detailed guidelines for social work practice than had previously been available (Howe, 1992). The bureaucratic theme is also associated with a tendency to move away from a medical model of abuse that implies treatment and 'cure' as an end-goal, towards managerial and legalistic approaches to child harm (Parton, 1991; Howe, 1992; Otway, 1996). A shift of emphasis from the *treatment* of abuse to the *management* of abuse is emphasised by the change in usual terminology in the 1980s from 'child abuse' to 'child protection' (Hallett, 1989a). However, the demise of medical, particularly 'psy' (psychiatric, psychological and psychotherapeutic), influences in front-line practice is debatable (White, 1998a).

The bureaucratic trend in assessment since the 1980s overlaps with other assessment themes identified above. For example, Howe (1992) identifies the bureaucratic assessment as a continued attempt to predict abuse in individuals. Many of the bureaucratic developments in social work assessment in England and Wales have also embraced the notion of a broad social assessment, rather than simply a focus on specific concerns. This may be seen in two separate Department of Health assessment guidelines (Department of Health, 1988, 2000a) and those designed for assessing the needs of Looked After Children (Department of Health, 1991). All of these combine high levels of prescribed activity with attention to a wide range of factors affecting the individual family or child.

Models of front-line assessment practice

The assessment approaches identified above are broad categories, relating to social policy and research trends. At a level concerned with individual exchanges at the front-line of practice, Smale et al. (1993) have identified three models of assessment practice. These are:

- *The questioning model*, where the professional-as-expert asks questions of those to be assessed, collates and analyses the information and produces conclusions.
- *The procedural model*, where the social worker follows a clear format to gather information and to assess whether standard thresholds have been reached.
- *The exchange model*, where the emphasis is on the assessed person as expert about their own situation and the need to aid them in planning on how to reach their goals.

Milner and O'Byrne (1998) note that each model may be of use in specific situations, such as child protection (questioning), where resources are scarce (procedural) and for assessments of need (exchange). However, these models are also likely to be used according to professional, team and individual cultures relating to theoretical orientation and relationships with local service users. It is noted below that the current Assessment Framework in England and Wales is broad enough in its conception that it could be administered using any of these models of practice. The model most strongly adhered to in this book is the exchange model, with the acknowledgement that the other models will be appropriate in some circumstances.

The Context of Child and Family Assessment Practice

Contextual issues form a vital part in understanding assessment practices. Whatever approach to assessment is used, front-line practices will be affected by the organisational setting. Political pressures arising after a child death, time and resource constraints, and poor staff morale will all affect decisions about thresholds of concern and eligibility for support services.

Although it must be recognised that there are wide variations in the circumstances of assessment practice between nations and within nations, it is possible to identify some common international themes relating to child and family assessment that cross national and continental boundaries. Current themes that consistently appear in the literature discussing child welfare practice might be seen as occurring in two main areas: issues relating to the management of professional practice (including staff shortages, training, assessment approaches and risk management); and key difficulties facing children and their families (including poverty, violence, substance misuse, homelessness and migration).

Managing increased demand for child welfare services

A key theme that crosses most international boundaries has been an increased workload for those providing for assessment and provision in the field of child welfare services. There are problems with staff shortages. In the UK, there has been a move to an almost totally qualified workforce in childcare social work. However, low morale, pay and status and the challenging nature of the work have led to staff shortages and a high staff turnover. Similar problems are evident in the US and Canada (Krane and Davies, 2000). Most Western countries have also seen an increase in child welfare referrals, due to a number of factors including increased public awareness, child poverty and substance misuse. Countries as far apart geographically as New Zealand and Ireland have seen rapid rises in child abuse and neglect reports (Duncan and Worrall, 2000; Buckley, 2000). In the US reports of child maltreatment have risen from a rate of 10 per 1,000 children annually in the mid-1970s, to 43 per 1,000 children in the mid-1990s (Brooks and Webster, 1999).

Key difficulties facing children and their families

Whilst there are significant differences in laws, service patterns and social provision internationally, and even within relatively small areas such as the UK and continental Europe (Pringle, 1998), there are some difficulties facing many children and their families that can be seen to present challenges to child welfare systems in many countries. *Poverty and unemployment* are, of course, acute concerns in much of the Southern hemisphere and Eastern Europe. However, they are also central concerns in all of Europe, with pockets of concern even in previously relatively equitable Nordic nations (Pringle, 1998). In the UK, despite policy changes to tackle child poverty since 1997, the vast majority of children coming to the attention of social services are poor, usually dependent on state benefits (Department of Health, 1995a). Abney (2002) notes that in the US there appears to be a close correlation between the over-representation of communities of colour living in poverty and their over-representation in the child protection system. This is undoubtedly also an issue in many other Western nations. The extent of poverty faced by families who come into contact with social work services presents a challenge to assessment services. These are often focused on individual problems and underplay the effect of the environment (Gambrill and Shlonsky, 2000). In child neglect cases, which are now the predominant category for child protection referrals in many nations including England, Ireland and the US (Department of Health, 2002; Buckley, 2000; Erickson and Egeland, 2002), social workers find themselves trying to assess the relative impact of poverty and parental acts of omission on the standard of child care.

A linked central concern for child welfare assessment work is the provision of adequate services for *migrant families, refugees and ethnic minorities*. In many Western nations, social services have recognised the oppression and discrimination faced by those marginalised from the predominant white cultures and attempts have been made to provide assessment and services that are more culturally sensitive. In the US, the rapid rise in formal kinship care arrangements has arisen as a response to the large numbers of African American children in the public care system and a recognition of the role of extended family in African American culture (Scannapieco, 1999). In New Zealand, the introduction of Family Group Conferencing was an attempt to use Maori methods of assessment and decision-making to stem the over-representation of Maori children in care (Lupton and Nixon, 1999). In England and Wales, the Assessment Framework (Department of Health, 2000a) aims to ensure a more culturally sensitive assessment than was previously in place.

A rising demand for child welfare services arising out of parental *substance misuse* can be seen in many parts of the world with, for example, alcoholism a major concern in Russia (Fokini, 1999) and illicit drug misuse in the US (Kelley, 2002). Both this issue and *domestic violence* pose challenges for a social worker assessing a child's welfare as both have been contested areas in terms of the causes and the best ways to intervene (see, for example, Forrester, 2000; Mullender, 1996).

Internationally, the assessment of children and their families is affected by institutional context, such as the development of social services and of assessment protocols, and by pressing social and economic issues, such as poverty and substance misuse. Following this broad overview, the discussion turns to consider, as case studies, the assessment practice in the US and then England and Wales. Despite some similarities in the approach to child protection practice in these countries, there are some differences in the approaches to assessment.

Assessment Policy and Practice in the US

In the US, assessment practice is determined at state level. The first state-wide assessment instrument was developed in Illinois in the early 1980s (Cash, 2001). Since then, a clear majority of states have adopted risk assessment tools to form part of state legislation governing child protection services (DePanfilis and Scannapieco, 1994; Gambrill and Shlonsky, 2000). Concerns were raised about the rush to adopt risk assessment schedules in the majority of US states before they had been empirically validated (Doueck et al., 1992). There has been more research carried out over the last decade into the effectiveness of the use of risk assessment tools. Gambrill and Shlonsky (2000) suggest that it is necessary to distinguish between systems that are based on empirical relationships between predicted variables and outcomes (actuarial) and those based on a range of factors agreed by experts (consensus). The authors note that over one hundred studies have shown that actuarial models are more reliable than consensus-based systems or individual judgement. Cash describes consensus models as 'nothing more than practice wisdom arranged neatly on a form' (2001: 818).

Proponents of structured decision-making tools for assessment, which are characterised by large numbers of closed questions and the use of scoring, point to the advantages in increased rates of consistency between workers and the potential to reduce cultural bias (California Health and Social Services, 2001). However, problems remain. There are difficulties in the empirical base on all systems, relating to the definition of key concepts such as neglect and a lack of baseline data from the general population (Gambrill and Shlonsky, 2000). Despite an aura of objectivity, most factors still require worker judgement. For example, on the *California structured decision-making model*, workers must comment on the primary caretaker's view of the situation by ticking boxes such as 'blames child' or 'justifies maltreatment' (California Health and Social Services, 2001). Without an acknowledgement of the subjectivity of the process, present even when using assessment instruments, there is a risk that attention to reflective and critical practice will be reduced. A further problem is the concentration on deficits rather than strengths in many systems (Cash, 2001).

It may be that, in practice, such limitations are recognised by the users of predictive tools. Research into how American child protection practitioners use the tools to assist decision-making suggests that they are being used to verify decisions already made (DePanfilis, 1996). Caseworkers continue to 'rely on intuitive processes based on supervision, experience and training to make decisions' (English and Pecora, 1994: 468). However, in the US the general thrust of assessment policy, at least in relation to child maltreatment, appears to be the need to reduce the ability of individuals to influence outcomes.

Current Assessment Practice in England and Wales

In England and Wales there have been significant changes in assessment practice in recent years. This is rooted in a 'refocusing' agenda that has attempted to shift child welfare work from a narrow child protection focus to a broader view on the needs of children.[1] The main outcome has been the development of the *Framework for the Assessment of Children in Need and Their Families* (the Assessment Framework) (Department of Health, 2000a).

'Refocusing' refers to a shift in emphasis in British childcare social work policy following the publication in 1995 of a series of 20 empirical studies by the Department of Health. These were collated by members of the Dartington research team into a guide known as *Messages From Research* (Department of Health, 1995a). The collective research studies provide quantitative information on the child protection process, including information on the 160,000 families subject to child protection enquiries in England and Wales on an annual basis (Gibbons et al., 1995) and on inter-agency co-operation (Birchall and Hallett, 1995). There are also several studies providing qualitative data alongside quantitative data on the processes of child protection practice (Cleaver and Freeman, 1995; Thoburn et al., 1995; Farmer and Owen, 1995; Sharland et al., 1995). Studies regarding parenting practices in the population as a whole (Smith and Grocke, 1995; Nobes and Smith, 1997) appear to have been influential in the collating document's statement that child abuse is a social construction (Department of Health, 1995a: 11–24). Further messages drawn by the Dartington team from the 20 studies include the need to work in partnership with parents and for social workers to avoid concentrating narrowly on incidents of abuse. Policing and coercive intervention with families should be reduced. Instead, social workers should be encouraged to see protection as one of the potential needs of a child and to concentrate on meeting the child's wider needs. This shift in emphasis has been labelled 're-focusing' (Little, 1997).

The Assessment Framework

One of the main outcomes of 're-focusing' in England and Wales has been the development of the *Framework for the Assessment of Children in Need and their Families*. The Assessment Framework consists of the framework itself and its voluminous companion publications: guidance, records (and guidance for completing the records), packs of questionnaires and scales, reader and training pack (Department of Health, 2000a, 2000b, 2000c, 2000d; Howarth, 2000; NSPCC, 2000; Cox and Walker, 2002). Together they constitute a comprehensive set of guidance for practitioners. The National Assembly for Wales has published versions for Welsh agencies. These are slightly adapted for the Welsh context and most are bilingual. As Government guidance, the Assessment Framework is not legally binding, but under the Local Authority Social services Act 1970 its implementation is expected unless exceptional local circumstances require adaptation.

The Assessment Framework is summarised in the form of a triangle (see Figure 2.1) in which three main domains impacting on the child's everyday experiences are laid out. These are the child's developmental needs, the parenting capacity of main carers, and family and environmental factors. The thrust is

Figure 2.1   The Assessment Framework

Source: **Department of Health, 2000a: 17**

the careful examination of children's broader needs. These may include child protection needs, but potential abuse should no longer be the sole focus of an enquiry. There are two stages of assessment: all accepted referrals should be subjected to an initial assessment, taking no more than seven consecutive working days; more complex cases will be followed up by a core assessment, lasting up to 35 working days, where the same domains are assessed in much more detail and depth.

The assessment approach might be seen as drawing on both the broad social assessment approach and the bureaucratic trend. The assessment model is primarily one of in-depth interviewing of family members, with scope for this to be along the lines of the *exchange model*, the *questioning model*, or, at a stretch, the *procedural model* (Smale et al., 1993) depending on the skills and approach of a worker and their agency, or perhaps the nature of the referral. Assessment work rooted in in-depth interviewing is similar to previous models in the UK (Department of Health, 1988). There is, however, much more emphasis than previously on the engagement of fathers and children in the assessment, consultation with other professionals and the use of broader assessment methods such as observation and scales. There is more overt inclusion of the views of family members into the assessment report. More attention is given to environmental factors such as poverty, housing and social networks. The impact of disability and of 'race' and ethnicity on children's lives are given careful consideration. The guidance is 'evidence based' (although not actuarial), with copious references to research findings in the guidance and even in the margins of recording forms. In sum, therefore, the Assessment Framework may be viewed as a welcome development in assessment practice. It is anticipated that the Assessment Framework may be adapted for use by other countries, as has been the case with the Department of Health's earlier *Looking After Children* materials (Jones, H., 2002).

Despite the welcome nature of the Assessment Framework in general, there are some questions that may be posed in relation to it, both of a general and specific nature. Of importance is the prominence given to the use of questionnaires and scales during an assessment. This has been reinforced by the publication of the HOME inventory, an instrument originating in the US, for use in the UK (Cox and Walker, 2002). In Chapter 8 of this book the use of scales in assessment is discussed in more detail (and generally welcomed), but here it might be noted that the use of such instruments represents a departure for childcare social workers in the UK. Garrett (2003) argues that this represents a commitment both to positivist social science and to the predominance of the 'psy' professions. It is possible that the evidence derived may become seen as the 'hard' evidence by judges, magistrates and managers, as opposed to the more qualitative information derived from general interviews. Yet it is clear to the writers of the Assessment Framework that such scales should not be used in isolation from other evidence (Department of Health, 2000d: 3).

The superficially solid nature of information gathered by the use of scales, or in the checklists that form much of the Assessment Framework's recording forms, may serve to promote an illusion of certainty and objectivity for assessors and the assessment report's audience. This may serve to undermine thorough analysis of all assessment material using a reflexive approach (see Chapters 3 and 9). Certainly, one of the key findings from the piloting of the Assessment Framework in England and Wales has been the continuing problem of poor quality analysis in assessment work (Cleaver, 2002; Thomas and Cleaver, 2002). Despite the copious guidance, the Assessment Framework's advice on analysis of large amounts of data is rather thin.

With any large document authored by many participants, it will be possible to find weak points in specific wording or advice. Thus Garrett (2003) notes potential class prejudice in instructions for social workers to note stale cigarette smoke and questions about whether children have been taken to county shows. He also suggests that there is an uncritical reliance on normalisation and conformity in the areas of social and economic relationships (this he locates within the broader New Labour agenda). Criticisms also might be made of the research summaries contained within the margins of the recording forms. Whilst (anecdotally) practitioners like them and they give a context and reasoning to the bald tick-boxes, they do not cite sources and are in such a pared-down form they are open to accusations of over-generalisation and misinterpretation. For example, in the margin of the Core Assessment Record for a young person aged 10–14 is the statement, 'Black children often underachieve at school' (Department of Health, 2000c: 10). No context is given, such as a discussion of different achievement patterns of different ethnic groups, links to poverty, racism and school exclusions and so on. The form is to be shared with the young person, and the message being given by the statement to a Black child and their family is questionable. Similarly, it is possible to question the wording of other aspects of the checklists on the core assessment records. It is possible to find further difficulties, omissions and ambiguities in the framework, but this is almost inevitable in guidance of such ambitious breadth. Some difficulties have been identified and are being remedied following the pilot stage (Thomas and Cleaver, 2002). Further discussion of aspects of the Assessment Framework is included through-out this book.

Risk, Postmodernity and Assessment Practice

The final theme of this chapter is that of risk. Risk to children (and to the prac-titioners who make decisions about those children) is a concern that pervades all of the approaches to assessment identified above and the everyday assessment practice of social workers in the field of child welfare. Risk *management* is an increasingly global concern, affecting almost every aspect of society. Many authors have located the preoccupation with risk management in broader trends associated with late modern society. In order to understand the place of risk management in child welfare assessment, it is necessary first to summarise some of the arguments about risk and postmodernity.

Postmodernity

The relevance to social work of debates about postmodernity has been discussed and debated in the social work literature in recent years. Despite its rather esoteric nature, this debate has clear practice implications that are particularly pertinent to assessment, including our understandings of subjectivity, relativism and expertise. Many commentators, such as Howe (1994), Pardeck et al. (1994a, 1994b), Parton (1994a, 1994b) and Martinez-Brawley and Mendez-Bonito Zorita (1998) have written about the applicability of a postmodern analysis for social work. The modern era has been characterised as one that has striven for ratio-nality, progress through human endeavour, reason, professional expertise and the ordered sovereign state since the seventeenth century in Europe and subse-quently much of the rest of the world (Giddens, 1990; Howe, 1994; Smith and White, 1997). A postmodern analysis suggests that this consensus has broken down, with a recognition that 'truth' is not discernible through reason, but is locally negotiated through language (Howe, 1994; Pardeck et al., 1994a). The grand narratives and theories no longer hold and expertise is questioned (Parton, 1994a). It is suggested that postmodernist trends in social work include the diversification of tasks and of theory, the diffusion of power, the concentration on actions rather than actors and a pre-occupation with risk (Howe, 1994; Parton, 1994a). These are exemplified in Britain by the marketisation and com-modification of community care and the legalisation of childcare social work (Parton, 1994a).

Others (Sheppard, 1995b; Ferguson, 1997; Smith and White, 1997) have questioned the relevance of postmodernity to a contemporary analysis of social work. Ferguson (1997) and Smith and White (1997) have drawn on Giddens's

(1990, 1991) analysis that society is in a state of advanced modernity that is more self-aware of the implications of modernity. He has labelled this 'reflexive modernity', that is, 'modernity coming to understand itself' (Giddens, 1990: 48). Smith and White (1997) argue that postmodernists exaggerate the erosion of social work's unifying knowledge and practice, such as realism and humanism. Ferguson (1997) argues that in an era of reflexive modernisation there is the potential for a more radical relationship between lay people and (social work) experts, with the social observers also becoming socially observed.

To some extent the debate on whether the current era should be labelled postmodernity, advanced or reflexive modernity is a matter of semantics. Both Parton (1994a) and Howe (1994) have written that they would not wish to exaggerate a break with modernity, with Parton (1994a, 1994b) emphasising this by using parentheses around the 'post' in (post)modernism. Despite some real differences in emphases around the implications for social work of the modern era, there are also many common aspects of the various analyses of current social trends. There appears to be agreement that the distinction between the expert and lay person is being eroded, with professional expertise increasingly open to challenge (Giddens, 1990; Beck, 1992; Howe, 1994). In social work this can be seen to have led to an increased managerialism and bureaucratisation, with social workers' tasks becoming more prescribed and less open to professional discretion (Howe, 1994). A corresponding legalistic trend has led to an emphasis on rights, contracts and responsibilities (Howe, 1994; Smith, 1999). Many have emphasised an increased wish to calculate, predict and manage risk (Parton, 1991, 1994a, 1998; Giddens, 1991; Ferguson, 1997; Scott et al., 1998).

The questioning of scientific and expert knowledge and of the nature of 'truth' has important implications for social work assessment. Whether the modern era has ended or is engaged in a period of reflexivity, it appears that the modernist rational agenda of seeking absolute truths through systematic means has been eroded. The implication for social work assessment is therefore that an attempt to discover the 'truth' about a client through assessment may be futile. It may be suggested that social work must recognise that there will be a series of competing explanations in any assessment. Abandoning a search for one external reality means that social workers conducting assessments may need to learn to sit with uncertainty. However, there is a need to be aware of the nihilistic dangers of pure relativism for social work (Parton, 1994a; Sheppard, 1995b; White, 1997; Martinez-Brawley and Mendez-Bonito Zorita, 1998). In Chapter 9 of this book, a method is suggested for working with competing explanations and developing assessment conclusions which are derived from a process that is rigorous, reflexive and critical and are those that are 'least likely to be wrong' (Sheppard et al., 2001: 881).

Risk

However we label our current era, it is clear that the management of risk is a major preoccupation. It has already been noted in this chapter how research has aimed to produce instruments that will accurately identify risk for children (from their caretakers) and how, in the US, such instruments are widely used to aid decision-making. Actuarial-based instruments appear to aid inter-assessor consistency and accuracy in predicting substantiated abuse. Difficulties with such instruments have also been noted, in that they are often based on unreliable research findings, they produce both false negatives and false positives, they are often deficit based and their use creates an illusion of objectivity and accuracy that discourages reflection and critical thinking. Krane and Davies (2000) note that a goal of scientific objectivity can serve to obscure the inherently moral and political nature of much decision-making about risk in the child welfare arena.

As the anthropologist Mary Douglas notes, risk is future-orientated, assumed to be calculable and associated with accountability:

> Within the cultural debate about risk and justice opponents seek to inculpate the other side and exonerate their own supporters from blame. *Risk* is unequivocally used to mean danger from future damage, caused by the opponents. How much risk is a matter for the experts, but on both sides of the debate it has to be taken for granted that the matter is ascertainable. Anyone who insists that there is a high degree of uncertainty is taken to be opting out of accountability. (Douglas, 1992: 30, emphasis in the original)

Yet, of course, in the child welfare arena, risk cannot be accurately predicted. As MacDonald and MacDonald (1999: 22) explain, the 'hindsight fallacy' suggests that because an adverse, but low probability outcome has occurred, it ought to have been predictable. Yet, sadly, sometimes an unlikely event will happen and still remain unlikely. The best we can do is to thoroughly analyse all available evidence against a range of possible explanations (see Chapter 9). If a child is thought to be at risk, this will include looking for evidence that supports this view, as well as actively seeking information about safety in the home environment. We need to pay attention to unremarkable events and details, as well as to vivid evidence (MacDonald and MacDonald, 1999).

The context of risk management will also affect decision-making about risk. Difficulties related to resource constraints and shortage of trained workers may lead either to the raising of thresholds about which cases are concerning (and so reduce the workload) or, perhaps, to avoiding time-consuming preventative and rehabilitation work. Local teams and area authorities develop their own understandings of risk, as reflected in the regional variations in child protection register rates in England and Wales. Scourfield (2003) notes how a child death associated with neglect raised child protection concerns about other neglect cases in an area team. There are also national differences in the way that risk is approached, arising from legal and cultural variations. For example, in the Netherlands, the confidential doctor system entails a less legalistic approach to risk than the UK approach (Hetherington et al., 1997).

Risk may also be assessed differently, according to differences between disciplines (Birchall and Hallett, 1995) and whether the assessment is carried out by individuals or in groups (Milner and O'Byrne, 1998). The influence of 'groupthink' may lead to group decisions that may not have been made individually by the participants at a meeting. As Gambrill and Shlonsky pithily observe:

Tolerating feeble inferences, rewarding gold and garbage alike, and the buddy-buddy syndrome (a reluctance to criticise friends) may dilute the quality of decisions in case conferences. (2000: 816–17)

It can be seen that risk is not a concrete concept and is, in fact, socially constructed according to organisational context, profession, culture and, indeed, on a case-by-case basis (Wattam, 1992). Authors such as Beck (1992), Douglas (1992), Parton (1996b) and Parton et al. (1997) have demonstrated how risk is constructed. It cannot be just a technical calculation. It might be seen as a way of thinking, rather than a 'thing' or a 'set of realities' (Parton, 1996b: 98). This does not mean, of course, that holding an intellectual stance that risk to children is socially constructed supports any acceptability of child abuse. Stainton Rogers and Stainton Rogers (1992) use the example that throwing boiling water on a child would be universally agreed to be a morally reprehensible act. However, a multitude of observers might differ in how they understood the causes for that act, who is responsible, and perhaps most crucially, what should happen next to the child, its parents, and in terms of professional intervention. The social worker then has to actively construct a view on how 'risky' an individual situation is. Whilst they may be helped by various scales and other assessment instruments, it has been seen that these are not watertight. A soundly based *judgement* must be made in each case.

A final note on risk management is the management of risk to professionals. It has been seen that Douglas relates risk to accountability. In the US (and more rarely in the UK) there is a risk of being sued for malpractice by aggrieved service users, including children who were left in an abusive situation or who were wrongly removed from home. There is also a risk of being the subject of a formal complaint or a public inquiry. In Chapter 9 it is noted that written records may be a form of prospective justification. Writing in the UK context, MacDonald and MacDonald (1999) suggest that practitioners should record outcomes that are possible but not likely, as well as the expected outcomes for a case. For practitioners in the US, Myers outlines in detail the best ways to reduce the likelihood of being the subject of a lawsuit, whilst noting: 'Although the number of lawsuits is growing, the likelihood that a competent professional will be sued remains small' (2002: 404).

Conclusion

This chapter has set the scene for a detailed consideration of child and family assessment by examining various historical and contemporary approaches to assessment, research into assessment, international themes affecting assessment and the relevance of current broader debates of postmodernism and risk. Front-line practitioners are confronted with day-to-day experiences of contemporary social challenges, including child poverty, homelessness and migrancy, substance misuse and staff shortages. Finding the best approach to assess and assist families in such situations is a challenge, and there is often a tension between the development of standardised systems for promoting equality of service and efficiency and the need to respond to very individual human situations. The ways in which social workers understand their task in such settings is the key theme for the next chapter.

Note

1 This re-focusing towards family support and prevention can also be observed in the US (Daro and Donnelly, 2002; Garrett, 2003).

3 The Nature of Assessment

Chapter summary

This chapter explores the following ways of viewing assessment of families:

- that assessment practice is concerned with maintaining a balance between rights and responsibilities and that partnership may be partly achieved through honesty and information sharing;
- that assessors should aim for strict objectivity and factual accounts; or
- that assessors should aim to acknowledge complexity and assess through a close engagement and reflection.

Practitioners feel that it is vital to be open, clear and fair in assessment work, but that true partnership is an impossible goal in many complex situations. It is noted that practitioners have a dominant tendency to describe their assessment decisions through language of objectivity and science, especially to other agencies. Informally, however, some also describe their decision-making as being based on reflective judgement.

This chapter examines the nature of complex assessment of families. In the last chapter different policy approaches to assessment were outlined. These included predictive and diagnostic approaches, the broad social assessment and the bureaucratic approach. In this chapter the understandings and practices of assessing practitioners are discussed. A number of key themes are explored: assessment as a legalistic task, maintained by a system of rights, responsibilities and openness about power differences; assessment as an objective, information-gathering task; and assessment as a process of reflective evaluation of competing explanations.

None of these is held up to be the 'correct' way of understanding assessment. Instead, the Coastal Cities practitioners' reflections on these understandings are presented, and these are compared with findings from other, international research studies. It is likely that many practitioners will understand assessment in all of these ways from time to time, depending perhaps on the nature of an individual case or the audience for a report. The limitations and possibilities for assessment suggested by these various ways of understanding the assessment task are explored.

Assessment as a Legalistic Task: Rights and Responsibilities

The first theme of this chapter explores the social workers' understandings of the nature of in-depth assessment as being based on legal duties and a system of rights and responsibilities, shared between the participants. The balance of power in the assessments will be discussed. It will be argued that the social workers perceive the assessment as being a rather neutral, legalistic task, underlined by rights and responsibilities for all parties.

An observation made of contemporary child protection social work has been that it has become increasingly legalistic (or socio-legal) in its orientation over the last two decades (Otway, 1996). It is argued that this is seen in the increasingly detailed procedures issued centrally, the use of court proceedings to intervene in child protection situations and an emphasis on forensic risk assessment of dangerousness (Parton et al., 1997). In England and Wales, the Children Act 1989 puts legalism at the heart of social work, balanced by the principles of rights, responsibilities, openness and honesty (Smith, 1999). In the guidance associated with the Act, partnership with children and families is named as an important principle (Parton et al., 1997) and partnership has been partly defined as being concerned with rights, responsibilities and an open, contractual form of working. For example, the Department of Health's guidance on partnership in child protection lists amongst its essential principles for working in partnership:

> Ensure that children, families and other carers know their responsibilities and rights.
> Be open and honest about your concerns and responsibilities. (1995b: 14)

In the Coastal Cities study, social workers emphasised the rights and responsibilities of all parties within a clear and open framework of working. The basis of the work is often laid out in a written agreement or contract. Such methods of working have been cited as contributing to a spirit of partnership (Marsh and Fisher, 1992; Department of Health, 1995b) where the overall aim would be to reduce the power difference between social worker and client (Pugh et al., 1987; Family Rights Group, 1991). However, in the context of in-depth assessment, an equality of power tends to be seen by social workers as neither possible nor desirable. The social workers have a legal responsibility to retain control of the process. Instead, an emphasis on openness and rights is seen as a just way to proceed. The use of rights and responsibilities language can be seen in the following extract from the Jones family assessment report:

> 'All adults, not only parents, have a *responsibility* to assert and protect the *rights* of children' [source not noted in original]. Where there is a conflict of interests between the parents and the child, the child's *interest* must be given first consideration. Parents have a *right* to expect careful assessment prior to long term decisions being taken. *Opportunity to challenge* information held on them should be given to parents and decisions taken that affect them should be taken in a framework within which the parent is always involved. Parents have a *right* to an *open and honest approach* from social workers and a *right to clear explanations* of the power, actions and reasons for concern of the agencies involved. Their views should be sought and taken into account, although engaging them in assessment and planning does not mean a total sharing of the agency's *responsibility* for decision-making. (Extract from first Jones family assessment report: emphasis added)

Here, children have rights, parents have rights and responsibilities, and social workers have responsibilities and power. Parents have rights to a 'careful assessment', openness and honesty and their views should be sought. Fairness is implied by the opportunities given to families to challenge information and to have their views taken into account. However, this statement does not include a promise of partnership and clearly states that the final responsibility for the assessment rests with the social worker.

In the following extract, one of the Hillside Family Centre social workers is discussing how he attempts to bring elements of partnership into his work with families:

> Partnership in this setting is slightly different than in other settings you know. I never talk of assessing a family, I never say to the family 'I am assessing this family'. I try to say that I am doing an assessment *with* the family. So for me you are looking to promote with whoever you are working with in social work a sense of value, that you value them as an individual and that you are looking to provide some sort of opportunity for them to take responsibility and to offer a view … Now, we can't involve partnership in all honesty but really, you know, at the end of the day we provide a report which can go a long way to influencing how those family circumstances result. So, the nature of partnership is different, but for me you have to look at other ways of doing it. (General interview with George, social worker)

Here, George can be seen to be expressing an ideal aim of working in partnership and he suggests that he carries this out by 'valuing' individuals and by allowing them to 'offer a view'. However, he admits that the work involves the worker in a powerful act, that of producing an influential report, and that partnership is not achievable 'in all honesty'.

Whilst the Department of Health in England and Wales has produced guidelines (1995b) on partnership, which include a chapter on assessments, it can be seen that there is some scepticism amongst the practitioners quoted above about how realistic partnership can be in an in-depth assessment. This scepticism is also reflected in the academic literature (Dingwall et al., 1995; Katz, 1997; Corby and Millar, 1997). Katz provides a description of the difficulties:

> The idea that assessment involves doing work 'with' rather than 'to' families must be questioned. Assessment is often a 'cat and mouse' game in which the parent's and worker's interests are unlikely to coincide. Indeed, it can be argued that doing assessments 'with' families is analogous to the 'cat' convincing the 'mouse' that being caught is good for it. The implications are that we should aim for clarity, 'transparency' and fairness in assessment rather than the unachievable goal of 'partnership'. (Katz, 1997: 8).

Katz's solution, that of clarity and fairness, is also that reached by the social workers quoted above.

It has been seen, then, that social workers perceive the assessment process as being fair through the promotion of clients' rights and responsibilities and a clear explanation of the practitioner's own responsibilities and powers. This language implies a rather distant relationship between social workers and their clients and fits with the conception of assessment as a neutral and objective information-gathering exercise, structured by bureaucratic guidance. Smith (1999) provides an analysis of the recent emphasis of 'rights-talk', arguing that it has eclipsed 'values-talk' in social work:

A rights discourse is based on a contractual exchange between persons with entitlements and duties. It does not require any semblance of a relationship, any belief in the innate worth of particular individuals, any engagement, any caring. There is no ambiguity or uncertainty other than that which is introduced by practical or resource issues. (1999: 21)

She is arguing that rights, as legally bound or formalised in laws, and guidance provide a form of certainty in late modern 'risk society'. She also argues that 'rights-talk' is based on notions of rationality, abstraction and impartiality. Whilst the assertion of rights has a potentially powerful influence on fighting the limitations brought about by deprivation and oppression, it tends to ignore the inter-relational aspects of human encounters.

Themes of depth of relationship, and objectivity, recur throughout this book. Later in this chapter it will be seen that the dominant discourse of scientific observation emphasises rationality and abstract aspects of assessments, whilst the discourse of reflective evaluation places more emphasis on the close engagement of the client. In Chapter 5 it will be seen that aspects of the developing relationship between assessor and assessed appear to play a central role in the assessment process, however objective and distant a social worker strives to be. Here it has been seen that some social workers see their task as impartial and structured by 'rights-talk' (Smith, 1999). Part of the distancing of the relationship implied by this stance is seen in the clear (and honest) assertion of the power of the social worker in the child protection process. In Chapter 8 it will be seen that some assessment methods have the potential to reinforce power differences.

Assessment and the Truth

It has been written that it is naïve of assessors to assume that it is possible to discover one set of undisputed, objective 'facts' about a situation. Practitioners should accept that their perceptions are mediated through their own values, experiences and occupational cultures (White, 1997; Parton et al., 1997; Clifford, 1998) and that there will be uncertainty when analysing complex situations (Parton, 1998). It has been suggested that, whilst child abuse scandals have shaken society's faith in social worker and health professionals' abilities to work with scientific objectivity, the current emphasis on risk assessment again hints at the possibility of objective assessment (Parton et al., 1997).

Lay understandings of family assessment might be that it is the social worker's task to uncover the truth about a family. Media criticisms of social workers following the death of children at the hands of their parents or carers often centre around the practitioners' seeming inability to notice key facts about a child's plight. And, indeed, some of these scandals do appear to follow the disregarding of basic assessment practices, such as observing and interviewing the child and checking case records. However, practitioners are dealing with messy human situations where behaviour is never entirely predictable and where, if there are eight key players, it is possible to have eight competing interpretations of the 'truth' of a situation.

> The traditional notion of assessment implies comparison with some sort of measure or norm and is therefore based on rationalist assumptions. It relies on positivist notions of being able to clearly know reality, and has therefore invited social workers to attempt to present not only data but also judgements *as if they were certain* ... In court, non-legal experts are under pressure to come to a consensus. There is a tendency for theories of child care to be given a certainty they never had originally. (Parton and O'Byrne, 2000: 134–5)

Certainty in assessment will be returned to in Chapters 4 and 9. The rest of this chapter continues the discussion about the nature of assessment work, presenting and discussing the Coastal Cities social workers' views on how they reach conclusions in assessments. In particular, their views on reflection and objectivity are explored.

Reflection and Objectivity in Decision-Making

The stage of assessment where the debates around the nature of assessment might be seen to emerge most strongly is that of decision-making and recommendation. Is the social worker making some kind of informed or professional judgement? Is a calculation of risk being made? Is the decision an entirely personal process, or would all professionals come to the same conclusion? The process of decision-making has been the subject of lengthy and extensive academic debate encompassing a wide range of disciplines (Cuzzi et al., 1993). Over the next few pages the processes of decision-making by the Coastal Cities social workers, as accounted by them in interviews, informal interactions and case records are set out. These processes often proved to be elusive to the social workers. Each case was complicated and with each the social worker had an in-depth involvement. However, upon analysis of the data, some patterns and themes of decision-making emerged which spun common threads between the assessments.

Two main patterns of decision-making are discernible. I have labelled these *scientific observation* and *reflective evaluation*. For the purposes of clarity, they will initially be described in the ways in which they differ from each other most sharply: the stance of the assessing social worker and the timing of the decision-making. However, to maintain in this discussion a framework of two separate decision-making models might risk exaggeration of the differences. There are many shared elements in the decision-making through the case studies as a whole. Instead, these two ways of deciding might be seen as tendencies or constellations of factors, rather than separate models with clear boundaries. As shall be seen below, the differences between these two ways of deciding relate primarily to how the social workers understand the process and how they explain or justify their decision-making to a variety of audiences. Foucault's concept of discourse provides a useful means of analysis here. He labelled the ways of giving meaning to the world and organising social institutions and processes as discourses or discursive fields (Weedon, 1997). I suggest that there are two main discursive fields of decision-making operating here. Within each discourse are favoured methods of decision-making, although some of these methods differ little in content. It is how they are understood and explained that places them within one discourse or another, as detailed in Table 3.1.

Table 3.1 Two discourses of decision-making

Decision discourse	Stance	Aims	Timing	Methods
Scientific observation	Objectivity.	Gathering information:	Decision delayed until the end.	Weighing up.
	Distance.	facts and evidence.		Decision tools.
		Making decisions.		Check with others.
Reflective evaluation	Independence, but expecting a close engagement with the family.	In-depth knowledge.	Ongoing evaluation.	Evaluation 'pulled together' at the end.
		Reaching judgements.	Outcomes emerge.	Decision tools.
		Providing explanation.		Check with others.

Scientific Observation

The key elements of this discourse may be summarised as follows. Social workers describe themselves as maintaining an objectivity and distance from the family under assessment. They see the key aims of the assessment as gathering facts and evidence about a family situation and making a decision based on the information gathered. They would avoid reaching a decision until after all information has been gathered and the decision would be made by weighing up the positive factors against the negative, using decision tools and validating their results by consulting with others. Each of these aspects will now be described in greater detail.

Stance and aims of the social worker

Within this discourse the social worker adopts a stance of neutral observer of the family situation. The social worker is the professional expert who will use methods such as observation and measurement in order to form a professional opinion about the family. One of the aims of the assessment is to ascertain the 'facts' about a situation. An analysis of these facts will lead to a clear decision about which course of action will be in the best interests of the child or children involved. Social workers emphasise the clear, planned and structured nature of their work. The clear structure is firmly in the hands of the social worker. In this discourse social workers are aware of their statutory power and use it overtly. Although the principle of 'partnership' between clients and social workers is dominant in official guidance in the UK (see, for example, Department of Health, 1995b), the social workers operating here will see themselves as 'realists' in terms of the nature of the power relationship between social workers and parents in child protection procedures. Here, it is seen as fairer and more honest to be clear about their power than to maintain a pretence about an equality of relationship. Fairness and justice in the process is created by an openness and clarity with families regarding the concerns about them and the expectations that they must fulfil during the assessment time period. Families thus have a clear opportunity to respond to the challenges laid out by the social worker. In a general interview about in-depth assessments, a social worker described an assessment she had completed a few months earlier:

> So it was a clear case of, 'Yes, I see what you say, but this is what you do. There were plenty of warnings, etc.' And in each of those *six components*, the mother *failed at being able to maintain* … you could get *to first base* in each of those six requirements as it were, so it was a sequential thing and she accepted the end of it: 'This is what we've done, Mrs X has been able to identify but not been able to actually carry through; the recommendations are blah, blah, blah.' That was very simple. (General interview with social worker, Laura, unidentified assessment: author's emphasis)

Here, the social worker is able to justify the fairness of the decision through the clear and open manner in which 'Mrs X' was treated. Parton (1998) argues that in the increasingly proceduralised world of social work assessment the underlying assumption is that risk can be calculated. In the extract above, notions of scientific calculation, measurement and testing are invoked through the use of phrases such as 'first base', 'failed' and 'components'.

A key aim for the social worker within this discursive field is objectivity, and this is carried out by maintaining distance between the social worker and the family being assessed, denying any feelings about the client family which might influence the resulting recommendation. This is a difficult aim for many social workers; therefore, sometimes a distance has to be created when the time for decision-making has arrived.

Timing and method of the decision

The decision of what to recommend is usually located at the end of the assessment within this discourse. The facts and observations have been gathered and brought together in a fair and neutral manner. The social worker will then make her decision about what to recommend. To do this she may weigh up the positives and negatives. This may be done by listing them side by side, although as Waterhouse and Carnie (1992) found, this will not mean that each element will be equally weighted. The assessment of Ms James provides an example of a social worker 'weighing up' in decision-making. She appears to have listed the 'positive signs' and 'areas for development' with the help of her supervisor.

> Interviewer: How did you come to your recommendation?
> Sunita: There were some positive signs the last session or two. It was difficult to get to a decision. Some work could be done before court. But when we came to summarise the 'areas for development' the list went on and on. (Interview with Sunita, social worker, James family assessment)

At the end of the assessment report for court 14 risks were listed as bullet points. The length of the list of risk factors made with her supervisor appears to have been central to the final decision. Similarly, Farmer and Owen (1995) found that the listing of concerns was the most common form of risk assessment in the cases in their study. This decision model bears some resemblance to a traditional *costs–benefits model* derived originally from economics (McGrew and Wilson, 1982) where it is assumed that the facts about a decision area are assembled and only then weighed up in order to reach a decision. Gambrill and Shlonsky (2000: 828) warn of the dangers in assuming that risk is 'additive' in that risk factors can be added together and strengths subtracted. Some risk or strength factors may have 'multiplicative' effects when combined, or there may be other non-linear effects.

Use of decision 'tools'

In some assessments a decision tool of some type will be used. Some of these consist of rather more elaborate ways with which to list the perceived positives and negatives, but factors are weighted or placed on a continuum or matrix. An element of calculation may be introduced. Such tools produce an aura of measure and scientific objectivity to the decision-making. However, social workers use them in the only way that is open to them: to lay out their opinions in a structured manner and to make a rough or best guess of a numerical representation of the child's safety. These tools do provide a means for the social worker to take part in structured thinking about a case, and to display their opinions about a case transparently. They do not provide a means to calculate the 'answer' to what should happen to a child and their family.

Finally, under this scientific discourse, the views of others are sought to confirm or reinforce the social worker's decision. The views of peers and supervisors are sought for private reassurance, the views of outside 'experts', especially medical professionals, may be invoked to add scientific credibility to the decision.

Reflective Evaluation

Social workers' ways of describing their decision-making using the discourse of reflective evaluation may be summarised as follows. Here, social workers are likely to emphasis their close engagement with the family under assessment. The aims of the assessment include gaining in-depth knowledge of the family and reaching a judgement about what should happen next. There is an emphasis on reaching an explanation for the family difficulties. The social worker's final judgement is one that has gradually emerged during the assessment. The method of decision-making is one of ongoing evaluation, 'pulled together' at the end. Like the previous discourse, social workers here describe the use of decision tools and consultation with colleagues, although their use will have different aims. Each of these elements is described in detail below.

Stance and aims of the social worker

This discourse of decision-making shares many elements of that of scientific observation. The social worker is still aiming for independence, but in-depth knowledge is mentioned more than distance and objectivity, and evolving evaluation more than suspending judgement until the end of the assessment. Although within this discourse social workers maintain that their value base in relation to the family under assessment is neutral, objective and fair, their position in relation to the parents is not one of distance but of in-depth knowledge and involvement. A key aim is an early and close engagement of the family in the assessment. As one social worker puts it:

> You are hopefully engaging with that person on such a level that they are able to share with you those darker sides or those areas of their life that there is conflict and difficulty. (General interview with Brian, social worker)

Through the scientific discourse the social worker cites the setting of clear boundaries and conditions as the means of being fair to families. The client is informed of the results of the assessment at the end of the structured process. Under reflective evaluation the fairness comes from providing feedback to the client about the evolving opinion of the social worker. George described this process when discussing the Myers family assessment:

> I like to give people a good opportunity but what I try to do is to try and make sense of, evaluate it as I go along really. Well, this concerns me, or this is positive, or this is negative. So when you come to the end of it, you know, it is still painful and I remember sharing the report with mum, it was painful for her. There should be no real surprises for either of you really you know. (Interview with George, social worker, Myers family assessment)

By utilising decision methods of in-depth knowledge and ongoing evaluation, the social worker will expect to be able to reach a professional judgement about a family situation and, at times, to be able to provide an explanation of how a family has reached their current difficult situation.

Judgement

Within the discourse of reflective evaluation the notion of reaching a judgement about a case often appeared to be stronger for social workers than the concept of 'decision'. Judgement appeared to be closely aligned to 'getting a feeling' about a case. Social workers found this hard to explain; there appeared to be less of an acceptable vocabulary in currency than when explaining processes using the scientific discourse. In the following excerpt, Laura has been asked how she reaches recommendations in an assessment:

> Right, yeah. Erm ... (pause). Draw a lot on my own experience. I don't rely on that but I must admit that's the things that tend – because I've been working with families in social work for 22 years – tend to sort of ... you get feelings about what's good enough parenting, but then back that up by looking at pieces of research. (General interview with Laura, social worker)

Similarly, to return to George and the Myers family assessment, he acknowledges that he too uses gut feeling or some sort of sense of the case to guide his recommendations:

It is just that when you are so closely involved with a case you get the feeling ... I know you have to offer facts and evidence but you do get a sort of sense don't you, a strange sort of ... it is hard to quantify but you get a sense of, a gut feeling almost of, well, you know this person isn't going to be good enough in the short term, you know. (Interview with George, social worker, regarding Myers family assessment)

For both social workers there appears to have been an element of insecurity in naming this aspect of decision-making. The statements about feeling were immediately followed by claims that one must also use 'facts and evidence' such as research findings. The social workers here use the language of the scientific discourse to qualify their statements.

The role of explanation

Whilst for some social workers the process described above, of getting a feel for a case through in-depth knowledge, will mainly reside in the spheres of the family's current and future situations, some social workers will also attempt to reach an explanation of how the family's difficulties arose. Howe (1996a) has argued that current social work practice is mainly situated at the 'surface', with a concentration on evidence and behaviour rather than explanation. However, within the discourse of reflective evaluation, social workers can be seen to be still acting as 'applied social scientists' (Howe, 1996a: 77) as they seek explanations of how and why the family has reached this point of crisis.

Timing and method of the decision

The intermediary evaluations provide a guide to further assessment lines of enquiry as well as an indication to both social worker and client of the likely direction of the final recommendations. Workers talking about their decision-making within this discourse, as with the social workers understanding their work within a scientific discourse, may use decision 'tools' to structure their evidence and thinking. However, they are less likely to employ scientistic language or attempt to calculate the level of risk within a family. Rather, decisions are seen to emerge. Within the reflective evaluation discourse, again, the opinions of other professionals are sought. The reflective evaluator's aims might be to check the internal consistency of her reasoning. Any attempt to seek corroboration of views might be seen as a common-sense reasoning device (Wattam, 1992).

The Relationship Between Science and Reflection

The discourses of scientific observation and reflective evaluation have been presented above as two ways in which social workers understand and explain the decision-making process. It is not suggested that all social workers consistently place themselves within one of these discourses and understand this as the way they carry out every assessment. Most of the Coastal Cities social workers seemed to understand and discuss their work through both discourses, switching from one to the other in particular circumstances.

In general, the discourse of reflective evaluation appears to be used when engagement of the adults in the family has been successful and in-depth discussion on a wide range of issues, especially those involving personal reflection on the part of the parent, has been possible. If the information gained about the case appears to mainly point in one direction, and the situation does not appear too complex, then the social worker may feel at ease to explain their recommendation through the discourse of reflective evaluation.

However, such cases are rare in child and family social work. Only four of the 20 cases in the Coastal Cities study met all of the above criteria, three of which involved children already living at home and where court proceedings were not in place. It seems that the discourse of scientific observation is dominant for many social workers, in particular when communicating with other agencies, especially the courts. If the social worker is concerned that her decision may appear impenetrable to the court, other agencies, her managers or the family, then the discourse and methods of scientific observation is used to understand and present the decision-making process.

During a consultation meeting between local authority solicitors and family centre staff, social workers appeared to receive the message that they should provide facts and evidence rather than relying on opinions.

> Solicitor: Research is very valuable [it] heads off the advocate who knows little about social work ... It's clear you are working to a body of knowledge, not just something you thought up last Friday night. It establishes expertise ... List the documents you have read, it's all lessening the chances of being caught out. (Fieldnotes, 25 June 1997)

There did indeed appear to be a fear of being 'caught out' amongst social workers who understood their work through the discourse of reflective evaluation; a sense that the use of scientific and objective methods and ways of explaining the work are superior and dominant.

It might be suggested that the discourse of scientific observation is the default position for social workers. It is the discourse through which they feel their decisions are more likely to be judged valid and which responds more closely to the expectations of the court and official guidance. However, in some cases, the social worker appears to be able to justify and explain her decision-making within the reflective evaluation discourse, to herself and others. In these cases the social worker engages the client early on in the assessment process, and is able to see a decision emerging which appears easily justifiable in the light of the in-depth knowledge gained by the social worker.

Assessment guidance in the UK (Department of Health, 1988, 2000a) has tended to suggest a largely verbal assessment, which includes the exploration of attitudes, feelings and the past. This might be seen to sit largely within the discourse of reflective evaluation. It also contains suggestions for the use of checklists and other measures that might be placed within the discourse of scientific observation. Therefore any social worker using such guidance may end up using a number of decision methods which might be understood in more than one of the discourses.

Reflection-in-Action

The two discourses of decision-making form close parallels to the dominant models in professional practice identified by Schön. He suggests that the dominant, but fading, view of the professional's role is that of 'technical rationality' described as 'instrumental problem solving made rigorous by the application of scientific theory and technique' (1991: 21). Here, the professional applies theory to practice through the use of professional skills. In an alternative model, named *Reflection-in-Action*, Schön argues that professionals act as researchers who are concerned with the issue of problem setting as well of that of problem solving. By reflecting through their practice they attempt to make sense of problems of uncertainty, context and complexity.

Perhaps the largest potential difference between the two discourses identified in this study might have been located in social workers' ontological positions, that is, their understanding of the nature of the status of reality. Schön suggests that the reflecting-in-action practitioner has an understanding that much of the world with which we are interacting is constructed: 'These inquirers encounter a problematic situation whose reality they must construct' (Schön, 1991: 165). The professionals who work within the model of technical rationality are applying objective theories obtained from controlled experiment research to problems that are objective and real. However, the social workers carrying out the in-depth assessments did not display a marked ontological split when discussing the status of the knowledge obtained. The scientific observation discourse emphasises distance and the assembling of facts. But to the social worker operating within the reflective evaluation discourse, with the stance of closeness to the client and in-depth knowledge, the information obtained is still real and factual. Indeed, the social worker has become closer to the 'truth' about a family because of her closeness to them.

Conclusion: the Nature of Assessment

This chapter has explored a range of ways in which assessment might be understood. There is, of course, no one correct way of viewing the task of assessment. The Coastal Cities practitioners were able to describe assessment in a number of ways. They were able to relate their work to legal duties and the rights and responsibilities of the individuals involved in the process. However, it seems that when attempting to describe how they approach the task of reaching conclusions in assessment, social workers perceive some tension between two broad approaches. Practitioners feel that the courts and other professionals expect a level of scientific measurement, objectivity and certainty in their assessment conclusions. In practice, whilst most strive for objectivity, many practitioners acknowledge that individual relationships, judgements and reflection play a central role in assessment. I label these two approaches (or discourses) as scientific observation and reflective evaluation.

At some levels, the two discourses might also be seen as linked to the traditional (although now rather outmoded) split in social research methods, that of quantitative and qualitative approaches. Indeed, the clearest divide in the social work literature on assessment can be seen between advocates of quantitative methods in assessment (Ayoub et al., 1983; Sheldon, 1987; English and Pecora, 1994) and those who favour an in-depth qualitative approach (Meyer, 1993; Franklin and Jordan, 1995). As was seen above, social workers using the discourse of scientific observation used the language of measurement and testing, whilst the reflective evaluators favoured in-depth knowledge. However, little discernible difference could be seen in assessment methods between social workers describing their work through different discourses. Essentially, the in-depth assessment overwhelmingly involves the use of qualitative methods to carry out the assessment and to make decisions. All of the assessments involved in-depth interviewing and observation methods, and all of the decisions appear to have been mainly made on the basis of some form of qualitative analysis of the material gathered. The use of decision 'tools' involves little more than the provision of structure for the social worker's thinking about a case, a way of laying out the qualitative data about the family. The final decision will not be a calculation or measurement, but a judgement reached by the social worker.

Social workers conducting in-depth assessments in child and family work often are faced with the responsibility of making recommendations that may have profound consequences for a child and his or her family. The discussion above has illustrated some of the complexities in the understandings of the assessment task in child welfare work amongst social workers, highlighting the challenge for those engaged in policymaking in contemporary social work. To aid practitioners in this task, policymakers have tended to provide increasingly structured assessment models that limit social workers' ability to reflect and seek explanations for the complex family situations facing them (Howe, 1996a). In England and Wales, the publication of the Assessment Framework has provided an important step forward in allowing for complexity and reflection. The blank page in the core assessment records in which social workers are asked to write about their analysis of the family situation could potentially be used to give a more transparent explanation to service users and other agencies including courts of this previously undescribed aspect of assessment. This could serve to give more credence to professional judgement, when it is based on sound analytic principles and a reflexive stance. It might even allow social workers to discard the goal of 'scientific' certainty and to acknowledge the complexity and uncertainty involved in decision-making of this nature.

Coming to a conclusion that social workers should abandon certainty and any notions of gaining the objective truth may serve to leave social workers feeling disempowered. I am not attempting to suggest that there will not be many important facts and pieces of evidence to gather in an assessment. The intention here is to remind practitioners that there will be many different ways of interpreting the meaning and significance of those pieces of evidence and it is important to avoid pretending that there is only one possible conclusion that may be drawn from the evidence. Instead, practitioners will want to ensure that they have reached a valid and thoughtful conclusion. Readers of the report, including service users, will want to know through what methods of analysis or decision-making these conclusions were reached. In Chapter 9, a method is described for analysing in-depth, qualitative material using thorough methods from the social sciences.

4 Time and Change

Chapter summary

This chapter contains discussion of some key issues relating to time and change in in-depth assessments. These are:

- changing guidance on the length of time an assessment should take;
- the need to allow time for a fair assessment, balanced by the need of children and families for decisions to be made;
- whether an assessment should aim to stimulate change, or to assess potential to change;
- the influence of permanency planning policies on assessment planning; and
- how assessment conclusions can accommodate future change.

Social workers' views on these points are explored, and it can be seen that the wish of some for a flexible timeframe to meet the needs of individual families might clash with some of the aims of government guidance.

The likelihood of this one change and the others following is very much open to doubt. Time might tell but time is what she and her two children have not got. (Assessment report, Brown/Roberts family assessment: the Coastal Cities study)

I mean it is easy for me to say don't worry about three, six months ahead, because she does worry. She worries that the baby will be in care for a long time and when the baby does come back that the bond won't be there, because that is what happened historically, she feels. One of her other children in care came back and there was no bond and that broke down. (Interview with social worker, Hood family assessment, the Coastal Cities study)

As can be seen from these quotations, issues of change, time and concerns about the future are important themes in the assessment process. Families do not remain static during an assessment period and many of the families involved in assessments are experiencing periods of turmoil. The length of time available for an assessment can have a significant impact on the participants. A short timescale has the advantage for children and their parents of decisions being made quickly. On the other hand it can mean that the assessment may lack depth, does not allow some families time to properly engage with the process and, if necessary, demonstrate change, and can be a pressure for social workers. A long time period allows for depth, the engagement of all participants and the observation of family situations that are often rapidly changing. A long time period can also be an agonising wait for families who are awaiting a decision about permanency. This chapter covers three main themes. First, the length and the timing of assessments are explored. Second, the area of families and change is discussed, in relation to change during assessments and predicting future change. The third theme is the future, and this is explored in relation to the complexities involved in making permanent plans for children. The chapter is concluded with a discussion of the recommendation at the end of the assessment, and whether it can be dynamic in the face of a changing family situation. As in the previous chapter, social workers' own views from the Coastal Cities study on time and change in assessments are included throughout.

The Length and Timing of Assessments

In recent years the social study of time has enriched our understanding of society, the environment, the economy and many other areas of study (see Adam, 1995, for a detailed overview). However, with a few exceptions (for example, Lee and Piachaud, 1992; White, 1998b), there has been little attention paid to the issue of time in social work practice. In the area of social work assessment, aspects of time become central, yet 'Careful analysis of the various ways in which time affects the choice or decision process has yet to be undertaken' (Tallman and Gray, 1990: 420). This claim remains valid over a decade later.

Many aspects of time might be seen as relevant to in-depth assessments and the scope of these is briefly surveyed here. The historical time (Tallman and Gray, 1990; Clifford, 1998) of an assessment affects the understanding of all participants, including that of the researcher. For example, the dominant current constructions of child abuse (Wattam, 1996) influenced by scandals, inquiries, legislation, research and fiction will affect the operating perspectives (Cleaver and Freeman, 1995) of both social workers and families. Similarly, an analysis of time in the assessments might include the personal time (in the lives of the participants) or work time cycles such as annual leave, waiting for training, sick leave, maternity leave and length of experience. Related to this might be gendered time (Adam, 1995) covering aspects such as pregnancy and the division of mothers' 'own' time and time for the children. Developmental time (White, 1998b) in relation to children may also be a central consideration.

In England and Wales, there have been changing norms regarding the timing of an in-depth assessment. The Social Services Inspectorate report (1986) that recommended that comprehensive assessments should take place before a decision was made to return a child home from local authority care, estimated that it would take 35 hours to complete a comprehensive assessment. To counter claims that social workers could not spare such a length of time on each assessment, the authors pointed out that longer than this was already spent in an unstructured way by social workers on each such case. The subsequent Department of Health guide, *Protecting Children,* suggested that the assessment should take up to 12 weeks, 'preferably less' (1988: 18) and include 6–10 sessions with parents. David Mellor, the minister responsible for the Children Bill during 1989, did not agree with the *Protecting Children* recommendations for assessments of up to three months when considering the introduction of an assessment order:

> Mellor finally concluded 'After careful consideration, I reached the conclusion that a sensible assessment could be made within seven days in almost every case.' (Hansard, 23 October 1989, column 594, quoted in Parton, 1991: 190)

A seven-day Child Assessment Order was included in the Children Act 1989 for cases where access to a child was being denied, but no changes were made at that point to the 1988 guidelines for comprehensive assessments.

The Assessment Framework, introduced in 1999 in England and 2000 in Wales, shortened the required timescales for assessments. The new initial assessments are to be completed within seven working days (and within eight days of having received the referral). The in-depth, 'core' assessments are to be completed in 35 days (and within 42 days of the referral). It is anticipated that reports from other agencies may take longer. It is also expected that core assessments will have to be regularly updated, and there is rather less of an air of finality about the core assessments than there was under the previous guidance. This issue will be returned to at the end of this chapter.

These tight timescales have been received with a sharp intake of breath by practitioners in the Coastal Cities teams. The initial assessments in particular are difficult to complete in seven days, especially when families are changing rapidly.

> My caseload at last check was 30 cases, with siblings to ask about as well. In terms of actual outstanding assessments I've probably got about 15 initials that still need to be written up, at least half of them I've been working with for three months … I have found also when it is time to come back and look at the initial, it is so different from a family situation six or seven weeks later. Sometimes your initial impressions aren't correct. (Interview with Carin, social worker)

Another social worker found that where she was keeping up with the required timescales, the courts were not, bringing delays for the family:

> We are often finishing our assessments and then waiting two to three months before the court date. The courts are not geared up to the speed of the new framework. (Interview with Edna, social worker)

Krane and Davies, in their analysis of the impact of the introduction of risk assessment systems in North America and the UK, suggest that the tight timescales imposed, coupled with the de-contextualised lists of risk factors present in some systems, might lead to social workers being unable to reach a sufficient understanding of their clients' circumstances:

> Social workers need time to develop sufficient familiarity with the child and his/her living situation. However, in the current practice context social workers' time is at a premium given the explosion of child abuse and neglect reports and referrals … With increasing use of risk assessment tools and heightened stresses and demands in child welfare settings, social workers

may thus become more distanced and more adversarial in their relationships with clients. (2000: 41)

One social worker in the Coastal Cities study suggests that speedy assessments under the Assessment Framework may lead to them lacking depth:

> We just do them really, really quickly and obviously people are picking them up and saying, 'this is not a proper assessment it is just a really good referral'. (Interview with Gaynor, social worker)

Different Time-scales for Different Parents

Many social workers in the Coastal Cities study commented on the restrictions imposed by a set time limit for assessments. Most of the assessments in this study were directed by the court and therefore subject to time-scales agreed and set in court. The judiciary itself must be mindful of the principle of 'least delay' as set out in the Children Act 1989. However, whilst some assessments passed smoothly and the timetable was adhered to without difficulty, many others were subject to timing difficulties, including parental non-attendance (due to illness, imprisonment, lack of interest and a wide variety of other reasons), staff sickness and unexpected issues arising in the assessment. Furthermore, as the following extract suggests, individual needs will simply differ in terms of appropriate timing of an assessment.

> So it is building on the positives that you can, building up self-esteem and very often we don't have enough time for that you know if you are working to a timescale. Some people need a different timescale from, you know, the one we work to. There was one person who was very negative, you know, hated being here, didn't want to know really what it was about, went away a few weeks and came back with a different attitude and I think that is why it was different. I don't know what that is about sometimes and I think the time limit can be very wrong for some of the families, if there are criminal proceedings going on, mental health problems. But because we are having to make a decision about children, you know we do it in the quickest time possible. But I think the time is wrong for some people. (General interview with Jane, social work manager)

Here Jane brings up three key issues. First, she suggests that there is not always enough time to carry out the intervention that she suggests should take place in an assessment: the building up of positive aspects of the family under assessment and increasing their self-esteem. Second, she states that in some cases it is not appropriate to assess the family at that period of time, for example, if they are facing criminal proceedings or a parent is ill. Finally, she introduces a major difficulty following on from both of the above points: delaying assessment decisions for any reason, however valid, means that any decision about the child's future is delayed. The issue of children waiting for decisions is discussed further below.

The relationship between the timing of court proceedings and child protection decisions and interventions has been a central concern in childcare social work. For example, in cases of child sexual abuse, it has been seen that the child witness's need for therapy has often taken second place to the requirements of a criminal prosecution (Wattam, 1992). As is suggested in the quotation from Jane above, social workers often feel pressurised to reach a decision within a certain time-limit and this is particularly the case when assessments have been ordered through the court. As Laura reflects below, sometimes she feels pressurised to come to a conclusion prematurely, due to an impending court deadline:

> That [the court deadline] is an external pressure, having to come to a conclusion of some-thing about a family that is in crisis or is not moving along at the same rate as the proceed-ings. You have got to come out with something, sometimes it can take a while to change and collect. ... they need to be longer rather than shorter, to get a better feel of how things are. (Interview with Laura, social worker, regarding Thompson family assessment)

The assessment of children and their families is quite rightly framed by the Assessment Framework as an evolving process, one that can be reviewed and changed as a family's circumstances change. Therefore, although there is a pres-sure to complete each assessment quickly, there is scope for later revision. However, where there are more serious concerns for the child's welfare and the assessment is informing court proceedings, the assessment conclusion may be informing decisions such as the permanent removal of the child from home. In such circumstances, the assessing social worker understandably will feel under pressure if the situation is in a state of flux throughout the assessment timescale. It is possible for more time to be applied for, or for conclusions to recommend further work before decisions about permanency are made, but there is increas-ing pressure in the UK and the US for permanency decisions to be made within short timescales (Barth, 1997; LAC, 2000).

Assessment as a Time of Waiting

In contrast to the discussion about flux and change in assessments above, assess-ment is seen as a static time by some participants. It is a time of waiting for a conclusion, of being in limbo. Parents are waiting for a conclusion to the assess-ment. Children are waiting, often in temporary foster placements, for a reunion with their parents or possibly the prospect of new, substitute parents. Waiting occurs before an assessment actually begins, and also after an assessment has finished before a court hearing or case conference makes a final decision. It is popularly recognised (and more systematically theorised by Adam, 1995) that we experience time as moving at different speeds. For example, whilst a client may experience the several weeks of an assessment as lasting for a painfully long time, to a social worker it might represent a brief burst of frenetic energy. Social workers talk of events moving quickly at time of crisis, but dragging if the client is not responding. In addition, some periods of time appear more significant than others. A child not going home by Christmas might seem a more signifi-cant separation than being away from home for a longer period at another time of year.

In the following extract, a social worker describes assessment as a time of waiting for the client:

Yes, there may be negatives but at the same time [I] offer some positives that what they are going through is going to be worthwhile. [That] there might be some conclusions and decisions made so people can, you know, once decisions and conclusions have been made *people can sometimes move on* for themselves or make a decision themselves, because for many individuals *their life is in some sort of limbo*. They have been *hanging around* or they have been *caught up* in the system for such a long time and they are *waiting* for this elusive assessment to be done on them. And then may be some decision can be made and then they *can get on* with their lives, then they can do whatever they want to do. (General interview with Brian, social worker, regarding assessments: emphasis added)

Here, Brian vividly invokes the state of 'limbo' for clients who are waiting for a decision of great significance to their family life. They are 'caught up', 'hanging around' and 'waiting' during the assessment process. This is in contrast to concepts in the previous section, of clients changing during assessments. Brian invokes a sense of time-stood-still for the client, as if they are prevented from carrying out any normal routine or 'do[ing] whatever they want to do'.

The theme of (adult) clients waiting during an assessment is a minor one in the Coastal Cities study in comparison to that of children waiting. This is a strong concept in the culture and literature of childcare social work, influenced particularly by the early research by Rowe and Lambert (1973): *Children Who Wait*. In their study of 2,812 children in long-term (over six months) local authority care, they found that the majority had already spent a large part of their lives in care. Over 60 per cent were expected to remain in care until they were 18 years old (Rowe and Lambert, 1973: 38). The Maria Colwell inquiry at this time (Secretary of State for Social Services, 1974) also highlighted an individual and tragic case of a child denied a permanent alternative placement. A move towards 'permanency planning' in childcare policy arose in the 1970s with the premise that children should not remain in temporary care for long without a permanent home being found for them (Hill et al., 1992; Colton et al., 1995). This permanent home might be with birth parents, other relatives or adoptive parents. The policy has had a significant influence throughout the Western world (Backe-Hansen, 1992; Smith, 1995; Testa et al., 1996; Barth, 1997).

There was much concern expressed by social workers in the Coastal Cities study about the impact on children of having to wait too long for a decision about his or her future. In other words, that a child is in 'limbo' until placed permanently at home or in a substitute family:

There is much evidence of the damaging effects on children of being allowed to drift in Local Authority care without appropriate attention being given to planning their future. Within the stated time constraints of the proposed further assessment work, a decision should be taken about the feasibility of the child's return to the parent. (Assessment report, Jones family assessment)

In the extract above, the agency formally states its position in relation to children remaining in care. To avoid a child 'drifting' without a permanent base, there should be specific time constraints laid down. In this case there was to be a further, short, period of assessment, following which a decision would be made whether to return the child home to his birth mother or find an adoptive home. The further period of assessment was to enable the assessor to establish whether the mother was able to change her behaviour and attitudes in the 'gaps' that had been identified. The question of whether parents could change 'in time' for their child was a key question in many of the assessments.

> The likelihood of this one change and the others following is very much open to doubt. Time might tell but time is what she and her two children have not got. (Assessment report, Brown/Roberts family assessment)

Here it is emphasised that a parent might well be able to change, but that she may not be able to do this within a timescale that is seen to be appropriate for children to wait. The time that children are seen as able to wait is strongly related to their age, and also to the length of time they had already spent in care. Very young children were seen as those most urgently needing a permanent home.

> With very young children, such as these, decisions have to be made quickly for their future. (George, social worker, discussing Myers family assessment, fieldnotes 11 June 1997)

Summary: Assessment Timing

It has been seen that in England and Wales there have been significant changes in relation to length and timing of in-depth assessments in recent times. A previous recommendation that such assessment should take up to three months has been replaced by a tighter timescale. Whereas previously the in-depth assessment was usually a one-off assessment, often with significant implications, current guidelines suggest a more fluid approach, with regular updating. However, where there are serious child welfare concerns, and the case is being heard in court, it is likely that any assessment, under any set of guidelines, has the potential to impact upon permanent decisions being made about a child's future. It is therefore not surprising that social workers express some concerns about whether a short timescale gives all families a fair assessment. There is also, though, clear recognition on the need for decisions about children's futures to be made fairly quickly, to avoid cases 'drifting' and children being left in 'limbo'. Of key importance in decision-making of this nature is whether families can be seen to change, or have the potential to change aspects of their care of their children that have given cause for concern. It is the issue of change that we turn to now.

Time and Change

In situations where an in-depth assessment of a child's circumstances is required, it is likely that there are aspects of professional concern regarding the care and behaviour of one or more adults in the family, including circumstances where there is inadequate control of a child's behaviour. It is therefore likely that some changes in the child's circumstances will be sought. This might include a positive response to extra help, support and resources. It also often appears to be the case that parents will be expected to change their behaviour and their attitude to professionals' concerns.

The social workers' understandings of change are closely connected with questions of time and assessment. For example, a longer assessment would probably be needed if families were expected to change during the assessment. A short assessment may be able to assess readiness to change. The main issues regarding change and time in the Coastal Cities assessments are:

- Should there be assessment of the *potential* of parents to change (in the future)?
- Should there be change *during* the assessment?
- How is change understood? Is behavioural (current) or attitudinal change (future potential) sought?

These three areas are closely interlinked. For example, behavioural change is often sought during an assessment, whilst attitudinal change is often related to clients expressing a willingness to change in the near future. On the other hand, a small amount of behavioural change during the assessment might be seen as predicting a potential for greater change in the future. Attitudinal change may relate to agreeing with the professional view of the causes for concern, rather than only referring to the future.

Potential change or current change?

Regarding the first two of these questions, there appears to be a rather unresolved tension for social workers of how they understand the significance of change in an assessment. Whilst some social workers appear to be looking for families to change during the period of assessment and regard this as an indicator for the recommendation, others talk about looking for families to show a potential to change sometime in the future. This question relates to wider issues about in-depth assessments in general. Are they assessments of families' current functioning? Are they the beginning of a therapeutic process with the aim of producing and measuring change?

On the subject of change, the guidance in England and Wales has shifted.

> It must be remembered that the primary purpose of the exercise is to provide a basis for planning and, though changes may occur during the assessment, change is not the main objective. (Department of Health, 1988: 22)

> Undertaking an assessment with a family can begin a process of understanding and change by key family members. A practitioner may, during the process of gathering information, be instrumental in bringing about change by the questions asked, by listening to members of the family, by validating the family's difficulties or concerns, and by providing information and advice. The process of assessment should be therapeutic in itself. (Department of Health, 2000a: 15)

It can be seen here that there is a rather significant shift in emphasis in the understanding of the assessment task that centres on the question of change.

Previous guidance appeared to construct assessment as one stage in a distinct process, a precursor to planning and then intervention. In practice, however, it is impossible to become involved with a family over several weeks for an in-depth assessment and not be intervening in some way. The very act of answering questions about their situation will cause participants to reflect on their lives and possibly change their understanding and actions. It will be seen in Chapter 5 that an important element of an assessment where a positive recommendation is made is that the parent and assessing social worker agree an explanation for the causes and solutions for the family problems. For that process to occur, then the social worker must intervene (probably mainly through talk), rather than simply observing a situation 'as it is'. Assessment has now been reconfigured as an intervention. Interventions by their very nature aim to stimulate change.

Angela, a family centre social worker, reflected on the differences that the new guidance had made to her understanding of assessment:

> We are looking at their capacity to change as we are carrying out the assessment. It is assessing that change and that continuing from day one, rather than [under the previous ways of working] we would gather all this information, make a decision and then at the end we would put in a programme, and I would monitor that programme. [now] It is all done at once. (Interview with Angela, social worker, Hillside Family Centre).

The differences between the two ways of understanding the role of change in assessment could also be seen as linked to two main ways social workers were seen to understand the assessment task in Chapter 3. The notion that assessment might be seen as 'scientific observation' fits with a view of assessment as a rather detached precursor to intervention. On the other hand, understanding assessment as an intervention in itself, and a potential time of change for families, appears to fit with the notion of assessment as 'reflective evaluation' where conclusions are reached after close engagement with the family.

In the Coastal Cities study, social workers tended to talk about assessment as a time of change. For example:

> *Cathy*: They need time to take it on board, *time for change to happen*. It can take a long time. They need time to consider what they need to do.

> *Laura*: We need time to test *whether that change is going to happen. How do they manage change*? How do they cope with the impact? It gives a more realistic picture for us. (Meeting between Hillside Family Centre workers and local authority solicitors, field-notes, 25 June 1997; emphasis added)

Here, Cathy clearly states that she would be looking for change during an assessment. Laura's statement is rather more ambivalent. She suggests that she may be involved in a process of testing for the possibility of future change, but her question of 'How do they manage change?' would suggest that she might also be expecting some change during the assessment to establish how well a family copes with change.

The issue of whether social workers are assessing families' potential to change or actual change during an assessment is fundamental to the nature of these assessments. If the social workers are expecting change during the assessment, then they are clearly acknowledging that the assessment is an intervention in the lives of a family. Here, the skills of the social worker to facilitate change becomes important and the assessment process is moved onto a different level from an understanding of assessment as a collecting and analysis of facts about a situation. An expectation that an assessment will reveal the *potential* to change suggests, as was stated above, that social workers may be looking for mainly attitudinal change. The different types of change that may be looked for in an assessment are discussed next.

Behavioural and attitudinal change

Closely related to the issues of current change, or potential to make changes in the future, is the question of the nature of the change sought. Theories of social work practice provide a range of bases from which to understand change. Pure behaviourists would seek changes only in behaviour (Hudson and MacDonald, 1986), but cognitive-behavioural theorists would also understand change in terms of changes in cognition and attitude (Berlin, 1982). Psychodynamic theory places an emphasis on change in terms of self-understanding rather than behaviour (Hollis, 1964). Other theories, such as Marxism or feminism, emphasise change in societal structures, rather than focusing on changing the individual (Langan, 1998). The understandings of change by social workers conducting the assessment were individualistic, reflecting the individual nature of the assessments. As suggested above, change was sought that was behavioural and/or attitudinal.

It is possible to draw up two groups of adjectives and phrases used with 'change' in the Coastal Cities study. First, there is mention of change that is 'demonstrable', 'measurable', 'real', 'tested', 'sustained', 'consistent', 'maintained' and 'positive'. A second group of phrases associated with 'change' includes: 'potential', 'capacity', 'prospects for', 'ability to', 'commitment to', 'motivation', 'acknowledgement of the need to' and 'to want to' . The first group of words is similar to those used when social workers are describing their work through the discourse of scientific observation, as described in Chapter 3. It might be suggested that this group of words, which appear to describe behavioural changes, mainly describe change that should occur *during* an assessment. This appears to construct the assessment period as a test, a time in which parents might prove themselves able to change their behaviour for the better. The type of behaviour tested might include keeping a home clean, attending contact sessions with children or abstaining from criminal or addictive behaviour. The second group of words relates to attitudinal change where parents might be seen to be expressing a (future) *willingness* to change their behaviour for the better. These are likely to be discovered during verbal interviews between social workers and parents, as will be described in Chapter 5.

It has been argued that social workers tend to seek change that is attitudinal rather than behavioural. For example, in a collection of essays published following the death of Jasmine Beckford and the subsequent inquiry, Sheldon criticised social work assessment thus:

Insight, even where it can be achieved, is one thing, manifest behavioural change is another … Less emphasis should be placed on changes in the verbal content of interviews and more on demonstrable changes in parental functioning. (Sheldon, 1987: 26–7).

Similarly, in Chapter 5 it will be proposed that in in-depth assessments, verbal reasoning may be central to the decision-making process. It is likely, however, that in areas of decision-making, such as permanency planning, behavioural change is seen as being as important as attitudinal. For example, a Scottish study of decisions of whether to return children home to their parents or apply for them to be adopted, found that parental failure to change behaviour was linked to decisions to free children for adoption (Hill et al., 1992).

The type of change to be assessed will, of course, be affected by the identified concerns about the family, and their strengths. If there have been concerns about chaotic substance misuse, then concerns about the child's safety might not be allayed by a simple pledge to change the behaviour. Concrete signs that the drugs or alcohol are being taken safely and at a manageable level, or not at all, might be sought. Regular attendance at a clinic or other treatment centre might be one such concrete sign. Where the concern might be due to the emotional scapegoating of a child, or beliefs about allowing a person with a criminal record of crimes against children access to a child, then attitudinal change may be as important as behavioural change. Parton and O'Byrne (2000) describe the use of a solution focused approach to work with service users to set goals that feel achievable to the client and are written in the client's own words. Part of the aim of an in-depth assessment might be to have agreed a set of goals that will answer the concerns of the family themselves and of the statutory authorities, and for the service user to have achieved success with some of these goals before the end of the assessment period.

Assessing the Future

In Chapter 2 it was seen that the notion of risk – a central concept in child welfare assessments – is essentially concerned with the future. When social workers assess risk they are being asked to predict the future behaviour of others and the future likely effect on children's lives.

Ryburn casts doubt on the ability of the traditional assessment to predict the future. On the issue of coming to a conclusion following the assessment of adopters, he suggests that:

All that this could possibly offer us would be a perspective relating to one particular point in time. Because we are living systems, each of us changes every day and our relationships are also dynamic and changing. Indeed the *raison d'être* for social work could be seen as centring in a belief in the capacity of people and systems to change. The traditional assessment process can be seen as an attempt to freeze time, as if a finite decision can be made that could be right for all future time. All future time for children or young people adopted today does not mean until age 18, it may mean 60 or 70 or even 80 years. Social work planning should have an openness of view that takes account of this fact. (1991: 24–5).

Here Ryburn exposes the dichotomy that exists in social work assessment: the belief and hope that people will change, sitting rather uneasily with the making of fixed recommendations for the long-term future of children. Packman and Randall (1989) acknowledge that the changing nature and complexity of family situations often defies social workers' attempts to assess accurately. However, the current system requires the social workers to express themselves with some certainty. The advice of writers such as Pozatek (1994) and Parton (1998), who argue that social workers should 'sit with' uncertainty in social work rather than prematurely reaching conclusions that are closed or narrow, does not fit easily with the requirements of court reporting.

Milner and O'Byrne (1998) suggest that assessment recommendations should make clear their timeframe. Are they intended to be short-term, long-term or episodic? Undoubtedly, the overall aim of an in-depth assessment for some court proceedings is to provide recommendations that will have implications for the long-term or permanent future of children and their families. Such court proceedings might include decisions regarding 'freeing' a child for adoption or an application by parents to revoke an order that requires their children to live separately from them. The need to make long-term recommendations for children's futures poses a problem for social workers. They often see that a parent may have some potential to act as a full-time parent to a child, but that their current circumstances, abilities or attitudes do not suggest that it would be wise at the current time to return the child home on a full-time basis. This brings us back to the issue of how long children can be expected to wait before their parents are seen as ready to provide parenting care.

In the following two extracts, two social workers grapple with these issues:

So, the assessment bit comes in putting that all together and making judgement on their potential for change. [Pause] but you also have to take into account that that is a period of assessment, it is based on time in a particular setting. *I think it is difficult to make a judgement that this will definitely be forever,* on that potential at that time. (General interview with Jane, social work manager: emphasis added)

I think you can use the phrase 'at this time' and I think I have probably used that in there (the report). I think that what we were trying to do is, we do look for some potential, but I think there has got to be some sort of time clock and think, well, we are talking about another year's work. I mean, is that fair to the child? I mean how long can we wait? I don't know really. (Interview with George, social worker, Myers family assessment)

In the first quotation above, Jane suggests that she is judging a parent's (future) potential to change their behaviour until it reaches a level where they will be able to care for their child. She acknowledges that, however in-depth the assessment has been, it represents a particular period in the family's life. The past and current events that have been discussed and assessed may come to be understood differently in the future. Jane states that it is difficult to reach a conclusion 'that this will definitely be forever'. However, as discussed above, the type of recommendation required from an in-depth assessment report often has long-term or even 'forever' implications for the child and the family. In the second quotation, George similarly is struggling with the issue of the timeframe of assessment conclusions. He reports that, in this assessment, he has used the phrase 'at this time' to suggest that his conclusions are not meant to provide a prescription of how it will be for that parent forever. He explains how he attempts to resolve the difficulty: by predicting approximately how long the parent will take to change and then judging whether the child or children will be able to wait that long until their permanent care is established.

Few social workers would claim that they are attempting to predict the long-term future for a child. The conceptualisation of assessment as a continuing process (Department of Health, 2000a) recognises that family situations may change rapidly following an assessment. However, what George was discussing above was the dilemma of trying to predict how long a parent might take before they were ready (or judged ready) to care for their child. Such judgements may be taken out of the hands of individual decision-makers by the introduction of minimum standards on permanency outcomes for children. Barth (1997) calls for performance targets to be introduced in the US to improve the likelihood of a permanent home being found for children in foster care. He suggests that this home should be reunification with parents, adoption or kinship guardianship. The US permanency *planning* timeframe is 18 months unless reunification is expected. Barth suggests that the *achievement* of permanency should be met within four years of a young child entering foster care. In the UK, following the Prime Minister's Review of adoption, new National Adoption Standards set clear timescales for decision-making about adoption (Department of Health, 2001).

One possible solution to the dilemmas caused by the difficulties of predicting future change, the need to allow time for families to engage with an assessment and intervention and the imperative that children should not wait too long, is that of concurrent planning (this is sometimes also known as 'twin-tracking'). In the UK, the planning for children looked after has tended to be sequential (Smith, 1995). This is reflected in the concerns expressed by the social workers in the Coastal Cities study. Concurrent planning was developed in Seattle in the US and involves the simultaneous planning of a reunification and a permanent alternative. This means that if a reunification is unsuccessful, then adoption (or a permanent placement with a relative or foster carer) might swiftly follow (Katz, 1996). Concurrent planning provides the potential for social workers involved in the most serious child welfare cases to 'sit with uncertainty' (Parton, 1998) for a period of time in which it might be seen if parents can indeed produce the changes necessary to care for their child. However, it must be acknowledged that almost all permanency decisions will be made on a basis of less than certainty. This is a message that is rarely acknowledged in public debates when cases end in tragedy. In less serious cases, particularly where children may safely remain at home, it is indeed possible for assessment to be a continuing process over a longer timescale.

Conclusion

When exploring concepts of time and change in assessments it can be seen that social workers and families face a number of potentially conflicting imperatives.

There is a need for children and their families to be clear about the timescales of assessment and decision-making. They should not be kept waiting over long periods for decisions of great importance, such as whether they are to be reunited at home or whether the child is to be settled into a permanent placement elsewhere. On the other hand, the pressure to rush such decisions may lead to families having difficulties in engaging with the process. There are also difficulties when families are in a state of flux (perhaps involving illness, imprisonment or marital separations) or indeed the social work agency is in a state of flux (perhaps involving staff sickness and staff turnover). Finally, there is the issue of how much time is required in order to assess the potential to change behaviour, whether change has actually been achieved and what continuing risks are likely to be present in the future. In England and Wales, the government response has been to impose clear (and tight) timetables in order to meet the needs of children and families for early decision-making. A notion of continual assessment, as necessary, has been introduced to recognise that families do often change rapidly. It has also been recognised that change can be facilitated during an assessment and that therefore the capacity for a family to change may become part of the assessment. It must be acknowledged, however, that whatever timescale of decision-making is achieved by social workers and other professionals, cases are subject to the timetable of the courts, which can lead to lengthy delays for some children.

The Coastal Cities social workers, understandably, have a more personal and individualistic notion of time than that imposed by government guidance. Some suggest that timing should be individual and tailored to the needs of a particular family. Policymakers fear that leaving such decisions in the hands of individual social workers will lead to cases drifting and stalling through lack of efficiency or prioritisation. Indeed, it has been seen in this chapter that social workers experience assessment periods often as times of frenetic activity, whilst families may experience the period as one of limbo – of time stood still. Of most importance appears to be the goal of avoiding premature and ill-judged conclusions whilst making decisions quickly enough for children. Smith (1995: 16) comments:

> Children's needs must not get lost. Their childhoods will not come again and they have a right to expect those with responsibility to act in a considered and decisive way in order to secure their future. (1995: 16)

How, therefore, can a set of assessment recommendations accommodate these dichotomies? How can conclusions be reached that are decisive for the child, but which allow for change? The answer may be to produce recommendations that are dynamic. 'Dynamic' can be defined as 'energetic and forceful' (OED, 2002). Thus, dynamic recommendations will have energy, in that they will meet immediate needs and be flexible enough to be able to accommodate changing circumstances. They will be forceful in that they set transparent goals and are clear about the likely consequences and actions if goals cannot be met. Assessment recommendations can be regularly revisited with family members and other important parties to see if they are continuing to accommodate the changing needs of a child and her family. In the most serious cases, concurrent planning for permanency is an important example of a dynamic approach to an assessment recommendation. Ways in which an assessment conclusion may be reached are explored in Chapter 9.

Suggestions for practice

- The timescale of an assessment may be experienced differently by the assessor and the assessed. For social workers it may feel like a hectic time, particularly when they are carrying out many assessments at once. For service users it may feel like a time of limbo, especially when children are being accommodated away from home
- Governments set timescales for assessments in an understandable drive to ensure minimum standards for service users. It should be remembered that some families will require much longer than others to understand and become involved in the process. Taking time to build a trusting relationship is an important part of an in-depth assessment.
- A distinction may be made between attitudinal change and behavioural change by families (or families saying they will change and actually doing it!). Part of the aim of an in-depth assessment might be to have agreed a set of goals that will answer the concerns of the family themselves and of the statutory authorities, and for the service user to have achieved success with some of these goals before the end of the assessment period.
- There will always be a tension between the need of the separated child for an early decision about permanency and the need for their birth parents to be given the opportunity to become ready to resume the care of their children. One method for reducing the timescale is concurrent planning.
- Assessment conclusions should aim to be decisive and yet flexible enough to accommodate potential future change.

PART II

PEOPLE IN ASSESSMENTS

5 The Assessment Relationship

Chapter summary

This chapter explores the assessment relationship: that is, the relationship that develops between the assessor and the assessed during the course of an assessment. It is argued that this relationship plays a vital role in determining the outcome of the assessment. It is noted that, in the Coastal Cities research, the most important indicator of a positive outcome was that the social worker and parent could agree a plausible explanation for the family problems and how they should be solved. The ability to reach such an agreement will be affected by the quality of the assessment relationship. It is therefore vital that the assessing social worker works to maintain a positive assessment relationship.

It is suggested that the practitioner maintain a reflexive awareness of the impact of herself or himself on the assessment relationship, and of the process of assessment upon all participants.

This chapter is about what I have labelled the 'assessment relationship'. This refers to the relationship that develops between assessor and assessed during the course of an assessment. In particular, I discuss the relationship between social worker and parent (or other adult carer). This is because of the centrality of that relationship in the Coastal Cities research. I will be discussing the role of children in assessments in the next chapter. This chapter includes considerations of gender, culture and language in the processes of engagement and working together. I go on to argue that the quality of the assessment relationship affects not only the experience of the assessment for social worker and service user, but also the outcome of the assessment.

The Practitioner–Client Relationship in Social Work

The relationship between social worker and client has been an important element in the social work literature in the twentieth century but has, like many other areas of social work, been subject to fluctuating popularity and interest. In the context of traditional social casework, the relationship was of central importance from the 1930s until about the 1960s (Coady, 1993; Petr, 1988).

Interest in relationships in social work in Britain has been muted since the 1970s (with occasional exceptions, for example, Howe, 1998). However, counselling practice and theory continues to place an emphasis on the quality of the client–counsellor relationship (Howe, 1993). Research, mainly from the US, into relationships between social workers/therapists and their clients has been concentrated in the 'psy' disciplines and on therapeutic interventions. It has tended to be quantitative and does not provide detailed information on the microprocesses involved. Findings from such studies appear to suggest that the working relationship between practitioners and their clients has an effect on the outcome of interventions. For example, a meta-analysis conducted by Horvath and Symonds of 24 quantitative studies (1991) found a moderate, but reliable, association between a good working alliance and a positive therapy outcome. Indeed, some of the findings from such studies suggest that, when predicting outcome, the type of therapy used in an intervention is less important than the quality of the therapeutic relationship (Coady, 1993). It is worth noting that the concept of the alliance in psychotherapy refers, in the main, to positive aspects of the therapist–client relationship. Negative aspects are seen to belong to other theoretical areas, such as transference and counter-transference (Gaston, 1990).

Within social work more generally, practice guides may list technical skills that aim to improve the relationship, but, as Payne (1996) points out, this often ignores political and theoretical implications such as covert coercion. In the general social work literature the relationship between social worker and client has been described in rather vague terms such as 'interaction', 'warmth' and 'respect' (Proctor, 1982). However, it may be argued that such terms are helpful in that they appear to be broadly understood. Drake (1994) describes research conducted with groups of child welfare workers and groups of their clients. When describing desirable relationship competencies, both types of group came up with similar lists including 'respect' and 'warmth'.

In recent years there has been an increase in policy-making and social work theorising which attempts to address the power imbalances between social workers and their clients through notions of 'partnership' and 'empowerment' (for example, Department of Health, 1995b; Adams, 1996). The concept of partnership has been criticised on some levels, including a suggestion that it ignores the emotional aspects of social worker–client relationships (Webb, 1994).

The Impact of the Worker on the Assessment Relationship

This part of the chapter will explore the impact of the worker on the assessment relationship. An awareness of the impact of various aspects of one's self on an intervention is part of being a *reflective practitioner* (see page 39). This term is also often used interchangeably with *reflexivity*, but reflexivity can be seen as taking reflection a step further. White (1997) emphasises that a reflexive awareness will not simply involve the social worker being aware of the impact of attributes such as gender and 'race', but also of the occupational constructs associated with their work. In child protection that may involve an awareness of the impact of influential theories, such as permanency in child placements and attachment theory. Payne (1998) emphasises that reflexivity is a circular process of thought and action, with our thoughts and beliefs interacting with and affecting service users, and their responses and experiences in turn affecting our thoughts and belief systems. Clifford applies notions of reflexivity to social work assessment thus:

> Both the reactions of the users to the assessment process *and* the changing perspectives of the professionals need to be scrutinised within this framework, so that the reactions of those being assessed can be understood as a specific response to a particular set of powerful relationships at a particular point in their lives, the life of the agency and its representatives, and wider family and social history. (1998: 20)[1]

A body of literature has also built up in the welfare professions regarding the influence of the professional on the helping process, especially within therapeutic fields such as family therapy (Anderson, 1990; Campbell et al., 1992). In social work, practice guidelines advising, for example, that careful consideration be given to the ethnicity and sex of workers when allocating work in specific cases (Department of Health, 1995b), suggests an interest in the possible effect of the worker's 'self' on the social work process. Farmer and Owen (1995) found that a matching of sex and ethnicity of worker and client appeared to be associated with the best outcomes, at least for clients from ethnic minorities.

In the Coastal Cities study there were examples of social workers working with clients of the same sex as themselves and also examples of social work across sexes. The majority of the social workers were white, with one Asian social worker and one dual heritage social worker, both from Hillside Family Centre. One of the parents being assessed was an Asian British man and children from two of the families were of dual heritage. One family was from the travelling community. None of the ethnic minority clients was assessed by a worker from the same ethnic background. Most of the white clients were assessed by white social workers, although some were assessed by black social workers.

An analysis was also carried out of social workers' understandings of their own contribution to that relationship. There was an awareness of the difficulties involved, including issues of power differential on grounds of class, 'race', gender and statutory powers. However, whilst social workers were able to *theorise* that they themselves could have an impact on the quality of the relationship with parents, most identified compensatory tactics they used to minimise the impact of self *in practice*. The two examples below are drawn from social workers' discussion of these issues.

> I am very much aware that I am a mixed race man. She is a white woman, I think we have some common ground in the fact that we both have small children and I can disclose things about my children and so on. ... I think, in a sense, the issues of class relate to the fact that I am employed, in full-time employment and she isn't, so I mean there is an imbalance there. I mean, I was brought up on a council estate and she is from a council estate and I am familiar with the situation that exists with single parents who have large families. ... I like to think that

I have used different approaches with her that she still feels able to talk to me. (Interview with social worker, Cooke family assessment)

Here, the social worker acknowledges that there are potential differences in cultural understanding between himself and the parent concerned, but he suggests that he has compensated for these differences through disclosing personal information and a variety of other tactics. In the next extract, another social worker suggests that there could potentially have been problems with the assessment due to her uncomfortable feelings in relation to the male service user. Like the social worker above, she consciously adopted a compensatory tactic.

Social worker: I'm uncomfortable with Mr Marsh, professionally and personally.
Interviewer: Did that affect the nature of the comprehensive assessment?
Social worker: No, I don't think so, except that because I'm so conscious of the difficulties with these parents I may have made more effort to communicate with these parents. (Interview with social worker, Marsh family assessment)

A reflexive approach to assessment work would *assume* that the worker and all that they represent (a culture, gender, age, profession, individual and professional history, institutional culture and so on) would have an impact on the assessment process. It is important for the worker to maintain an awareness of the potential effects of himself or herself and to discuss these in supervision and, where, appropriate, with the service user.

The Impact of the Service User on the Assessment Relationship

In the Coastal Cities study, social workers were asked to describe the main factors that influenced their decision-making in the assessments. The key decision-making factors cited by social workers were largely consistent across both City Social Services Department and Hillside Family Centre. In addition, the core evidence for decision-making did not differ according to severity of behaviours labelled as abusive or different types of abuse. Their answers can be grouped into three main areas: parent-related factors (including parenting skills and the relationship between parents); the ability of parents to change their behaviour and lifestyle within an acceptable timescale; and the verbal interactions between the assessing social worker and the parent being assessed. It is the last area which is under consideration in this chapter. Whilst all the areas were regularly cited as core evidence, it was often the case that the area relating to verbal interactions appeared to be given the highest status. This area is inextricably concerned with the assessment relationship; that is, the relationship that develops between social worker and parent during the course of the assessment.

Verbal Interactions as Evidence

Major areas of evidence in the in-depth assessments centred on the perceived personalities of the parents and their attitudes to the assessment. These were mainly assessed through verbal interactions within the assessment and were seen to influence the ability of the parent to enter into a constructive working relationship with the assessing social worker. Equally, the ability to form relationships was seen to be an indication of the personality of the parent and ultimately perhaps their ability to care for their children. Parents who could work well within a relationship were seen to share many of the following attributes: they were articulate, plausible, co-operative and motivated. On the other hand, parents who were seen to provide a negative contribution to the assessment relationship were viewed as inarticulate, inconsistent and passive.

In the extract below, a social worker summarises some of the core evidence to be sought during an assessment:

> I am looking for commitment and motivation. For her to be able to demonstrate that things are different, that she has some awareness of the issues. That she can step back and say, 'Yes', you know. The minimum has to be that she can step back and say, 'Yes, in itself that would be concerning', you know. (Interview with social worker, Hood family assessment)

This worker suggests that, as a minimum requirement, the parent should be able to admit that her type of actions give rise to concern. The attributes of motivation, commitment and awareness of concerns could be seen as existing also outside of the assessment relationship, that is, as attributes of the parent independent of the relationship with the social worker. However, I would argue that they are also integral parts of the relationship with the social worker and his or her social work agency. For example, commitment and motivation appear to be judged by the parent's willingness to co-operate with the social work agency, willingness to accept concerns about themselves as laid out by the agency, and willingness to accept the assessment methods. Parents must provide explanations for their behaviour and situation that are plausible and insightful to the social worker. Such explanations may be linked with the parent's ability to be articulate. A parent who is articulate, plausible and co-operative possesses the attributes that lead to a successful and positive assessment relationship. I will now consider some of these characteristics attributed to parents in more depth.

Co-operation and motivation

Parents who are viewed positively are willing to co-operate with what is acknowledged as being a difficult process for them. In the assessment of the Baker family, for example, the willingness of the family to accept all of the demands of the local authority, such as supervised contact sessions and the father living away from the home, was seen as important evidence that the family might be reunited:

> The plan is for rehabilitation. He's now in a hostel. They're working hard, sticking by everything, sticking by the contract. They've worked with us, right the way through. I was really sceptical in the beginning – looking at the injury – but they've been really committed, abiding by the rules. (Interview with social worker, Baker family assessment)

By way of contrast, other parents were seen to be unco-operative with the assessment. Some families withdrew from the assessment completely and others co-operated only partially; for example, by attending most contact sessions with their children, but missing assessment interviews. These families were seen as lacking the ability to prioritise the assessment.

> They've been attending the sessions with the children only ... She said there wasn't much point in coming if the children weren't there, which says something about her attitude to the assessment. (Interview with social worker, Lewis family assessment)

Handelman (1983) suggests that a co-operative service user signals that the bureaucracy's reasoning is valid and that the social worker is confirmed in her viewpoint that she is helping the client. However, the Coastal Cities social workers tended to argue that commitment to the assessment process equated commitment to their child. Some suggested that if a parent co-operated with an assessment, then they would be more likely to co-operate with future interventions and monitoring by social workers.

A further element of co-operation is the willingness to accept the concerns expressed by the social services department. Parents are expected to accept responsibility for the risk they pose to their child and to accept social work explanations of that risk. A parent who accepts responsibility in this way is often attributed with having insight. By way of contrast, the mother under discussion below was seen to be lacking insight due to her lack of acceptance of the concerns presented by the local authority.

> There was just sort of no real insight or acceptance of the concerns that were presented. Her replies were often characterised by sort of deflection, objection, denial. And now that is fine to a point if you can move people on and say, 'Let's not look at your situation, let's look at another situation', but she couldn't even make that leap really, so she had little insight into the concerns, she didn't accept them. (Interview with social worker, Myers family assessment)

This social worker is here describing how he had tried to approach the discussion in another way by asking the woman if she would be concerned about another person who was acting in the way she had done. But, according to him, she was unable to make any connection with her own situation.

Plausibility and shared values

In the Coastal Cities study, a further element was important. The parent was required not simply to co-operate and accept concerns, but to provide an adequate explanation to the social worker of how those concerns arose and to show contrition for past acts. Such interactions can take on a nature that is almost confessional, with the worker rewarded for their sensitive questioning through disclosures made by the parent of feelings of shame or with the parent changing their story to acceptance and explanation of their wrong-doing. On the other hand, explanations were inadequate if they were made implausible due to inconsistencies and denials. The ability or otherwise of the parent to provide a plausible explanation of their behaviour or family situation appears to play a central role in the process and outcome of the assessment. As will be discussed below, a merging of the social worker's own explanation and that of the parent appears to be a necessary precursor for the reunification of families.

To summarise, according to the accounts of some social workers, a parent who is co-operative with the assessment methods and accepts agency concerns possesses the attributes that contribute positively to the assessment relationship. He or she is also someone who provides a plausible explanation for the concerns and who is able to demonstrate contrition where appropriate. A further element that may be seen to follow on from the above is that of parental articulacy.

> It's still looking fairly optimistic. He is able to describe the boys and I can see them there, he describes them well. He's quite articulate. (Interview with social worker, Cross family assessment)

> He demonstrates insight into the child's needs. He can put himself into the child's position. I think that's a prerequisite, to be able to empathise. For many of the parents we work with that's a problem. His values and attitudes I identify with, they seem appropriate. He doesn't say unrealistic or dubious things about his parenting. (Interview with social worker, Moore family assessment)

Whilst there is no suggestion that the decisions to return the children to Mr Cross and Mr Moore in these cases were related to their articulacy alone, there is the possibility that a parent who is articulate will be better able to perform well in an assessment that is strongly based on verbal statements. This is perhaps seen even more clearly with parents who are less articulate. Many of the other relationship attributes listed above, such as co-operation, motivation and the ability to explain in a plausible manner, might be more easily discerned in an articulate parent. It is possible to distinguish a few assessments where the parents' lack of ability to express themselves well becomes a key theme in the assessment process. These 'inarticulate' parents might also be described as 'passive'.

Passivity and aggression

The passive parent in the Coastal Cities assessments was always a woman. It is possible that men who were not able to respond articulately to the assessment process responded in a different way, for example, by not attending sessions or by being aggressive. The passive parent was seen as co-operative, but only superficially so and gave short answers to questions, such as 'Yes', 'No', 'I don't know'. As discussed above, many assessments are both verbal and intensive and one of the social worker's key aims is to elicit detailed, 'confessional'-style statements from the parent. If the parent does not provide verbal responses, then the social worker is disarmed and frustrated. A parent who is passive and inarticulate is seen as lacking insight. Also, she is not providing the expected emotional response to the real or threatened removal of her child from her care. The social worker cannot identify with her or find any point of connection. Unlike with some of the parents discussed above, the social worker does not perceive any shared values on which to base their discussions. Ms James was one of the 'passive' parents:

> Ms James presents as a passive young woman, expressing little change in her emotions. Engaging with her has been difficult, not only due to her missed appointments, but her

personality is such that she does not initiate and maintain conversation. However, once given the attention, she can appear co-operative, she holds no strong views or opinions on matters relating to her life circumstances. Factors of her background, her motivations, the concerns she has, or her plans for the future are not known. (Extract from assessment report, James family assessment)

The two social workers assessing Ms James expressed their frustration at their inability to elicit any information which might be seen to form a plausible explanation for why Ms James had silently witnessed her partner severely injuring her baby over a period of time. In the case of Ms Cooke, a mother of four and accused of neglect, again she was unable to provide a plausible explanation for her situation. Her social worker expressed his frustration at being unable to induce an emotional response from her.

I find it very difficult that she's not angry. When people are angry I find it easier, well not easier, but there's something to hold on to. I find her very passive, that's difficult. (Interview with social worker, Cooke family assessment)

Social workers conducting core assessments, particularly where there are child protection concerns, are often faced with trying to engage and work with parents and other family members who are unwilling to be assessed. This might result in refusal to participate at all, or in a parent taking part on what feels like a superficial level. As will be discussed in the next section, there is a tendency in social work to expect engagement and involvement by mothers, but involvement by fathers is not always seen as a central necessity. It is possible that some reluctant mothers do take part in assessments because they feel that they have no other option, but they are unwilling to take part in all methods and topics of the assessment. 'Passivity' may also be related to learning disability and it might be argued that an assessment that relies heavily on verbal questioning may well discriminate against those who are less articulate. It is also possible that many of the women being worked with in in-depth child welfare assessments may be experiencing clinical depression. This may have a severe impact on their self-esteem and ability to engage with the worker, and the assessor will need considerable sensitivity to form a positive working relationship with these women (Sheppard, 2002).

Gender and the Assessment Relationship

The pressure on women to bear the responsibility for child protection assessments has been noted in the social work literature (Farmer and Owen, 1995; O'Hagan and Dillenberger, 1995; Davies and Krane, 1996). It is not uncommon to come across assessment reports where fathers or father figures appear to have been barely consulted. This is particularly the case where the father is living outside of the home. This tendency may be related to several factors, including the general tendency of society to assume that parenting is women's work, because women have been historically easier to engage with, because men are seen as having little to contribute, or because men are seen as potential threats. This last point is not an inconsiderable one in cases where there are child protection concerns. In such cases there are high levels of domestic violence (in the Coastal Cities study there were current or historic concerns of domestic violence in more than half of the families). Men are also often reluctant to take part in interviews and interventions relating to child welfare and parenting, seeing both the staff and venues as women's spaces (Ghate et al., 2000).

In Scourfield's (2003) study of the attitudes of social workers' constructions of men in child protection work, he found that men were seen in the following ways:

- men as a threat;
- men as no use;
- men as absent;
- men as irrelevant;
- men as no different from women; or
- men as better than women.

Men are often seen as threatening to social workers, to children and particularly to their women partners. They are also often viewed as being of no use, either as carers or as clients. Perhaps because they are so little involved in everyday family life, they are seen as providing little information or insight to the assessment process. Men are often absent from the social worker's gaze, because they absent themselves when the social worker visits, or because they are with a new partner or are in prison. Social workers, who are stretched in terms of time, often will not involve men who do not hold legal parental responsibility for the child. Men are therefore sometimes seen as irrelevant, both to their children and to social work intervention. Scourfield did observe some less negative constructions of men in child protection work, although this was usually in the context of a mother who was seen to be failing. For example, in some cases, men were seen as no worse than the woman in a family or, on occasion, as performing better than a mother.

Social workers build up much more experience of working with women than with men. It has been noted that child and family social work is an overwhelmingly female task, with (mainly) female social workers working with (mainly) female clients (Hallett, 1989b). Family assessments are often, in effect, an assessment of *mothering* (Parton et al., 1997; Scourfield, 2003). The mother's co-operation, then, can become a central feature of an assessment, especially when co-operation is not forthcoming or when she is seen to contribute at only a minimalist level. The *Framework for the Assessment of Children in Need and their Families* (Department of Health, 2000a) has been criticised for not putting enough emphasis on the engagement and role of fathers (Featherstone, 2001).

Where men are known or thought to be violent, there can be an element of fear on the part of the social worker. In such cases, two social workers often assess together, in an agency building equipped with panic alarms. Whilst it is vital that practitioners prioritise their personal safety, many men (and women) will feel defensive and/or threatened by such an environment. It may be helpful to co-work with a practitioner trusted by the service user, such as a probation officer or health professional, particularly in early sessions where the terms of working are agreed. Both men and women may feel concerned about what is written about them, and making arrangements to spend time during each meeting to review progress and share records may help build trust. In my experience, a 'straight-talking', overtly honest approach can help to engage aggressive or suspicious parents.

The Relationship Between the Assessment Relationship and Assessment Outcome

Several empirical studies have highlighted users' attitudes towards the assessment process, or to the assessing professionals, as playing an important role in social work decision-making (Handelman, 1983; Waterhouse and Carnie, 1992; Fernandez, 1996). Two quantitative studies in North America found significant relationships between maternal non-compliance in the assessment process and decisions not to return children home (Jellinek et al., 1992; Atkinson and Butler, 1996). However, both studies demonstrate that some 'complying' clients do not have their children rehabilitated and vice versa. In reviewing the individual cases in the Coastal Cities study, a similar pattern can be discerned. Parental co-operation, the key aspect of relationship as found in the studies above, was used to divide the assessments into categories. An additional aspect, the social worker's opinion of the overall assessment relationship, was included as a further indicator. This led to the assessments being broadly grouped into four categories:

1 The parent co-operates and the social worker speaks about the assessment relationship in broadly positive terms.
2 The co-operation is variable and the social worker makes mixed comments about the assessment relationship.
3 The parent co-operates, at least superficially, but where the social worker is unhappy with the overall quality of the relationship. These are the 'passive' parents as described above.
4 There is no co-operation and no effective working relationship. These cases are marked by aggression and sometimes violence on the part of the parent.

The social worker did not recommend the rehabilitation of the children home to their parents in any of the last three categories. In most of the cases in the first category, the recommendation was for a reunification between parents and children (or in two of the cases that the child should continue to be cared for at home). In this small study, then, co-operating and possessing other positive relationship attributes appear to have had rewarding outcomes for the parents under assessment. However, this explanation is not complete as it does not explain the few cases where the parent co-operated and the social worker rated the relationship positively, but the recommendation, nonetheless, was that the child or children should not be cared for by that parent. These latter cases had a specific element of verbal interaction in common with those from the other three categories. This was that the parents were either unable to offer any explanation for the concerns about them or that the explanation they gave appeared implausible. *The ability to provide a plausible explanation* emerged as one of the most important factors in the analysis of positive parent attributes. In those cases where the parent co-operated and where most of the other relationship attributes were positive, one element was still missing: that was, the lack of an explanation agreed between social worker and parent to satisfactorily cover the concerns about the family situation.

Bull and Shaw (1992) write about the causal explanations social workers might use in re-telling their work in a variety of settings, calling these 'causal accounts'. Taking the standpoint that it is through language that much of social reality is constructed, they suggest that recounting an event serves to provide it with a conclusion through the selection of incidents in the re-telling. Whilst Bull and Shaw in this instance only refer to social workers providing such causal accounts in the context of interactions with other professionals, it is possible to suggest that social workers are engaged in a similar process with the parents they are assessing. They are developing a causal account of how and why each family situation arose.

The social workers will have derived some explanation before the start of the assessment from a variety of sources: personal experience, practice experience, the information contained in referrals and theory. Parents, too, will probably begin the assessment with their own explanation of their situation. A parent who is able to provide a plausible, alternative causal account might be able to persuade the social worker to adapt or broaden their own account.

Handelman (1983), in his analysis of child protection work in Newfoundland, links service user co-operation with causal accounts. He suggests that if there is user opposition to social work intervention, then workers will respond by imposing their understanding of the case with coercion, but that where a user is co-operative, the social worker will comply with his or her viewpoint. Whilst, in the Coastal Cities research, to suggest that workers *complied* with parents would be to over-state the case, it seems that social workers were more willing to adapt their causal explanations if parents were co-operative. Whether the parent simply accedes to the social workers' causal explanation or is able to provide a persuasive alternative, one element appears clear: in order for an assessment relationship to be judged successful and for a recommendation to be made for family reunification, social worker and parent must share a common understanding or causal account of the family situation.

Here is an example from the Coastal Cities study. Rather unusually, a single father is being assessed by a male social worker. In the following extract from the transcription of an assessment session, the social worker and parent have been discussing the parent's understanding of the social services intervention. The social worker has commented on how the parent has moved his opinion from one in which he bore none of the blame for the children's neglect, to one where he agreed that he should share the blame with his ex-partner. He was able to provide an explanation, that the social worker found plausible, for how he had failed to understand the harm being done to the children at the time, whilst expressing contrition for that failure.

Social worker:	Yeah, but it sounds to me like you have clearly thought a lot about the events leading up to the removal of the children and, like you said last week, it's a really sad time but, also like you said last week, you can understand it, it's a time to make a new start …
Parent:	Since they've been removed, like, things have been put into perspective, haven't they? Things have been grouped out or whatever, haven't they? For want of a better word, like. So we've been made aware of difficult areas, like, you know. Because, before, it was all like one big problem, like [draws in air], but now it's been broken down like [draws on table]. So we've been able to tackle or to look at the difficult areas, sort of separately like, you know, which has been useful like and we've sort of worked on those areas.
Social worker:	Good.
Parent:	… Because, I mean, the situation now is far better than it was, obviously we don't have the babies, or …
Social worker:	Sure, sure.
Parent:	They're where they are, but the overall situation is far better apart from the fact that they're not home, like, and [pause], yeah, we're working on some areas. (Assessment interview, Cross family assessment)

The parent shows that he accepts the agency's explanation that removal of the children was a necessary precursor to any improvement in the situation. Interestingly, he is seen here to have adopted phrases usually associated with social workers, such as 'working on' and 'look at the difficult areas'. He and the social worker have reached a stage of the assessment in which they share a causal account for the family situation. The social worker subsequently recommended a return of the children to their father.

Conclusion

It has been noted in this chapter that social work assessments tend to be verbally based and often centre on parents' performance in interview. In the Coastal Cities study, one of the main areas of evidence cited by social workers was the way that parents responded to the social worker–parent relationship. Co-operation, a positive relationship, articulacy and an agreed plausible explanation for the family situation were all important factors in determining whether a recommendation for family re-unification was made.

Social workers might be seen to be carrying out a necessary part of a comprehensive assessment when differentiating between parents who are co-operative, motivated, insightful and able to explain their situation, and those who are not. Practice and lay wisdom suggest that the return of children to the former group is likely to be a safer option than to the latter. However, it seems necessary to sound a few notes of caution. Many of the areas mentioned above, particularly the ability to give a plausible account and to appear insightful, are likely to come more easily to the articulate. As was seen, some of the inarticulate are labelled 'passive'. Some might argue that articulacy itself might be a plausible ground for assessing parenting, particularly if that person's response to an inability to express themselves tends to result in violence. On the other hand, it is possible that an over-emphasis on verbal skills might be a less than fair attempt to assess the parenting skills of those who are not so verbally proficient, particularly those with learning disabilities. In the Coastal Cities study, all of the parents labelled 'passive' were women. The pressure on women to bear the responsibility for child protection assessments has been noted in this chapter. In the setting of an assessment, 'passivity' might be seen as a response to such pressures, a form of resistance or a function of learning disability. These possibilities could be explored with a service user and alternative methods of assessment might be considered.

Additionally, the ability of parents to express themselves verbally will also be linked to the quality of the developing relationship between social worker and parent. It requires a reflexive practitioner to analyse and maintain an awareness of the contributions of both the parent and the social worker to the forming of this relationship. Careful attention must be paid to areas such as cultural background, gender, organisational culture and the practitioner's own social skills in order to provide an environment in which a parent may express himself or herself freely in the manner expected. If the assessment relationship is not developing well, and resources allow, then consideration could be given to allocating a different social worker to the assessment. It is sometimes too simplistic to assume that an unco-operative service user lacks motivation in regard to his or her children.

It is also possible that those parents who succeed in the assessments (that is, they have their children returned to them) are those who have adapted their behaviour to conform to the expectations of the assessing social worker and their agency. It was noted in the last extract from the empirical data above that Mr Cross was using some speech that was similar to that of social workers. Howe writes that:

> Today's emphasis demands that actors change their acts, not by curing faulty minds but by showing obedience ... The disobedient are required simply to conform. The individual's social performance is all that matters. (1994: 527)

It might be suggested that, especially in an in-depth assessment, it is particularly important for parents to conform verbally, due to the verbal emphasis of these assessments. It seems likely that a parent who conforms to these expectations will be more likely to form a positive relationship with the social worker. And, as has been suggested above, it is this relationship that appears to be central to the outcome.

It might therefore be suggested that those conducting in-depth assessments should avoid any tendency to *over*-rely on verbal interactions between adults when making decisions about children's futures. Whilst the verbal presentation of the parent will be important, a balance with other aspects of assessment should be maintained. This should include a systematic, reflexive analysis of both the information gathered and the processes of assessment themselves, careful observation, and a greater role for the child's needs and perspective. It is this last aspect that is explored in the next chapter.

Suggestions for practice

1   Practitioners should aim to be reflexive about the impact of themselves (including gender, age, culture, class, education, disability/ability, agency culture, belief systems and legal powers) on the assessment relationship.
2   Practitioners should consider, at the planning stage, the likely issues that might impact on their ability to respond and relate to those to be assessed (see Chapter 9 on conducting a 'cultural review').
3   Consideration could be given to a new social worker joining or taking over the assessment if the assessment relationship is faltering.
4   Co-working with someone of the opposite sex or a different age or cultural back-ground might maximise the possibility of engagement with a range of family members. Co-working with a person from a different agency, who is trusted by the service user, may also help the assessment relationship.
5   Those being assessed should be able to express themselves in the language in which they are most comfortable.
6   Assessments that rely too heavily on interviewing should be avoided where the service user has difficulty expressing herself or himself verbally.
7   Parental attitudes to the assessment process are not as important as their attitudes to their children. Children's experiences should remain the focus of the assessment.

Note

1 In this book the terms 'reflection' and 'reflective practice' are used to imply critical thoughtfulness about practice experiences both during and after practice events. 'Reflexivity' is used to imply a more fundamental examination of the discourses and knowledge systems that underpin interactions in social care (Taylor and White, 2000).

6　Children in Assessments

Chapter summary

This chapter examines how children are assessed and enabled to participate in assessments. Findings from the Coastal Cities study and other research suggest that children are often marginalised in decision-making. The chapter explores how children are represented in assessment reports. The way in which child development is portrayed is discussed through the example of attachment behaviour and theory. The chapter summarises positive practice with children along the themes of listening to children, encouraging participation and representing children.

In the previous chapter it was seen that there has been a tendency in assessments to concentrate on the adults in the family. This has been encouraged by the concentration on the interviewing of parents, where their verbal performance, especially their ability to provide a plausible explanation for their family problems, has been important to the outcome of the assessment. Such interviews are necessary, of course. One of the most important tasks of assessment is to listen to participants' accounts of their situation and their thoughts about their futures. However, an over-concentration on the adults can lead to the exclusion or marginalisation of children. This might be viewed as ironic, considering the usual assumption that child and family social work is 'child centred'.

Fernandez (1996) suggests that phrases such as 'child-centred', 'the child's needs', 'risk to the child' and 'in the best interests of child' are often simply rhetoric in social work talk. She argues that they are used as if they are universally understood terms, without any analysis of who decides the meanings of such phrases for an individual child. In this chapter it is argued that, in spite of a tendency for social work rhetoric to claim that children are at the centre of the work, there remains a tendency for children to be represented as objects rather than as subjects and for only partial aspects of their lives to be reported. Some older children are given a voice and their views are sometimes directly reported. In this chapter it is seen how some children are represented in assessments, both in the Coastal Cities study and in research findings from a range of other studies. The second half of the chapter draws together current practice ideas on how to include meaningfully children's perspectives in assessment work.

Children and Participation

Over the last decade or two there have been some broad changes in how we view children in society. For example, a sociology of childhood has emerged that has challenged our understandings and representations of childhood (Alanen, 1994; Corsaro, 1997; James et al., 1998). 'Childhood' is not a universal, unchanging phenomenon. The need to listen to children's subjective experiences has been acknowledged (James et al., 1998) in the recognition that much of what we 'know' about children has been found out by measuring them and observing them from a distance (Stainton Rogers and Stainton Rogers, 1992). A range of new social theories relating to childhood view children as 'being' rather than 'becoming' (adults) (James et al., 1998). Children are therefore social actors with rights regarding their participation in society.

A large programme of research commissioned by the Economic and Social Research Council in the UK between 1996 and 2000, the 5–16 Programme, has increased our knowledge both of children's views and on methods of consulting children. The wide-ranging studies have highlighted issues such as the increasing diversity of children's lives, their increasing sense of self and their need and wish to be involved in decision-making at a range of levels.[1]

Children's rights to be involved and represented in decision-making have begun to be established in law and practice in recent years (Franklin, 1995, writes that as late as the mid-1980s the idea was ridiculed in many mainstream organisations). The United Nations Convention on the Rights of the Child declared that:

> [The child shall have] an opportunity to be heard in any judicial or administrative proceedings affecting the child, either directly or through a representative or an appropriate body in a manner consistent with the procedural rules of national law. (1998: Article 12)

The Children Act 1989 was the first piece of legislation in England and Wales overtly to attempt to address the issue of children's rights (Lyon and Parton, 1995). The Act and the associated guidance included provision that children should be consulted during court proceedings and before reviews (according to age and understanding) and should be informed of decisions made about them. The 1989 Act includes a Welfare Checklist that must be considered before a decision is made about making a Care or Supervision Order. This includes 'the ascertainable wishes and feelings of the child concerned' S.1 (3) (a). However, although progress has been made, in practice there has been a reluctance to fully involve children and young people (Thomas, 2000). There has been a particular reluctance to allow them to be present in court or to have their views upheld when professionals have disagreed with those views (Lyon and Parton, 1995). The Assessment Framework (Department of Health, 2000a) gives children's voices a much more central place in assessment work.

Children's Voices in Assessments: the Coastal Cities Study

> The focus of comprehensive assessments I should say is the child, so it's about getting a picture of the world from the child's perspective: how safe is that child, what needs to

change, what are the indicators of concern for harm, etc., etc. (General interview with Laura, social worker)

As Fernandez (1996) has noted, much has been said in recent years about the central place of the child in family social work, and this is reflected in the quotation from Laura, a social worker. However, in most of the assessment reports in the Coastal Cities study, children were, in fact, minor characters in the narrative. Parents were often portrayed in an in-depth, lively manner and it is possible for the reader to develop a vivid image of the adults from the narrative. In general, the children were represented quite differently. They were described rather two-dimensionally, which tended to make them *objects* of the assessment rather than the *subjects*. Children were discussed most frequently in relation to their parents. For example, there were often detailed descriptions of their responses to parents in periods of formal family contact, but no description of the child in other environments such as their foster home, school or playing with friends. In the assessment of one family, the 25-page assessment report contained eight pages of detailed description and analysis of the mother, a single parent. The four children, whose ages ranged from ten years down to two, were portrayed in just over two pages in total. The two-year-old was described in just four sentences.

In many of the other assessments, especially where the children involved were under five, the assessment report often contained a fairly detailed description of how the children have performed in accordance to the Sheridan developmental charts contained within Department of Health guidance (1988, 2000b). This portrayal, which will be discussed in detail in the next section of this chapter, serves to emphasise a rather detached objectivity in relation to the children, which is not present in the lively, subjective, descriptions of adults in the assessment reports.

It was stated earlier in this chapter that, despite the increase in rhetoric regarding children's rights to participate in decision-making, there is evidence from social welfare research that children's views are still routinely absent in decision-making that concerns them directly. In the Coastal Cities study, it might be suggested that there was an ambivalent attitude from the social workers conducting comprehensive assessments towards the worth of children's opinions in contributing towards decision-making. In a few of the cases children's views were given some prominence in the assessments, but the weight given to these views varied. Most assessments regarding children aged nine and over tended to contain some record of the children's views (with the exception of the Cooke family assessment discussed above). Social workers appeared to find it very difficult to know what weight to put on children's opinions. In the following four extracts social workers report children giving their opinion about their situation:

Greg then brought over an envelope (sealed) carefully positioned on table and said that it was for me and that mother did not know what it said inside. I asked him to read it to me, not in mum's presence (initially). It appeared that Stacey [mother of the children] did not know – she said it took him three hours to type. The content was that both boys want to be with her and that she is 'not guilty'. The language used was exactly like Stacey's. I praised both boys. I was left with a feeling that Stacey could have typed this when they were out.

Nevertheless, the message was clear. (Case recording of home visit, 1997, from Smith family assessment case file)

It may be the case that Mrs Gray and Mr Gray [mother and stepfather of the children] have effected [*sic*.] the children' views; nevertheless, they are as expressed to me together with a wish to remain at home. I consider that Angela and Elizabeth's views should be accepted. (First assessment report, Marsh family assessment)

I have had various sessions with Paul on his own and with his family and he has remained consistent in his expressed wish to have Mr Taylor return home ... Paul presents as a very sensible child who I feel would not hesitate to voice any feelings of unease, etc. (Assessment report, Taylor family assessment)

Elizabeth presents as whimsical and materialistic and may not be impressed by the current accommodation and area, or another for long ... It is clear that Elizabeth has changed her mind about with whom and where she wishes to live on a number of occasions ... Elizabeth has demonstrated that she lives in a fantasy world and has indicated that her expectations of being with her family are of holidays, presents and outings. (Second assessment report, Marsh family assessment)

In the first two extracts the social worker discusses the possibility that the children may have been directly influenced by their parents to give a message to the social worker that they wish to stay with their parents. Indeed, with Greg Smith the question is raised as to whether his mother encouraged him to pass off a letter written by her as his own work. It has been noted that a fear of children being pressurised or influenced by adults has often been used as an argument to deny children the right to participate in decision-making (King and Piper, 1995). Nevertheless, for a social worker assessing a situation where children are already thought to have been subjected to harm by their carers, the possibility that a child will be subject to further pressures is an important consideration.

The latter two extracts highlight how children's views can be represented in different ways. In the second Marsh family assessment, Elizabeth is expressing a wish to live with her father, a carer judged unsuitable by social services. Elizabeth's character is described in such a way as to imply that her opinion is less reliable than that of another child of a similar age. She is 'whimsical and materiaistic' and lives in a 'fantasy world'. This might be contrasted with the description of the similarly aged Paul Taylor above, who is described as a 'sensible boy'. Parton et al. (1997) have noted that children who do not fit the stereotype of innocent victim are not always regarded as victims of abuse. Similarly, here it is possible to see that some children's voices appear to be valued more than others. Whilst it is not possible, due to the small numbers involved in this aspect of the findings, to identify any characteristics of children portrayed as sensible or not sensible, it might be noted that the views of the 'sensible' Paul coincided with those of the assessor, whilst those of 'whimsical' Elizabeth did not. Social workers conducting in-depth assessments of children's situations face a difficult task of judgement when children's views do not appear rational or sensible to adults. It can be seen here that it is possible to make quite dramatic changes to the credibility of children's views through the choice of wording in assessment reports.

One assessment stands out from the others because of the vivid and direct manner in which the child is portrayed – the Johns/White family assessment.

Unusually for the assessments in this study, a relatively young child, six-year-old Paige Johns, is consulted in depth about her situation during play sessions. Three-and-a-half pages of the assessment report are devoted to detailed descriptions of Paige's life and perceptions. This is only a slightly shorter space than that written about each parent (in other reports the difference is usually much greater). Paige's relationships and activities at school and in her family foster placement are described. Her perceptions on her family situation are directly reported:

> Paige has talked at length about the baby expected in August, she is looking forward with enthusiasm to becoming a 'big sister'. Paige does, however, have fears regarding this child's birth, and these focus around her place in her mother's affections. She has stated that she hopes her mother will 'still love me' when the baby is born, and she has expressed her anxiety that her mother will 'look after the baby properly' … Paige has expressed very mixed feelings towards Mr White; she has told me that she 'wants to go home', but that she is scared when 'Mr White gets cross'. Another significant issue for Paige is her belief that both her mother and Mr White blame her for the events within the family. (Assessment report, Johns/White family assessment)

This report (from which this is a short extract) stands out from the others in the study because of the weight given to the child's perceptions. It is also unusual in that no attempt is made to place an opinion on whether the child's perceptions should be given credence or not.

Children in Assessments: UK and International Perspectives

It has been seen that in the Coastal Cities study, children were sometimes only minor characters in the assessment reports. This finding is shared by many other research studies into the workings of childcare social work in the UK and internationally. Scott (1998), in an Australian study of assessments involving child sexual abuse, found that little emphasis was placed on the meaning of the sexual abuse for the child. Assumptions tended to be made about the children's feelings regarding the abuse and the focus appeared to be on whether or not the case should be labelled as child abuse rather than the central question being 'How is the child?'. Egelund (1996), in a study of child protection work in Denmark, describes the involvement of children in decision-making as a 'lesser rule' for social workers (as distinct from a set of 'core rules'), whilst Kähkönen (1999: 594) describes children as 'invisible' in placement decisions in Finland. Thomas (2000), researching in Wales and England, found a wide variety of children's participation in review meetings about their care. Involvement ranged from some children being totally excluded, through some being invited to participate but without preparation or support, to some being full and active participants in the decision-making process. Whilst only 38 per cent of 8-year-olds were invited to all or part of a meeting, 85 per cent of 12-year-olds were. Masson and Oakley's (1999) study of the representation of children in British public law proceedings found that guardians *ad litem* were sensitive and skilled with children, but that children were still often distanced from the legal process.

Whilst the research findings cited here paint a rather gloomy picture of the involvement of children in decision-making in social work, it can be seen as positive that there has been attention paid to this area, both in research and in practice. Influenced by findings such as these, and the changes in perceptions brought about by the children's rights movement, legislative changes and the UN Convention, policymakers and practitioners have brought about important changes to social work practice involving children. It has become increasingly common to find accessible leaflets for children explaining the systems they have become involved with. There are many children's materials for use by social workers, including jigsaws, books and CD-ROMs, and children's rights in the welfare systems are being upheld by local and national ombudsmen, rights officers and commissioners. Later in this chapter some specific practice points regarding the involvement of children in assessment work are suggested.

Child Development

Having discussed the general portrayal of children in the assessments, including the way that children's opinions are represented, this section of the chapter considers the representation of children through the language of child development. One of the main ways in which children are represented in assessment reports is through their progress according to developmental charts, and this was the case in the Coastal Cities study. The reporting was usually aligned with Sheridan developmental charts, included in both previous and current assessment guidance in England and Wales (Sheridan, 1975, in Department of Health, 1988, 2000b). Several of the assessments, where the children were babies or toddlers, included descriptions like that of Arran Lewis below:

During the assessment period Arran has been observed to be developing at an age appropriate level of 12 months as outlined in the Sheridan developmental charts.

Posture and Large Movements – Arran sits well and for indefinite periods. He is able to pull himself to a standing position and has now started to walk unaided.

Vision and Fine Movements – Arran is able to pick up small objects with precise pincer grasp of thumb and index finger. He throws toys deliberately and watches them fall to the ground, whilst looking in the correct place for toys which roll out of sight.

Hearing and Speech – Arran knows and immediately turns to his own name and babbles loudly and incessantly and imitates adults' playful vocalisation with gleeful enthusiasm.

Social Behaviour and Play – Arran is able to drink from his bottle with little assistance and waves 'bye, bye' and claps hands in invitation or spontaneously and is able to put wooden cubes in and out of boxes. (Assessment report, Lewis family assessment)

It is undeniable that most children develop and grow and one important method of assessing children's general wellbeing is to judge whether they are growing and developing along expected 'norms' according to their age. The report into the death of Jasmine Beckford (London Borough of Brent, 1985) records how she physically grew during periods in foster care, and stopped growing or lost weight during periods spent at home. However, the domination of 'developmentalism' in social work, psychology and related professions has been strongly criticised in the last decade (Stainton Rogers and Stainton Rogers, 1992; Walkerdine, 1993; Burman, 1994; James et al., 1998). The roots of developmental psychology have been located with Darwin and evolutionary theories and became strongly established as a scientific field of study in the early part of the twentieth century (Stainton Rogers and Stainton Rogers, 1992). Theories of child development emerged which tended to be prescriptive, rational and universal in their assumptions. No variations according to culture and location are expected, and deviations from the norm are treated as problems (Burman, 1994). Indeed, White writes that:

> The tempo of biological changes have become normalized to the point where tiny deviations are rendered measurable and are imbued with significance. (1998b: 69)

Developmental psychology as a discipline risks being unfairly portrayed as rigid and uncritical, a picture that is out-dated and often based on second-hand readings of major theorists (Hobbs, 2002). However, attention to developmental norms can be seen as playing a major role in lay and applied professional understandings of childhood. It has been suggested that the dominance of developmental milestones leads to parents' and others' observations and images of children being organised and structured by developmental expectations (Burman, 1994). Walkerdine suggests that professionals *produce* the developing child by using:

> ... a calculating and classificatory gaze which, both in the provision of play and its classification, produced the very object it claimed to describe. (1993: 454)

In the Coastal Cities assessments, a child's development was reported in an unproblematic manner. Often, a detailed description of the child's development is given. Yet, in the way that Walkerdine describes, the use of the Sheridan developmental charts in the assessments of younger children provides the lens through which many of the children in these assessments are viewed and then portrayed. The descriptions of the children were often direct quotations from the Sheridan developmental charts. For example, the description of Arran Lewis quoted above was entirely structured and worded in this way. To take just one example:

> Hearing and Speech – Arran knows and immediately turns to his own name and babbles loudly and incessantly and imitates adults' playful vocalisation with gleeful enthusiasm. (Assessment report, Lewis family assessment)

This description of Arran on first glance appears highly personal and vivid. However, on looking at Sheridan's chart for a child of 12 months under the section 'Hearing and Speech', she writes:

> Knows and immediately turns to own name. Babbles loudly, tunefully and incessantly ... Imitates adults' playful vocalisations with gleeful enthusiasm. (Sheridan, 1975, in Department of Health 2000b: 25)

Arran appears to have been viewed according to how he fits with an assessment tool, rather than observing him closely, and then using an assessment tool to aid in the analysis of his behaviour and experiences.

In this chapter so far, three main ways of representing children in the assessments in the Coastal Cities research have been identified. It has been seen that some children are barely mentioned in the assessment report, with the result that they appear to be minor characters in the process. Some older children are directly represented in that their opinions are asked and recorded. The weight given to those opinions by social workers appears to vary. Some younger children are described in detail. Descriptions of children tend to be structured by developmental norms and assumptions. In the next section the representation of children's attachment behaviour is discussed.

Attachment Theory

Whilst it is not within the scope of this book to attempt to provide a discussion of the range of child development theories relevant to the assessment of children and their families (and this is done well elsewhere, for example, Daniel et al., 1999; Colton et al., 2001, Ch. 2), it is necessary to pay particular attention to attachment theory. Attachment theory is important first because it provides a framework for understanding the emotional development and behaviour of both children and adults being assessed, who may have experienced many losses, disruptions and unpredictable relationships. Second, it is important to discuss it here because of the theory's strong influence on practice and policy in child and family social work.

Drawing on the work of Bowlby, Ainsworth, Belsky and others, Howe et al. (1999) describe how our varying attachment experiences, starting from infancy, lead to us forming internal working models of our own self-worth and of our expectations of others' behaviour towards us. These internal working models may be confirmed or modified according to our experiences as we develop. Whilst this theory therefore is applicable to individuals throughout the lifespan, attachment theory has been particularly used to explain the behaviour and emotions of children. Patterns of attachment behaviour have been observed and mapped and Ainsworth and colleagues' (1978) typology of secure attachment behaviour and three types of insecure attachment (anxious avoidant, anxious resistant/ambivalent and disorganised disorientated) has been used as an assessment framework by many front-line practitioners.

As with all theories, we need to be thoughtful and critical about how we apply attachment theory. The potential problem with such an important concept is that it may be used to form powerful arguments about a child's needs and/or parenting capacity, but using a flawed or overly narrow evidence base. We therefore need to examine first the evidence base of the theory itself, and second the manner in which it is sometimes applied to analyse the relationship between children and their parents.

Howe (1996b and Howe et al., 1999) notes that theory based on the premise that the quality of our childhood relationships affects our ability to make and maintain relationships in adulthood appears well supported by clinical and empirical evidence. Others have criticised aspects of attachment theory and its application by practitioners. Burman (1994) has noted the rather contradictory nature of attachment theory. For example, she discusses how, in the typology of attachment associated with attachment theory (Ainsworth et al., 1978), the securely attached child explores his or her environment confidently. A 'clingy' child is seen as insecurely attached. Yet, in addition, the secure, exploring child is expected to protest when his or her mother leaves the room. In other words, 'Polar opposites of behaviour can ... be read as pathology' (White, 1996: 75). It has also been noted that attachment theory was originally developed by observing children in strange environments in the company of strange adults or by experimenting on caged rhesus monkeys (Burman, 1994).

Whilst valuable insights might be obtained from such methods, they do not provide a holistic picture of children's daily lives in natural environments. Attachment theory may also be criticised for its cultural bias (Robinson, 1998). The patterns of attachment commonly used to classify attachment behaviour (Ainsworth et al., 1978) were developed through observation of white North American infants. Numerous studies have found children from other cultures (including European) showing different forms of attachment behaviour (Rashid, 1996). Even amongst North American infants, only 65 per cent display behaviour labelled as secure attachment (Berk, 2002). Thus 35 per cent of children are seen to be living with less-than-ideal attachment relationships. It is therefore statistically not unusual to display insecure attachment behaviour, and one might question the rather pejorative language used to describe the behaviours of 35 per cent of the population. Despite these criticisms of attachment theory, it appears to be a useful framework for understanding the experiences, behaviour and attitude to relationships of children, young people and adults. There is no reason why it should not be applicable to most assessment work, as long as its potential for cultural bias is allowed for, it is not applied too rigidly to diagnose behaviour patterns and that observations are not too narrowly based. It is this last point that is discussed next, in relation to the Coastal Cities study.

Children's attachment to their parents was a strong theme in the Coastal Cities assessments. All of the assessment reports referred to this area, directly or indirectly. The following examples illustrate some of the ways in which attachment behaviour is described:

[Terry] is generally a happy and contented boy who is pleased to see his parents, but equally shows no distress at separation (apart from one occasion with his father) ... Arran, at the age of 13 months, although he recognises and responds to his parents, does not demonstrate a strong attachment to either parent, and this is concerning particularly in the light of Ms Lewis's primary carer status for the first seven months of his life. (Assessment report, Lewis family assessment)

She only waves to mum when parting. She'll show excitement when seeing Mr Reid, then just sort of just sits there in silence. It's hard to know whether it's a sign that they're not really a family or if she's missing mum. There's never a tear, never a cry. There's been a few times when they haven't shown up. The first time there was no reaction, the second time there was a sulky face for a minute, then nothing. (Interview with Hayley, social worker, Reid family assessment)

John's attachment to his father appears to be developing, e.g. John looks for him when he leaves the room, becoming upset occasionally. (Assessment report, Cross family assessment)

As can be seen, the first two examples are of families where it is implied that there are some difficulties with attachment. The last example illustrates a more positive description of attachment. In the first two extracts, the attachment descriptions serve the function of demonstrating the lack of primary significance of the parents to their children. In the case of both Arran and Terry Lewis, their lack of distress at parents leaving the room is highlighted. Similarly, in the Reid assessment, the four-year-old girl is described as sitting in silence after her father has arrived for contact (at this point her mother was out of the country). The social worker speculates on whether this means that 'they're not really a family'. Similarly, her lack of reaction to parents failing to arrive for contact is highlighted. In a similar line of argument, John Cross's distress at his father leaving the room is seen to be a sign of developing attachment.

The social workers here have carried out an important aspect of an assessment in that they have paid attention to the emotional bonds between parents and children and have closely observed the children's behaviour. However, I would argue that in these cases, only a partial aspect of the children's attachment behaviour has been observed. The children's responses to their parents when they arrive and leave contact sessions cannot be understood unless placed in the context of the children's behaviour elsewhere and other life experiences. It is much rarer to see descriptions of children's developing relationships with their foster carers, extended family, teachers and peers. Such information might lead to a more rounded understanding of the child's internal working model (Howe et al., 1999) of their expectations of relationships with others. Additionally, contact with parents, where children are living elsewhere, can be an emotionally charged and rather artificial situation in which to make judgements about relationships. All of the children mentioned in the quotations above were in foster care and some of them had been looked after by other primary carers for several months. The 13-month-old Arran Lewis had not lived with his mother for almost half of his life and had experienced changes of primary carer since being accommodated. It is perhaps unsurprising therefore that he did not display strong attachment behaviour towards his mother.

In the assessments in the Coastal Cities study, attachment behaviour appears to have been used as part of the decision-making process. The weight of scholarly opinion pointing to its usefulness in understanding the behaviour and emotions of family members would suggest that this is rightly so. However, I would argue that practitioners should approach attachment theory reflexively, given the potential for subjective and cultural bias in its application. Additionally, attachment theory, when used for assessment, risks being applied in a partial manner. As was stated earlier, it appears that social workers are, at times, looking at the child's attachment behaviour within a rather narrow arena, for example, by concentrating on children's behaviour when parting from their parents following contact sessions.

Assessing and Representing Children: Best Practice

The first point that may be noted when considering our practice in assessing children is that there is a considerable potential impact on family inter-relationships of intervening in this manner. When an outside adult wishes to speak to a child, the usual power balances of a family are overturned. O'Quigley (2000) notes that some children feel concerned about the undermining of their parents' authority implied when such professional involvement takes place. We are reminded yet again that assessment is an intervention, not a neutral act.

Over the years some foundations for good practice have been developed from a range of sources. First, individual practitioners have developed tools and methods of engaging children through practice experience of communicating with a wide range of children facing difficult experiences. Second, pressure groups, such as those comprising care-leavers (Voices from Care is one British example), have campaigned for, and themselves developed, accessible and age-appropriate information for children and young people. The voluntary agencies in particular have developed methods of advocacy and helping children to express their views. Third, methods developed in the therapeutic services, especially play therapy, can be used by practitioners for everyday communication with children (such as sand and water play, use of dolls, puppets and other figurative play). Finally, research with children has not only provided us with direct information from children themselves about the types of communication that they find most useful, it has also developed a wide range of methods of engaging children that are transferable to practice. Three main areas of practice are discussed next: informing children, listening to children and representing children.

Informing children

Children may be harbouring many fears about the implications of their participation in an assessment. It therefore appears important to provide attractive and accessible information for children on the meaning and implications of their involvement with assessment. Children and young people have become used to accessing high-quality, attractive information from television, the Internet and advertisers. There are many good examples of practice that have emerged in recent years. For example, the *Power Packs* produced for children involved in the court system (NSPCC, 2001), the video produced by the Family Rights Group for children and young people and their families involved in Family Group Conferences (Family Rights Group, 2001) and the UNICEF youth rights website are examples of different ways in which information can be produced for children and young people.

Listening to children

Many practitioners become skilled at communicating with children of various ages and abilities, using a range of communication methods. It seems important here to re-emphasise the individuality of children and the need for careful observation and relationship building before beginning to explore in-depth issues with children. Like adults, children of course have a range of interests and abilities, and some will express a strong preference for, or dislike of, imaginative play, drawing or written exercises. When using drawing it might be noted that pictures may be over-interpreted. Following a systematic review of the research evidence concerning the use of drawings in the assessment of children who have been maltreated, Veltman and Browne conclude that:

> The evidence ... appears relatively inconclusive as to the use of drawings for identification purposes in terms of possible maltreatment suffered ... However, it does appear that drawings have their use in terms of easing recall of important events ... as well as being a useful strategy in 'breaking the ice' between child and professional. (2000: 34)

There are some themes that emerge from several research studies of what most children are looking for in terms of communication skills in their social workers. These include confidentiality, non-judgementalism, honesty, accessibility, humour and listening to children's everyday concerns (Butler and Williamson, 1994; Thomas and O'Kane, 1998; O'Quigley, 2000). Here are some examples of children's views about social workers, the last two of which also emphasise the importance of continuity for children:

> They're nice, they try to help you, but they don't listen. They just do things to you. I would like them to listen to me a bit more (boy, 8). (Butler and Williamson, 1994: 93–4)

> The one I liked best I had for a long time. She got to know me and I got to know her. We understood each other (boy, 15). (Butler and Williamson, 1994: 97)

> I think they should like to have a talk with them and be really friendly to them and try to get to know them. I think after a while because they would know you and trust you, they would be able to say, 'Well, I have been hiding it for a long time, but I really don't want to live here'. (Thomas and O'Kane, 1998: 29)

Many textbooks and sources provide detailed and imaginative ideas for helping children to express their views and experiences (for example, Brandon et al., 1998; Clark and Moss, 2001; Colton et al., 2001), many of which derive from the experience of practitioners and therapeutic services with children. There is not enough space in this book to provide discussion at that level of detail. However, it is interesting to note that a growing range of methods are being developed in research into children's lives that are potentially useful for practitioners. Some of those researchers may in turn have developed ideas that had proven useful to them in their previous roles as practitioners (Thomas and O'Kane, 2000). Researchers (who often have more time and space to think these things through than front-line practitioners) have used methods such as statement sorting, topic cards, group discussions, 'pots and beans' and advice giving to others, to enable children to express themselves (Hill, 1997; Sinclair, 1998; Thomas et al., 1999). The last reference listed here is a resource and training pack for practitioners aimed at providing them with the means to enable children to participate in meetings and express their views.

Clark and Moss (2001) outline how they used a 'mosaic approach' when researching with nursery school children. They explored the experiences and perspectives of the children by bringing together information from a range of sources and co-constructing understandings of the children's experiences with the children and adults. Methods included short interviews with children and adults, observation of the child, and mapping the child's view of the nursery through their own photography and child-led tours. A further perspective on pre-verbal children's lives was gained from their siblings' insights. The focus is not on gaining any one 'truth' but on exploring the meanings that the child ascribes to aspects of their life. Such methods might aid a practitioner in ensuring that even young children's perspectives of their situation might be included in an assessment.

It has been noted that disabled children are often excluded from decision-making (Westcott and Cross, 1996). Principles of communicating with disabled children are foremost the same as those for communicating with any child, including the need to learn about the individual child's skills, interests and preferred play and other communication means. All children, but perhaps particularly disabled children, often lack choices in their everyday life (Westcott and Cross, 1996) and it is advisable therefore to consult them directly about how they would like to be communicated with, where, with whom and when. Disabled children's ability to express a view can be underestimated by those who value only verbal or other conventional means of expression. Russell (1998) cites both research projects and consultation activities by practitioners that have used multi-media means, including drama, video and photography, to allow disabled children to express themselves. An eclectic approach increases the possibility that each individual will find an appropriate means of expression. She comments that even the children's parents can be surprised and delighted to find that their children are able to express their opinions in such ways.

Representing children

The *Framework for the Assessment of Children in Need and their Families* (Department of Health, 2000a, 2000b) in England and Wales provides some useful information on the principles of good practice for communicating with children (see pp. 45–7 of the Framework and pp. 8–9 of the *Practice Guidance*). There is also, built into the recording proforma, space for young people to record their views. This has the advantage of them being able to express their views directly, without the social worker editing and choosing from the discussions (which will also happen, for the social worker's section of the report). In typical assessment reports the social worker has been in control of reporting the child's view and, even if direct speech is reported, this could potentially be highly selective. With the Assessment Framework, there is the potential for young people to choose for themselves the wording and selection of their views. They could possibly even contradict the social worker and their parents' or carers' views. However, it must be remembered that the power of producing the assessment report is in the social worker's hands and it is possible that the young person may edit what they say according to what they think the social worker and other adults want to hear. Also, the social worker and or parents/carers could pre-empt the content of the children's views by the questions they ask or by giving advice as to the sorts of thing they might want to record there. It should be noted that children's voices are curbed further in that there is no space for the direct recording of children's views in the core assessment record of those under the age of 10. Even very young children are often able to communicate wishes and feelings (Alderson, 2000). Schofield and Thoburn note that:

> ... children can express 'wishes and feelings' about all aspects of their life at a much earlier age than they can 'form a view' in a more formal sense about legal opinions ... there is no age and stage limit to participation. (1996: 12)

In all of the core assessment recording forms, there is a space for 'Parents/Carers comments on the assessment' but none for the child or young person's comments, even for those aged 15 and over. In contrast, within the brief initial assessment pro-forma there is a space for the child/young person and parents/carers views on the reasons for the assessment, for all age-groups (there is one pro-forma for all).

Despite the inclusion of principles of practice in communicating with children, there is no formal guidance in the Assessment Framework on how then to *represent* those children's views. There will be more discussion of the principles of reporting assessment findings in general in Chapter 9, but from the Coastal Cities research it is possible to draw the following conclusions about representing children in particular. A two-dimensional picture is more likely to emerge if children are viewed only according to how they fit with checklists, such as developmental milestones. Portraying a child's whole world, including friendships, activities and interests, may promote a more holistic picture. These areas are often of more pressing concern to children than some of the longer-term concerns of adults (Thomas, 2000). Representing children's views is a difficult area. As has been seen in research findings (O'Quigley, 2000) children are concerned about confidentiality, loyalty and the consequences for their parents of expressing a view. Social workers who both provide children with their own spaces to record their views (through any medium, including audiotape, writing, drawing, diary keeping) and agree in advance with children what they will themselves write about the children's wishes and feelings may help with some of those fears. It must be remembered that children's wishes may change as circumstances change or after they have had the chance to experience a new living situation or contact arrangement.

Conclusion

At times the discussion about the role of children in assessment work presents a rather polarised argument. On the one hand there is the argument that children have the right to have their voices heard and to take an active role in decisions being made about their own lives. They should be regarded using a competence model of what they *can* do rather than a deficit model that highlights what children *cannot* do. On the other hand, a child's welfare perspective might emphasise the need for children to be protected from harm and from the burden of making decisions. However, as Schofield and Thoburn (1996) have argued, such perspectives need not be in opposition to each other. Children themselves often take a balanced view on the issue, with many suggesting that they wish to have their opinions listened to, but that they do not want to be responsible for a final decision about difficult issues such as where they should live (O'Quigley, 2000). Schofield and Thoburn (1996) note that, when individual cases are looked at, it can be seen that each of a range of options might meet some, but not all, of a child's needs and fulfil some, but not all, of his or her wishes.

Whilst a few children will not wish to take part in decision-making at all (O'Quigley, 2000), most want their opinions to be heard and acted on, where possible. However, in the Coastal Cities research it could be seen that children were often marginalised or minimalised in the assessment reports. Hall et al. (1997: 182) suggest that voices are silenced in social work narratives in the following ways:

- by not reporting the voices when recounting stories about them;
- by objectifying them;
- by presupposing what they might say rather than letting them speak; or
- by presenting the voices as subjective, biased or untrustworthy.

All of those processes can be seen to be operating in relation to the children in the assessments. Some children's voices are not reported and the description of children through developmental norms might be seen to be objectifying them. The children's wishes were often presupposed rather than discovered through asking or reporting children's opinions. And, in some cases, children's views were reported as being untrustworthy. Therefore in the Coastal Cities reports and, it seems, in social work practice internationally (Egelund, 1996; Scott, 1998; Kähkönen, 1999), we come to know partial aspects of these children's lives, and these revealed aspects are those that are mediated through adult perspectives and actions.

Fortunately for practitioners our knowledge and awareness of such issues are increasing through research into what children themselves say about their role in assessments and through gradually improving practice and policy guidance. Hopefully future research studies will find that children are playing a clearer and stronger role in assessments of their and their families' lives.

Suggestions for practice

Pages 80 to 84 contain detailed suggestions for practice in relation to involving and representing children in assessments. These may be briefly summarised as:

- Children should have access to clear information about the assessment process and its implications, in addition to verbal information.
- Children should be consulted about assessment methods.
- Children's preferences for expressing themselves verbally, through, play, art or writing will vary enormously. Relationship-building in order to become familiar with a child's individuality is important.

- Children report that they are looking for honesty, reliability and assurances about confidentiality in a social worker.
- Pre-school children's participation can also be encouraged using a 'mosaic' approach (Clark and Moss, 2001).
- When portraying children's lives it is important to give a holistic picture including experiences in school, relationships with peers, siblings and extended family and individual character.
- Children may be given the space to express their views directly, or be consulted at an early stage about how their views will be represented.
- All of the above applies equally to children of all abilities, including disabled children.

Note

1 Details of the research programme can be found at http://www.hull.ac.uk/children5 to16programme.

7 Assessing Parents: Parenting Skills and Parental Relationships

Chapter summary

This chapter explores several aspects of assessing parenting. It is seen that current research into parenting in the general population suggests that beliefs and behaviours are diverse and likely to change with time. Additionally, behaviours that are of concern to social workers, such as severe physical punishment, appear to be carried out by a significant minority of the population (Nobes and Smith, 1997). Social workers therefore do not have any firm guidelines of parenting behaviour that is acceptable. Instead, the focus is on the needs of children.

In examining how social workers assess parenting in the Coastal Cities teams, it is seen that direct parenting behaviours are observed in detail but that this is rarely a deciding factor in assessment conclusions. Parental lifestyles and co-operation with the assessment process are more important. Coastal Cities workers' approaches to assessing parental relationships are considered, particularly where there is domestic violence.

Assessing levels of competency in parenting is a tremendously complex, but vital, element of in-depth assessment in child welfare. This chapter will explore how social workers attempt to gauge adequacy in parenting during assessments. Social workers see parental 'lifestyle' issues as central to the experience for children of family life. This chapter also examines the assessment of parental relationships and domestic violence. The discussion covers two broad areas. First, there is discussion of some general concepts and research findings regarding parenting. Second, the chapter explores how social workers assessed parenting behaviour in the Coastal Cities study. This includes discussion of parental relationships in general and domestic violence in particular.

Parenting Norms

In order to develop an idea of whether parents under assessment are reaching a standard of parenting that is seen as adequate, or in Winnicott's famous (1965) phrase, 'good enough', then it is essential that we reach some understanding of norms of parenting amongst contemporary cultures. Observations of parents have been carried out over last century, particularly of mothers and babies, concentrating on child development and the parent–child relationship (Smith, 2001). Recent studies have often highlighted family members' own views about parenting and family life. For example, a study of children aged 8–16 who had experienced the divorce of their parents found that children, on the whole, hoped for a 'democratic family'. This would be one where children are both cared for and loved *and* given respect and the chance to make some of their own decisions (Neale, 2001). Sidebottom's (2001) qualitative interviews with parents (mainly mothers) of eight-year-olds in the Avon area explored the impact of contemporary culture on parenting. The parents reported stress arising from balancing work and home, commercial pressures to buy goods and entertainment for their children, difficulties when single or not supported by a partner, and the expectation that their children be engaged in a range of activities. Whilst the parents were positive about their children, they found parenting to be a difficult task.

Studies in the UK have been carried out by Marjorie Smith and colleagues from the Thomas Corum Research Unit into the extent and range of parental behaviours in the general population. Nobes and Smith's (1997) study of the physical punishment of children by parents was the first of its kind to interview *both* parents and therefore to be able to provide a picture of the total amount of punishment received by their children. A study of 99 two-parent families in England found that physical punishment in these families was almost universal, with only one child in the sample having never received any physical punishment. Younger children were more likely to be hit or smacked than older children, with 52 per cent of one-year-olds and 11 per cent of eleven-year-olds smacked or hit at least weekly (1997: 276), and 21 per cent of both mothers and fathers had inflicted punishments rated by the researchers as 'severe' (1997: 277). Whilst the rate of physical punishment of children in England appears to have decreased in the last 30 years (Newson and Newson, 1989), the physical punishment of children is still very common. Research by Thompson et al. (2002) of 67 mothers in the New Forest area of England reported diverse behaviour management tactics. Behavioural problems amongst children were reported no more frequently by mothers who use physical punishment than by those who use reasoning (although the authors acknowledge that the children's emotional experiences may differ). A further study by Smith and Grocke of family sexuality and children's sexual knowledge found a wide range of acceptable behaviours and topics of discussion within families. Levels of acceptability were related to the children's age, social class and, to a lesser extent, gender (Department of Health, 1995a).

Whilst most of the studies cited above have taken care to gain a socially stratified sample, they are mainly (although not wholly) studies of parenting by the majority white culture in the UK. Studies of parenting by ethnic minority families in the UK are rarer. Dosnajh and Ghuman's (1998) research with Punjabi parents in the UK emphasises the dynamic nature of migrant cultures in the UK. Singh (1997) emphasises the need to assess Asian parenting in a manner that is relevant and acknowledges particular strengths of aspects of Asian cultures. It appears that any assessment of ethnic minority parents in a Western nation should acknowledge the individual nature of their relationship with the cultures of their parents and also with the dominant white cultures and avoid trite generalisations. Many aspects of parenting cultures are likely to be specific to nations, religions, localities and generations. Birchall and Hallett (1995) found that their study of UK practitioners' perceptions of abusive parenting differed from the perceptions reported from studies conducted in the US. They speculate that this may indicate different levels of tolerance in different societies, or the fact that the studies were conducted with the time lag of a decade.

The Task of Parenting

Given the knowledge that parenting is a stressful role, that there is a wide range of acceptable behaviours and that the physical punishment of children in the UK may be almost universal, how do social workers know what behaviours to look for when assessing parenting during an in-depth assessment? One way of answering this, and in line with the Assessment Framework and the Looking After Children (LAC) materials in England and Wales, is to examine whether parents are meeting children's actual needs. Each child's needs are different and this is why we assess these needs as part of a family assessment. Needs will change as the child grows older (Daniel et al., 1999), most disabled children's needs are far higher than average (Roberts and Lawton, 2001) and children living with substitute carers will often have extra needs related to separation, trauma or deprivation (Parker, 1999). Children of all ages are themselves often able to give valuable insights into their needs (Thomas, 2000). Despite the individuality of children's needs, there are common elements that appear to be generally accepted as necessary for all children. The contributions of many authors on this topic are collated by Lloyd as:

- basic physical care;
- affection and security;
- stimulation of innate potential;
- guidance and control;
- responsibility and independence; and
- self awareness, a sense of identity, social acceptance and personal history. (1999: 28)

Lloyd also comments that black and minority ethnic children may need to be equipped with strategies to deal with racism. Meanwhile, Coleman (1997: 47) suggests that the four main roles for the parents of adolescents are:

- meeting core needs;
- guiding and supporting development;
- protecting; and
- acting as advocates. (1997: 47)

Just as children's needs change and develop, so do parents' abilities to meet them. Woodcock (2003), drawing on psychological parenting literature, notes that although parental characteristics such as their own experiences of being parented are relevant, their *current and changing* psychosocial state will be very important in determining their parenting capabilities. Belsky and Vondra (1989) provide a multi-dimensional model based on Bronfenbrenner's (1979) ecological system to remind us that parenting behaviour is multiply determined. The model is developed from mainly North American studies of abusive and non-abusive parenting. The authors state that parenting behaviour will be influenced by an individual's childhood experiences, their personality, the social context and the child's own characteristics, and that these elements can combine and interact with each other. One of Belsky and Vondra's central arguments is that positive parenting is related to psychological maturity in the parent. This is seen in attitudes and behaviour such as being empathetic, nurturing, not being overly egocentric and having good self-esteem. One potential criticism of Belsky and Vondra's argument is that they present aspects such as the parent's history and the characteristics of the child as rather fixed elements. The parents' *beliefs* about their child (for example, that they are difficult, clever, special, naughty) may influence parenting styles and, in turn, the child's behaviour, as much as the child's innate characteristics. The parental behaviour will also be strongly influenced by how they *interpret* and understand their own childhood experiences as much as the experiences themselves. Often, negative beliefs and interpretations of self and child can be changed with skilled intervention.

Socio-environmental Factors

It cannot be ignored that most of the parents and children coming to the attention of social work services are living in poverty (Green, 2000; Jones, C., 2002). It can be argued that much of this is due to the fact that parents living in poor communities are more monitored than wealthier parents. However, it also likely that those living in poverty are more likely to require support than others. It is known that living in poverty provokes stress, due to factors such as overcrowding, lack of play facilities, fewer leisure opportunities and the lack of means to purchase respite from caring responsibilities. Ghate and Hazel's (2002) comprehensive survey of parenting in poor environments in the UK reveals that such parents typically experience significantly higher physical and mental health problems and there are widespread severe problems with poor quality accommodation. However, they also noted a general optimism amongst respondents that led to most parents feeling that they managed their limited finances well and that their neighbourhoods were friendly. There is no doubt that very many parents cope well, despite poor environmental conditions and there is a challenge to policymakers and case workers to find the best way to identify and build on such strengths.

In accord with Belsky and Vondra's multi-dimensional model of parenting is the increasing awareness that the presence of social support systems (from partner, family or community) is linked with successful parenting (Jack, 2000). Both informal and formal sources of social support appear important, and Gilligan (1999) reports on a successful Canadian intervention that appeared to reduce child abuse risk in vulnerable families. Parental networks were mapped and the intervention concentrated on strengthening informal supports, reducing sources of stress and linking formal and informal systems. Gilligan notes that children's and parents' networks should be analysed separately, as there will be some differences in their social networks. Coohey (1996) argues that such mapping should not be too simplistic and that the *quality* of supports, especially in terms of emotional support and help with childcare, are more important than the quantity.

Despite the general awareness of the importance of social capital for successful parenting, it has been difficult to identify how the community environment impacts on poor parenting and child abuse. Coulton et al. (1999) found a great deal of difference in terms of child abuse risk within neighbourhoods, as well as between neighbourhoods. This may suggest a complex interaction between the individual and the environment in keeping with more ecological approaches to understanding parenting. What does appear clear is that parents identified as abusive towards their children, or at risk of being abusive, tend to see themselves as more socially isolated than their neighbours in the same communities (Korbin, 2003). This has been found in cultures as diverse as North America, Columbia and Spain (Coulton et al., 1999; Gracia and Musitu, 2003). Additionally, the absence of social supports appear to weaken the effects of factors that often act as protective buffers against child maltreatment (Coulton et al., 1999).

Intervening to Improve Parenting

As was discussed in Chapter 4, in-depth assessments usually have the aim not only of assessing current behaviour but also the potential for that behaviour to change for the better, if necessary. Research into parenting education is well developed, although not in the areas of children's views, parenting older children, ethnic minority families, substitute carers and gay and lesbian parenting (Lloyd, 1999). Parenting training appears to be effective and helpful for approximately two-thirds of families, helping with child behaviour, parental depression and unacceptable parental behaviours (Golding, 2000). Both group and individual programmes can be effective, but group programmes help with support, building networks, raising confidence and are more cost effective (Richardson and Joughin, 2002). The theoretical base has broadened from largely behavioural origins to include social learning theory and relational theories, such as attachment and a family systems perspective (Webster-Stratton, 1999). The one-third of families who do not respond to parenting programmes tend to be those with multiple problems and disadvantages (Golding, 2000). These are also the characteristics of many of the families we may be working with on an in-depth assessment. Such families may well require individually tailored interventions to help them attempt to achieve positive changes.

How do Social Workers Assess Parenting?

Howitt suggests that social workers (and people in general) understand others through a process he labels 'templating' (1992: 123). He argues that this is a broader and less crude process than stereotyping, which involves checking an individual's characteristics against a social template to determine whether they fit a pattern. For example, he argues that social workers will hold a mental picture of the patterns within a typical abusing family. They may search for characteristics in the family that might match a pattern or 'template'. Equally, it might be argued that social workers conducting in-depth assessments might be seeking to identify characteristics of families which might match a template of 'good enough parenting' (Winnicott, 1965) or possibly an 'ideal model' of parenting (Campion, 1995). However, it is unlikely that the process in which social workers are engaged in these intensive assessments is a simple matching against a fixed 'template' of normal family life:

> Deciding on 'normal' is a moving, and negotiated, feast between practitioner, the subject(s) of reports and any other relevant people on any relevant occasion. (Parton et al., 1997: 91)

Similarly, it might be suggested in the Coastal Cities study that the overall assessment of family situations is a complex task mediated by aspects such as the quality of the relationship between assessor and assessed (see Chapter 5) and the individual family experiences of the practitioner. However, it has been seen in previous chapters that some aspects of the Coastal Cities assessments were common across assessments, for example, the need for co-operation by parents and the developing of a plausible explanation agreed between social worker and parent. What are being examined here, in addition to the individual circumstances of the assessor and assessed, are the elements of occupational and cultural socialisation that may lead to some common expectations (or templates) amongst the social workers of what is 'normal' (or at least acceptable) in families.

Parenting Skills

Most of the assessment reports in the Coastal Cities study included a section on parenting skills. In these, both physical tasks and emotional aspects were emphasised, although the physical tasks such as feeding, dressing and washing received more emphasis when the children were babies or toddlers. For children of all ages the quality of adult–child play and social interaction was described. The extract below represents an example of the way in which parenting skills were reported in assessments:

> During the practical assessment, Miss Hood demonstrated her ability to meet Kaylie Marie's needs, both physical and emotional. Miss Hood initiated all the routine care tasks and showed competence in sterilising, bottle preparation (milk), feeding (milk and solids), nappy changing and bathing. Miss Hood has consistently promoted Kaylie Marie's development, through encouraging floor play, physical contact/comfort and age appropriate independence skills e.g. holding a spoon. In promoting floor play, Miss Hood provided Kaylie Marie with a range

of age appropriate toys. Miss Hood shows an awareness of safety issues relating to Kaylie Marie e.g. moving toys to prevent her rolling on them. (Assessment report, Hood family assessment)

This extract provides a positive example of the detailed nature of this aspect of many of the assessments. It can be seen that this parent was seen to provide appropriate physical and emotional care for her child. Yet it is quite possible for parents to be assessed as possessing sophisticated parenting skills and for the parent and child to not be reunited. This was indeed the case in the Hood family assessment above. Parenting is seen more widely to include parental lifestyles, behaviour and attitudes. These are discussed later in this chapter.

Verbal skills, planning and consistency

In the Coastal Cities study, whilst both the physical and emotional aspects of parenting were central aspects to the assessments, verbal skills, planning ahead and consistency were also highly valued by social workers. It shall also be seen below that similar areas were remarked upon regarding relationships between adults. In the following paragraphs from assessment reports, aspects commented upon include the verbal responsiveness of parents towards children, planning play and reliability:

The provision of stimulation and new experiences have been observed during the play between Mr Moore and John. Praise and approval was demonstrated, responsiveness to questions and exploratory behaviour was achieved. Mr Moore had thought and prepared for contact at the Family Centre, providing toys which were appropriate and offered educational opportunities. (Assessment report, Moore family assessment)

Miss Cooke has shown consistency with time-keeping and attendance for contact. However, she fails to plan ahead or have any ideas for playing with the children, relying on them to produce toys or games for themselves. (Assessment report, Cooke family assessment)

A further theme in the assessment of parenting skills in the Coastal Cities study was the ability (or inability) of the parent to be adult in their behaviour and to maintain the child in the position of a child. In particular, parents were expected to put their child's needs before those of their own. For example:

Ms Jones places her own needs before those of the child and has poor impulse control. Considerable work needs to be done in this area to enable her to prioritise [son's] needs before her own. (Assessment report, Jones family assessment)

The expectation of parents to be 'adult' in their behaviour and responses to their children might be linked to the expectation of rationality, forward planning, consistency and verbal skills, all of which might be associated with 'adult'-like behaviour.

Shared parenting

Another theme that arose in the Coastal Cities assessments, particularly where there was more than one parenting figure, was the issue of gender roles in parenting.

There was, on the whole, an expectation of shared and equal roles between male and female parents in terms of carrying out most parenting functions. For example, in the assessment of the Lewis family, both parents were criticised for not being able to share the parenting tasks between them. The researcher had asked the social worker why she had concerns about the family:

> Their lack of ability to share tasks around the children. She criticises how Mr Lewis does things. There would be a lot of responsibility on Mrs Lewis which would lead to more arguments. We're encouraging them both to take an equal role. That's all very well here in the family centre, but may not be feasible back at home. (Interview with social work manager, Cathy, regarding Lewis family assessment)

Few adults involved in the assessments were in paid employment and, therefore, even if they had wished it, a traditional model of family relations with the father as paid earner and the mother as child carer was not the norm in the families typically seen by the social workers. It appears unlikely, however, that it was simply the absence of the traditional model that led social workers to an expectation that parents would share childcare tasks on a more or less equal basis. It is possible that this illustrates the acceptance of some feminist ideas into the mainstream of social work. Whilst no social workers in the Coastal Cities study mentioned feminism overtly when asked about theories that had influenced them, there was evidence of a critique of traditional male roles in family life that would broadly fit with a mainstream feminist critique of society. In particular there was overt criticism of men who did not play an equal role in the upbringing of children. For example:

> We spent some time with Mr Cross exploring the significance of his past relationships. As a partner he insists that he always took responsibility with tasks and chores, although he now accepts that this may not be as much or enough as he thought it was. This is certainly the case in relation to him not taking appropriate responsibility in relation to the situation when living with Ms Myers, Craig and John. (Assessment report, Cross family assessment)

> Mr Brown clearly had a sense of himself as Kathleen's father, but in practical or emotional terms was not able to illustrate what this meant. By his own admission Mr Brown has little understanding of what constitutes good parenting. He maintains that he does not know what to do with children, finding contact longer than half an hour difficult with any child. (Assessment report, Brown/Roberts assessment)

In both of the above extracts, fathers are criticised for their lack of involvement in home and childcare tasks. There is a clear expectation of involvement and ability in childcare on the part of men. This might be seen as, to some extent, challenging the criticism that women are usually held responsible for childcare by social workers (O'Hagan and Dillenburger, 1995).

Both male and female social workers were critical of men who were uninvolved in parenting. Indeed, one of the most overt critiques of an uninvolved father in the data came from a male social worker during an assessment session with a mother. The mother (Ms Cooke) lives separately from Kevin, the father of her three youngest children.

> Brian: And you said he's supportive of you and he says he's got no fault with you, and they [the children] were fine and you looked after them well. [Pause] The words sound

	hollow to me. You know he says these words and it doesn't sound like there's anything behind it. I might be wrong, I haven't met the guy [Ms Cooke smiles], but you know he shirks responsibility very easy [Ms Cooke nods] ... Kevin declined to get involved in the assessment because he hasn't got time. Yet you described him as a good father. And I asked you what that means. And you said, 'He plays with them, he gives them money. He sorts the children out, puts them to bed. They don't mess about when he's there.' He gives you money when you need it. He doesn't really help around the house. You said he's useless [Ms Cooke gives slight laugh] and if anything needs fixing or breaks you tend to get a neighbour in. Kevin visits about 3–4 times a week. Usually in the evenings? Or days?
Ms Cooke:	Well, it varies.
Brian:	It varies. And he stays for about three hours and usually watches TV.
Ms Cooke:	[Nods]
Brian:	I mean, basically he's a single man isn't he? He's got, I mean he comes across to me as a single man. He's got no responsibilities. He tells you what a good job you're doing, but at the same time the children have been removed and it seems to me he's [pause] he's got things wrong there a bit, in the things he's saying, you know he's very hollow in the things he's saying. (Extract from video recording of assessment session, Cooke family assessment)

Much of Brian's wording suggests criticism of Ms Cooke. He suggests that Kevin is 'wrong there a bit' when he says that Ms Cooke is doing a good job of parenting. But the stronger message conveys an undisguised critique of the male role in the family. Kevin is particularly criticised for escaping responsibility in terms of involvement with the children and for not taking part in the assessment.

Setting Standards for Parenting: Good Enough, or Good, Parenting?

There have been surprisingly few studies of social workers' assessments of parenting, particularly of the specific behaviours and attitudes expected of parents (Woodcock, 2003). Daniel (1999, 2000) has noted a tendency for assessments of parents to focus on specific events rather than the overall parenting environment. Encouragingly, in her research with 92 Scottish childcare social workers [using 50 statement cards] Daniel found a link between practitioners' views about children's needs and their views about appropriate decision-making. There was a centrality placed on children's emotional wellbeing, with examples including the importance of secure attachment and the emotional impact of witnessing violence in the home. Interestingly, she found a strong disagreement amongst social workers with the controversial statement drawn from Thorpe that:

> The vast majority of children in child protection systems have been neither harmed, injured nor neglected, but come from homes where their carer or carers are judged as unconventional in their child rearing practices. (1994, cited in Daniel, 1999: 87)

This suggests that, although the social workers acknowledged the difficulty of identifying appropriate standards of parenting, they had some faith that the system can identify unacceptable parenting levels. Daniel's study examined social workers' beliefs about their assessment of parenting in general. Woodcock's (2003) study, like the Coastal Cities study, examined social workers' perceptions of parenting in specific child protection cases. Her exploratory research with 15 social workers discussing 27 cases found that, although social workers implicitly drew on some psychological theory such as social learning theory and psychoanalytic theory in assessing parenting, their main view was legalistic or drew on idiosyncratic yardsticks such as their own children's progress. Furthermore, their strategies of intervention tended to rely on exhorting the parents to change, rather than providing them with tools to do so. She labels their approach as reflecting a 'static surface' model of parenting.

It has been suggested above that there were similarities in the expectations of parenting skills by a variety of social workers in the Coastal Cities study. If it were possible to characterise a possible 'template' of parenting as held by these social workers, it would include elements of competence in physical tasks as well as emotional care, sharing parenting between mothers and fathers and putting the child's needs before the adult's. On a more micro-level these would include making up baby feeds, changing nappies, providing consistent care, being verbally responsive, and being 'adult' in their responses to children. These themes were similar to those identified by Woodcock (2003). She suggests that the social workers in her study had four key expectations of parenting. As in the Coastal Cities study, these were the need to put the child's needs ahead of the parent and to provide routines and stability. She also found that parents were expected to hold knowledge of child development and to prevent harm.

A question that could emerge from these findings would be, 'Are these expectations of *good enough* parenting or of *good* parenting?' It has additionally been argued that 'good enough' parenting has become associated with a 'lesser' form of parenting (Edwards, 1995, cited in Daniel, 2000). These are issues that have dogged attempts to produce standardised checklists or proforma for assessing parenting in social work and medicine (Swift, 1995). One well-known attempt to provide a checklist for assessing parenting set standards which might be seen as belonging to an earlier generation and culturally specific to the US (Polansky et al., 1981). To take a few examples, positive points were scored for a prayer being said before meals, the child being immediately spanked for running into the street and the mother (*sic*) planning meals with at least two courses. In more recent years the emphasis has been on a minimum standard in which children's basic needs are met and children are free from significant harm (Minty and Pattinson, 1994; Swift, 1995). However, arguing from a legal and children's rights standpoint, Dwyer has suggested that standards set for parents should be raised: 'children have a right to relatively demanding parenting standards' (1997: 173). Campion (1995) argues that many of our idealised models of parenting are rooted in 1950s models of the traditional nuclear family that are increasingly irrelevant and that there is no clear conceptualisation of what constitutes good parenting in current British society. Following LaFollette (1980, cited in Campion, 1995), she explores the concept of issuing parenting licences to parents and carers who meet the required 'job specifications' of parenting.

Due to the lack of agreement on what constitutes 'good enough' parenting, it is difficult for the assessing social workers to analyse whether they are requiring standards that are too low from the parents under assessment, whether their expectations are minimal, good-enough standards, or perhaps something more. Dingwall et al. (1995), carrying out fieldwork 20 years ago, argued that social workers lowered their expectations of parents when the parents were social work clients. They suggested that a belief in parental love led social workers to over-look poor parenting standards within a general, institutionalised (and, they claim, much misquoted) 'rule of optimism' (1995: 250). Reder et al. (1993), in their review of child abuse inquiries, suggest that:

> Sometimes, workers became desensitised to poor standards of caretaking in the family and, over time, they tolerated conditions of hygiene and care that were later described as appalling. (1993: 90)

On the other hand, Howitt (1992) and Hill et al. (1992) suggest that once parents are under the scrutiny of social workers, then standards are set higher than for their neighbours. Certainly the expectation of shared gender roles might be seen to be above the norm for contemporary society, but this expectation does not appear to have been a crucial influence on social work decision-making in these cases. It simply formed part of the detailed background description of the families.

The Coastal Cities social workers refuted any suggestion that they were expecting more than 'good enough' parenting:

> I am not expecting the perfect parent to go away from here and there isn't such a thing, I don't think, as a perfect parent. I can hopefully see a good enough parent, an appropriate parent. (General interview with Brian, social worker)

> There's things I'd like to see, like more fresh vegetables, but we're talking about ideals, lots of people bring up their children without fresh vegetables. (Social worker in review meeting, Cross family assessment, fieldnotes, 21 July 1997)

In the two extracts above, social workers used the terms 'perfect' and 'ideal' to reinforce their belief that they do not have unrealistic expectations of parents. The first social worker emphasises that it is not possible to reach perfection with parenting. The second justifies her reasoning by explaining that there are others who maintain the same level of parenting as the parent in question. The impli-cation is that these numerous other parents are bringing up their children in the same manner successfully, or at least without statutory intervention.

These two social workers gauged their assessments of parenting skills in two ways: first, one social worker suggested that he was not looking for 'perfection', only for 'good enough' parenting; a second practitioner said that she would compare a parent to what other (presumably successful) parents do. A third way of assessing parenting might be to compare with personal experiences of par-enting. In the Coastal Cities study another social worker drew on our (assumed) common experiences as parents in order to bring about an unfavourable com-parison with the parent being assessed:

> The interactions [with the baby] have been OK, but you know when you have your baby and you hold him and talk to him and cuddle him? There's none of that. I mean OK, you under-stand that he's in foster care, but you'd still expect her to show some emotion, but there is none of that. (Interview with social worker, Sunita, regarding James family assessment)

It has been suggested that social workers carrying out assessments tend to be 'verificationist' (Scott, 1998) in that they subscribe to the human tendency to search for evidence to support their existing hypotheses (Sheldon, 1987, and see Chapter 9 of this book). This tendency could be provided with rich pickings in the area of assessing parenting skills. The detailed assessment of this very broad set of behaviours, parenting, might mean that it is relatively easy to find areas to criticise many of the parents under assessment, particularly perhaps those who do not fit a broader template of 'good enough parents'. However, as was suggested above, the social workers did not appear to be looking for 'perfect' parenting. The knowledge that perfect parents do not exist allows for parents who are having some difficulty with some parenting skills, but who are successfully completing other aspects of the assessment, still to receive an overall positive assessment. Conversely, many parents who are able to meet basic (or good) standards of childcare may still be negatively assessed in terms of their overall ability to care for their children. This is due to wider issues of lifestyle and, as was seen in Chapter 5, difficulties with aspects of the assessment relationship such as co-operation or commitment. An example from the Coastal Cities study is that of the Lewis family. With this family there were concerns about instability, domestic violence and drug misuse.

> I think it's quite sad in terms of there have been good bits in terms of the relationship that they have got with their children. Sometimes seeing the four of them together in the play-room it has been good, it has been positive. But I think it is quite sad that you know their lifestyle, their commitment, their inability to put the children's needs first really. (Interview with social work manager, Cathy, regarding Lewis family assessment)

In the Coastal Cities study, the assessment of practical parenting skills (including emotional engagement) seems to have had little effect on the assessment decisions. Positive assessments of parenting skills were associated with all types of assessment recommendation. For example, some parents who were assessed as having good parenting skills had recommendations that they be reunited with their children, whilst others faced recommendations that they should not be reunited. Even fairly negative assessments of parenting skills led, occasionally, to decisions to rehabilitate children. It therefore might be suggested that, whilst parenting skills featured strongly in all of the assessment reports, this area was not seen as representing the decisive core of the assessment.

Adult-to-adult Relationships

The ability to parent is, inevitably, not simply assessed through practical parenting skills, but also wider aspects of the parents' lives. In this section a further element of parents' roles within families is explored in detail: that of relationships between adults in the family. General expectations of parental intimate relationships are discussed first, followed by a discussion of domestic violence.

In the Coastal Cities assessments, many of the expectations of adult-to-adult relationships were along similar lines to the expectations of them as parents.

Social workers appeared to be looking for consistency, rationality, planning ahead and being adult-like rather than child-like. Some of these expectations were not met in the first two extracts in this section:

> The couple's subsequent re-unification was surprising, given what had been said by Ms Roberts at this time … She was never really able to give an adequate explanation for this reversal. (Assessment report, Brown/Roberts family assessment)

> During the assessment process, issues around lack of trust, poor communication, inability to compromise, negotiate and share roles and responsibilities have been very prevalent within the relationship and the couple appear to have no acceptable way of resolving differences. (Assessment report, Lewis family assessment)

The two extracts above draw together the range of difficulties which social workers may find with the adult relationships in many families where there are concerns about child welfare. In the Coastal Cities study, many couples underwent numerous separations and reunifications, without being able to provide rational explanations for these. They were seen as unable to negotiate everyday living or to discuss and plan for major life events. As has been seen in other areas of the assessments, verbal skills were emphasised. In the two extracts below it can be seen that parents were expected to be able to give verbal descriptions of their relationships:

> Mr Cross had most difficulty in describing in specific terms his relationship with Ms Myers. (Assessment report, Cross family assessment)

> When discussing her relationship with [her ex-partner], Ms James is vague and seems very detached. (Assessment report, James family assessment)

Social workers were also confronted with relationships that appeared to be irrational and unplanned. For example, there was often commentary in the reports about the decision to co-habit being undertake without much discussion or thought:

> There is nothing to indicate that Ms James and [her ex-partner] planned their relationship and appeared to drift into co-habitation as the opportunity arose. (Assessment report, James family assessment)

Similarly, Ms Jones's method of finding a partner in order to conceive a child appeared to transgress social norms:

> Ms Jones explained to the assessors that she planned to become pregnant following her arrival in town. This was her decision. It was also her decision not to inform Mr Ali, the father she had sought for her yet-to-be-conceived child, of her intentions, 'I liked him and told him when I was about three months pregnant.' Ms Jones explained to the assessors why she chose Mr Ali, known as 'Big Mac', as the father of her child. She explained that she was attracted by his reputation for violence, 'shooting, knee-capping, and other offences'. (First assessment report, Jones family assessment)

In assessing parents such as Mr Brown, Ms Roberts and Ms Jones, social workers are confronted with relationships that do not fall within everyday expectations of the 'normal' progress of romantic relationships. They must make a decision about whether these unusual relationships fall within their template of *acceptable* family relationships. Social workers see many complex family situations in the day-to-day course of their work, and there is no attempt to suggest that these social workers held rigid or overly traditional expectations of parental relationships. Social workers may have held as an ideal that relationships should be equal, rational and verbal, but many social workers were at pains to point out that they did not intend to be prescriptive when assessing relationships.

It has been noted that social workers in the Coastal Cities study expected adults to plan ahead, be rational, consistent and to give verbal accountability both in regard to their parenting and their adult-to-adult relationships. There are two key points to be made here about these observations. First, such expectations might be seen to be linked to the concept of 'psychological maturity' in adults. There appears to be evidence, as discussed above, that psychological maturity is associated with positive parenting and may act as an important 'buffer' against child maltreatment (Belsky and Vondra, 1989). Therefore it might be argued that the Coastal Cities' social workers' expectations of parents fit well with research evidence. Second, as discussed in Chapter 5, it should be noted that more articulate and educated parents may find it much easier to demonstrate skills such as rationality, consistency and planning ahead than other parents, particularly those with some degree of learning disability. If such skills are mainly assessed through verbal interviews, then this may compound difficulties for less articulate parents who wish to demonstrate their parenting abilities. With both parenting skills and parental lifestyles, the assessor's priority is likely to be the assessment of how children experience everyday life with their parents, rather than how parents are able to explain their lives.

Domestic violence

It has been noted that competence in relation to direct parental care is not, and cannot, be the only key indicator of whether a parent may provide an adequate home environment for their children. Inevitably, other aspects of broader family life are crucial and domestic violence is a key example of this. Domestic violence violates many of the above expectations of rationality, verbal methods of problem solving and stability. It was also an issue in the majority of the Coastal Cities assessments. Domestic violence is therefore an interesting example of how factors relating to parental lifestyles and relationships affect social workers' assessments of parents.

Whilst recognising that domestic violence (also known as domestic abuse) is a contested area in social research, theory and policy (Gelles and Loseke, 1993), I use the term here to denote men's physical, verbal or emotional acts of violence against a women partner. I do so in recognition of what I consider to be the weight of research evidence (for example, Dobash et al., 1992; Nazroo, 1995) and the apparent nature of the violence encountered in client families in the Coastal Cities study. Domestic violence debate has been summarised as reflecting the different approaches of functionalism and conflict theory (Malloch and Webb, 1993), with feminism being the most influential conflict theory. Featherstone and Trinder (1997) claim that what they call the 'radical feminist' approach to domestic violence (which they criticise) has reached hegemonic status in current social work practice and thinking. This feminist approach foregrounds men's coercion of women to maintain power in the domestic sphere as the explanation of central importance (see, for example, Dobash and Dobash, 1979). Despite Featherstone and Trinder's claim, such an approach was not strongly evident in the social work practice in the Coastal Cities study.

Domestic violence as an issue in the assessments tended to be approached in a broadly similar manner across a range of assessments. The violence is at times referred to euphemistically. The woman is seen as partly to blame for the violence, or mutually responsible. The violence is sometimes seen as being caused by alcohol or drugs, or by the man's frustration at his family situation. Women's accounts of violence are sometimes not believed. Such approaches might be aligned with what has been labelled a 'functionalist' approach to domestic violence. Malloch and Webb (1993) describe such an approach as being individualistic and normative. Such traditional attitudes towards domestic violence, which do not include a gender and power dimension in their analysis, were, according to Mullender (1996), common amongst practitioners up to the 1980s in social work. They were also to be discerned in these assessments in the late 1990s. The following quotations and extracts illustrate this. In the first two extracts, violence is mentioned euphemistically:

> Mrs Baker's relationship with Mr Baker has also been *volatile* in the past. However, since the *'incident'* involving Paul [her son] and Mr Baker's subsequent prison sentence, Mrs Baker advises that she has become much 'stronger' and more able to protect herself and her children. (Assessment report, Baker family assessment, emphasis added)

> There had been *a domestic* on the Sunday. He ended up in the police station and in court. It doesn't look too good if they're already having *domestic incidents* during the assessment period. (Discussion with social work manager, Cathy, regarding Lewis family assessment, fieldnotes 20 August 1997, emphasis added)

The neutrality of words such as 'volatile', 'domestic' and 'incident' (in the first extract 'incident' is used regarding physical violence against a child) can serve to soften the impact of the message for the audience and to shift some of the responsibility for the violence away from the perpetrator. This is perhaps reinforced in the first of the two extracts above, where Mrs Baker is reported to be the partner whose behaviour has changed for the better. In the next two quotations a further aspect of a functionalist approach to domestic violence can be seen:

> She [Mrs Lawrence] stated that in March 1995 she received 'The beating of her life' ... The couple insist that violence is not an issue now and Mrs Lawrence has spoken of 'setting boundaries for Mr Lawrence'. Throughout the assessment the couple have stated that there is now better communication between them and that they are 'more of a united front now'. *Violence within the relationship* is clearly unacceptable when the welfare of the child is being considered, and *the couple acknowledge a need to identify more appropriate ways of dealing with differences between them.* (Assessment report, Lawrence family assessment, emphasis added)

> Domestic violence continues to be a factor within the relationship and although both feel it should not occur, *equally both accept it* as part of their relationship and justify it in comparison with more violent relationships they are aware of. (Extract from Lewis family assessment report, emphasis added)

In the two extracts from assessment reports above, the tone suggests that responsibility for domestic violence be shared equally between the man and the woman in a couple. For example, violence is described as being 'within the relationship' rather then inflicted by one person on another. The *couples* are seen to be accepting the violence, or recognising that it is wrong. In both of these cases the allegations were, in fact, of physical violence inflicted by the man on the woman. Mullender (1996) describes how interactional approaches to couple counselling and family systems theory (the latter of which has been particularly influential in social work) have tended to view violence as being caused by circular or interactional processes within the family, thereby attributing blame and causation equally with all parties. However, many therapists within these areas have begun to acknowledge and act on feminist critiques in recent years.

A final example of a traditional approach to domestic violence in the assessments provides an example of a woman's account of domestic violence not being believed by the social worker when recounting abuse from her partner:

> [Ms Thompson] said that she had left Tim, that the emotional abuse had been horrendous, that he used to make her crawl in bed like a dog and she wouldn't be treated like that anymore, he was drinking heavily and all this sort of stuff, prior to the visit ... As I said to her, 'Well, you know, you have given no indication at all and you have had plenty of opportunity to tell us' ... I sensed that she was fibbing, I still sense this because they are still together. (Interview with social worker, Laura, regarding Thompson/Turner family assessment)

Despite the tendency in these assessments to approach domestic violence in a manner which does not fit with the feminist discourse, one aspect of an (arguably) feminist approach to domestic violence could be seen in some of the assessments. Mullender (1996, 1997) suggests that, whilst previously women were encouraged to stay with their violent partners for the sake of their children, such relationships are now seen as unviable arenas in which to raise children. This belief may be influenced by a feminist understanding of domestic violence that suggests that violent men are unlikely to change, as well as an increased understanding of the impact for children of living with domestic violence (Mullender and Morley, 1994; McGee, 1997). Women are now often told that they must make a choice between the man and the children (Humphries, 1999; Scourfield, 2003). Similarly, in the assessments in the Coastal Cities study, women were sometimes expected to make a decision between choosing to stay with a man or to separate from him and therefore have some chance of having the children returned to her. Here it might be noted that, despite separation from violent men being associated with a feminist standpoint, the burden of responsibility for the woman's and her children's safety is placed on the woman. Mullender describes this as '[replacing] one set of controls, the abusive man's, with another from the local authority' (1997: 59).

Aside from the specific issue of requiring women to leave abusive partners, in only one case was a social worker seen to be applying what might be interpreted as an overtly feminist understanding of domestic violence during an assessment. Here the social worker suggests that the perpetrator of domestic violence is attempting to minimise his role and lay an equal share of the blame on his female partner:

His relationship with mum, the violence within that, I think he seeks to minimise his own role, he talks of the mum initiating it, he talks of him just defending himself and if you sort of see him and know him, he is a big lad, you wonder really how true that could be. Now I have met mum and I have worked with mum and she is no quiet person let me tell you, but equally you have to understand the power of the relationship there. He also has a history of violent relationships. (Interview with George, social worker, regarding Khan family assessment)

This type of analysis stood out in the data because it was unusual. As suggested by the other quotations above, a more typical response to domestic violence in the Coastal Cities teams fitted with 'functionalist' and other traditional approaches, rather than a feminist or 'conflict' approach (Malloch and Webb, 1993).

Domestic violence and children's welfare

These social workers' practice did not, then, appear to fit with Featherstone and Trinder's (1997) suggestion that a radical feminist discourse is prevalent in social work approaches to domestic violence. It is possible that these authors would also argue, as others have (Wise, 1995), that there can be difficulties in marrying a radical feminist position in social work practice with a child protection or indeed a children's rights perspective. Social workers can be placed in a double bind by authors such as Stanley (1997). She emphasises the link between domestic violence and child abuse, yet argues that women should not be threatened with care proceedings as a means of encouraging them to end a violent relationship. If a woman is reluctant to separate from a violent man, or repeatedly unable to maintain a separation, then the child protection social workers' duty to consider the welfare of the children involved may have to lead to coercive action of some kind. Social workers tend to resort to threatening care proceedings, or to not return children if care orders already exist, because that appears to be the only way forward. Even social workers who maintain a feminist understanding of societal relations are faced with such dilemmas in front-line practice (Wise, 1990, 1995). Whilst Stanley (1997) does argue that a partial solution in cases of domestic violence is to concentrate on challenging abusive men rather than coercing women, this will not necessarily provide an immediately safe environment for the children.

There are clear and established links between domestic violence and negative experiences for children. Many potential effects are similar to those experienced by children who have experienced neglect, physical abuse and sexual abuse (and indeed all of these may be experienced in addition to domestic violence for some children). The experience of witnessing or being caught up in domestic violence and often unstable living arrangements may lead children to experience a range of behavioural, physical and psychological effects. These include physical injury, behavioural difficulties, developmental delay, self-harm, poor social skills and educational difficulties. The impact differs according to age, gender and ethnicity, but not always in predictable patterns (see Hester et al., 2000, for a more detailed discussion). A growing body of evidence suggests that, in addition to the emotional harm suffered by those witnessing violence, children are also at increased risk of other forms of abuse, including physical injury, sexual abuse and neglect (Hester et al., 2000). There has been increasing attention paid to the voices of children themselves who have lived in situations of domestic violence. A recent study in the UK included a survey of school children's views of domestic violence and qualitative interviews with 45 children who had experienced domestic violence (Mullender et al., 2000). The findings from the latter aspect included:

- the wide range of coping strategies used by children;
- the shared experience of the loss of the familiar and of disruption;
- the widespread experience of not being believed or listened to, except by refuge workers; and
- the wish to be safe, with their mothers and with their own belongings.

There appears to be a growing consensus in the literature that, as with any aspect of an assessment, when considering the impact of domestic violence on children's experiences assessors should not assume that there are universal or assumed ways in which children will be affected. No situation of domestic violence is identical, nor can children's responses be predicted (McGee, 1997). There will be differences of severity and duration and of how children perceive and experience their situation. Belsky and Vondra (1989) write about 'buffers' that may offset negative aspects of parenting. Buffers in these situations may include levels of attachment, trusting relationships with siblings, peers, extended family and adults in the wider community, positive experiences of school and outside activities and access to places of safety. An assessment of a family where there is domestic violence could explore family members' perceptions of family relationships and positive aspects to the family, as well as risk to the children and adult members of the family. Women may feel fear, love, hope, despair or helplessness and perhaps all of these at various times (Abrahams, 1994). It is only by forming an understanding of economic, cultural, historical and any positive aspects of family relationships that we may come to understand and work with women's (and sometimes children's) reluctance to leave situations of violence.

There is therefore no intention of suggesting there is a clear-cut right or wrong way to approach domestic violence. As Malloch and Webb (1993) suggest, the various approaches to domestic violence can be seen as serving different professional- and gender-based interests. Featherstone and Trinder (1997), arguing from a postmodern feminist perspective, suggest that the dominant feminist discourse on domestic violence has become fixed and unyielding. For example, they, like Alanen (1994), argue that women's and children's needs have too often been assumed to be unified, and that there has been a fixed view of one form of masculinity, rather than a recognition of a range of masculinities (Connell, 1995). Featherstone and Trinder (1997: 156) state that 'families are more complex than the simple dichotomising of abuser/abused, powerful/ powerless'.

What appears important in considering domestic violence is that the complexity of family situations is acknowledged and that over-simplistic solutions are not imposed. This, of course, must be done with maintaining children's physical and emotional safety as a priority. In the US in recent years, programmes for training child welfare workers in domestic violence issues have emerged. These have varied theoretical orientations, but the three reviewed by Mills and Yoshihama (2002) all combined a feminist understanding of domestic violence with some individual psycho-social elements. Evaluation of such training is encouraging, with workers showing increased confidence in assessing domestic violence, a more proactive approach to intervention and less victim blaming.

Conclusion

Assessing parents' childcare abilities and the impact of parental lifestyles or personal needs on their parenting abilities is fraught with difficulty. Social workers risk ignoring difficulties if an attitude of total cultural relativism prevails. This might be a fear of imposing values associated with dominant white, middle-class, educated cultures on those who are socially excluded for a variety of reasons. There is also a risk of stereotyping those with minority, stigmatised or downright undesirable lifestyles as being universally unfit parents. In this chapter the core principles of looking at each child's situation individually, determining whether the parents are capable of meeting *this* child's needs, seeking specialist advice and knowledge and listening to the perspectives of all family members have been outlined.

Suggestions for practice

- Parenting is multiply determined and affected by the parent's personality (especially psychological maturity) and history, the child's characteristics and the social and cultural context. Strengths in one of these areas might act as a 'buffer' against weaknesses in others.
- A focus of an assessment of parenting should be on whether the parents are able to meet *this* child's needs. Demands on parents' skills can be greater when the child is disabled or has a history of trauma or separation, and will change as the child grows and additional siblings join the family. Parents' abilities will be affected by many external supports and stresses and are therefore likely to be changeable.
- Broad-based parenting training is effective in helping around two-thirds of parents.
- When assessing families facing particular issues, such as domestic violence, mental health or substance misuse, it is useful to maintain an awareness of your theoretical approach to the issue and the impact that may have on your assessment. It is usually necessary to draw on expert knowledge in the form of research findings and professionals from other disciplines.
- When assessing parents from minority ethnic communities, it should be remembered that their relationship with their own heritage and the dominant culture is likely to be individually experienced. Migrant cultures are usually dynamic and statements regarding typical behaviour are rarely helpful.
- As with all aspects of assessment, it is important to listen carefully to the explanations, experiences and hopes of parents and children.

PART III

The Assessment Process

8 Assessment Design

Chapter summary

This chapter provides a discussion of central elements to be considered when designing an in-depth assessment. Contents include:

- Participation: who to involve, co-working and inter-agency working.
- Methods: interviewing, observation, using documents and non-verbal methods.
- Power issues in assessment design.

This chapter explores the key elements of an assessment design and provides a critical discussion of some potential assessment methods. The range of people that may be involved in an assessment is described and, in this chapter, emphasis is put on the involvement of other professionals in the assessment. Whilst this chapter is written with in-depth assessments in child welfare in mind, most of the principles in the chapter could be applied to a range of settings and levels of assessment.

The content and method of planning for an assessment will differ according to the assessor's view of the purpose and nature of assessment work. It was suggested in Part I of this book that there are a range of ways of understanding the nature of assessment, and the practitioner's stance on these will affect her or his approach to the planning of the assessment. A simple summary of two key ways of understanding assessment is that an assessment might involve, on the one hand, an objective uncovering and measuring of the facts of a case or, on the other hand, an attempt to reach an understanding of a range of perspectives through close engagement with key participants. It was seen in Chapter 3 that few practitioners are likely to view assessment solely in one way or the other. It seems sensible that any reasonable assessment would incorporate both approaches in the child welfare arena. For example, there are factual elements that both the statutory services and family members will wish to agree and establish, such as whether a carer has a criminal history of violence or child abuse, the nature of housing need, a family's refugee status or the diagnosis of an illness. Other aspects of evidence gathering that are mainly factually based and useful for assessment include the setting of baselines and measuring change. For example, with areas such as home conditions it can be useful to carry out a detailed survey with parents, agree action for change if necessary (by family and/or agencies) and then measure any improvements using the same instrument as before. No assessment would be complete, however, without some sort of discussion with key participants on how they view their family situation and what could help make a positive difference. Such discussions do not simply involve facts and here it would be a fallacy to suggest that the assessor can decide which opinion is 'real' or 'true'. Instead, it is hoped that a systematic analysis of both the 'factual' evidence and of the usefulness and robustness of various explanations will lead to a balanced assessment conclusion (see Chapter 9).

Designing the Assessment

The word 'design' is used here deliberately instead of 'planning' to suggest a link with research design. Several social work writers have commented on the useful parallels between social research methods and assessment for the purpose of both interviewing methods (Thomas and O'Kane, 2000) and analysis (White, 1997; Sheppard, 1995a; Clifford, 1998). Whilst many former social work practitioners-turned researchers have used some social work skills of engagement, listening and reflecting in their research style, so too have they commented on how some of the rigor of research could be applied to assessment, which can be seen as in some respects analogous to research with an individual or family.

The key elements of an assessment design is likely to include consideration of the assessment questions, who should participate (both in doing the assessment and being assessed) and what methods of assessment should be used. When social research is being designed the most important starting point in determining the method of research is the research question(s). Similarly, with an assessment it seems sensible to begin with a consideration of what the assessment aims to discover or establish. It would be surprising if a routine procedure with set questions and methods were suitable for the assessment of all family situations. Some areas of family life may be irrelevant to the issue at hand, or the area might already have been thoroughly explored by an earlier assessment. The assessment question may have been set in broad terms by a case conference recommendation or at the request of a court. In all cases a more detailed set of questions will require consultation with family members and often other professionals and may need to shift in focus as the assessment progresses. One important principle to retain is that any assessment should endeavour to look for strengths in families as well as difficulties and problems. Almost all families will have been achieving some aspects of childcare successfully and the identification of these areas are as important as the identification of weaknesses.

Once the assessment questions/areas for exploration have been agreed, the assessor may find that she needs to conduct some preparatory work to increase her knowledge base of a particular area. For example, if the question was about the effect on a child's wellbeing of a parent's heroin use and involvement in prostitution, the assessor may need to research the evidence base on this topic before beginning the assessment. Here it can be useful to look for recent research overviews, or preferably 'systematic reviews'. When researchers conduct systematic reviews they search the world's databases for relevant research findings on a particular topic and assess the quality of the research studies. A report then summarises the most important and consistent findings in the field (Cochrane Collaboration, 2002). Such overviews are more useful to the practitioner than one solitary research study. Assessors may also wish to complement their knowledge of the latest research findings with a familiarity of guidelines to best practice in relation to a particular topic (these will usually have emerged from research). When considering their knowledge base in relation to any specific circumstances relating to the family situation, assessors may also wish to undertake a cultural review. This is the first stage of assessment analysis and is described in detail in Chapter 9.

The assessor can also at this stage begin to plan the practical aspects of the assessment. In doing so it may be remembered that a sound assessment generally should aim to include a number of viewpoints, take place in a range of settings and over a period of time (Gilgun, 1988). Gilgun's advice, whilst drawn from social work practice, might also be seen to have close parallels with one of the best known (although sometimes contested, see Silverman, 2000) principles of social research, that of *triangulation* (Denzin, 1970) Triangulation involves exploring something using a number of different approaches. Denzin outlines a number of types of triangulation, including data triangulation. Here it is suggested that data be collected at a variety of times, in a range of settings and from a range of participants. It can be seen that this principle is very similar to Gilgun's. The principle of investigator triangulation, where more than one researcher (or assessor) is involved, is explored below when co-working and multi-disciplinary working is discussed. Denzin also describes a principle of methodological triangulation and in this chapter it is suggested that the use of a range of assessment methods, including interviewing, observation, scales and elements of self-assessment is also likely to contribute to a well-rounded assessment. In the next section the question of who to involve in the assessment is explored, before a more detailed consideration of assessment methods.

Participation

Nearly all assessments will involve more than one professional and one service user and it is necessary to identify the likely participants at an early stage. In most circumstances, all immediate family members should be involved in an in-depth assessment, including those who are sometimes not the immediate focus of a family assessment: men and children. Sometimes, extended family members and friends are important to a family circle. Early discussions with adult or child family members about their support and other networks (see ecomaps, p. 119) may reveal the names of important people to be included in an assessment. Seeing people singly and in groups will give rise to different sorts of information. This is discussed further in the section on interviewing below.

The second important area to consider is the involvement of other professionals. This may include, at the simplest level, accessing written records such as school reports, but may well also include multi-agency meetings and one-to-one discussions between the assessor and other professionals. An alternative approach would be to plan and conduct the assessment alongside others. The first I term 'interagency working', the second 'co-working'.

Interagency working

It has been suggested that a key principle of assessment is to explore a range of perspectives regarding a family situation. The aim of this would be to avoid one explanation dominating the assessment before other potential explanations have been explored. A major way in which social workers might potentially come into contact with others' perceptions of the status and meaning of information known about a family would be through interagency and/or multi-disciplinary involvement in the assessment. Involving other professionals in the assessment provides the opportunity for practitioners to be challenged in their emerging viewpoint of a family situation and, perhaps, to problematise the notion of information gathering as a neutral activity. A rather more obvious advantage of assessing in an interagency context would be that contributions might be made from the specialist knowledge bases of a range of disciplines.

Despite the theoretical advantages of assessing on an inter-professional basis, research findings suggest that, in practice, interagency relationships are often fraught with difficulty. In the child protection field in the UK (covering a range of interventions, including assessment), there have been recorded difficulties in co-operation between social and health services, particularly between social workers and general practitioners (Birchall and Hallett, 1995; Murphy, 1995). Gould's (1999) qualitative audit of child protection work in one local authority area found problematic systems and record keeping in all key services, but particularly in general practitioner (family doctor) records. Research into the pilot implementation of the Assessment Framework in Wales suggests a more positive picture of interagency co-operation for the assessment of children in need than previously reported in the child protection arena in the UK (Thomas and Cleaver, 2002).

Stevenson (1989) suggests that there are some major barriers to collaboration that impede our ability to work across disciplines. There are different structures and systems in each discipline. Professionals are often working to different standards and have varying professional histories and cultures. In the UK, health professionals have traditionally worked within geographical areas that have different boundaries from those of social services staff. This can lead to difficulties in assigning responsibilities and in strategic planning. There are different understandings in different organisations about information sharing and confidentiality. Some professionals have a higher perceived status than others, and this is often related also to age, gender and ethnic profiles of various professions. There is also the range of prioritisation of child welfare within different organisations. Whilst some professionals provide a universal service, others specialise in child welfare considerations and this can impact on thresholds of concern and prioritisation of cases.

Despite such potential and actual problems with interagency working, it is a way of working that is increasingly becoming the norm in the US and in the UK (Alaszewski, 1997). In the UK, established multi-disciplinary co-ordination, assessment and intervention is more common in specialist services, such as those for disabled children (Yerbury, 1997) and domestic violence (Hague and Malos, 1998). There are examples of special inter-disciplinary assessment teams that work together to assess child welfare and protection situations. In the UK these are sometimes situated within the voluntary sector. Gilgun (1988) reports on a successful model for assessing families in the US where there are concerns about child sexual abuse. The professionals each dedicate one day a week to working together in assessing these families, and a range of disciplinary perspectives are brought together without the family having to undergo multiple assessments by different services.

Where such formal structures do not exist, social workers may need to agree methods of assessing together with others on a case-by-case basis. This may be particularly important when working with professionals who are rarely involved in this type of work, such as teachers. Teachers are a vital and rather neglected resource in in-depth assessments of children and their families, due to them having a greater depth of involvement with children than any other professional (Gilligan, 1998). When working with those more often involved in child welfare, such as paediatricians and health visitors, collaborative relationships between individual professionals across agencies may develop over time. Most importantly, the perspectives of all involved professionals should be integrated into an assessment at a meaningful level. This is best achieved where there is a mandate for collaboration at institutional levels (Morrison, 1996).

Interagency working in the Coastal Cities study

The assessments in the Coastal Cities study tended to be solo or dual exercises carried out by social workers. Whilst other professionals' views were canvassed, the planning, execution, decision-making and writing of the assessments was almost entirely a social work activity. Most assessment reports and records list the other agencies and individuals involved in the assessment. All assessments involved another professional or informant at some stage. The professional most commonly involved was another social worker. Others commonly consulted were foster carers (who also might be seen as part of the 'social work' stable), day-care workers and teachers. The day-care workers were, in these cases, always employees at social services nurseries, where parents and children had contact sessions. It can be seen then that liaison with professionals inside the social services departments was the most common form of working with others. Liaison with health professionals often involved a simple exchange of written reports rather than verbal consultation. In most cases, where consultation was cited by the social worker, it was impossible to discern from the written reports whether this had involved a brief telephone call or perhaps a more involved face-to-face meeting.

In the Coastal Cities study therefore, multi-disciplinary working tended to be limited, with little evidence of co-operation at the level of planning the assessment or analysing the findings. Interviews with social workers provide some insight into why this might be the case. It was suggested above that multi-disciplinary working might provide the potential to introduce a range of interpretations to an assessment, allowing for a more complex view of the assessment process to emerge. However, such a system would require a more reliable and co-operative system than that seen to be operating in the assessment settings in this study. Social workers report both poor liaison systems and distrust and different viewpoints between agencies:

> I think there may have been some sort of mental health issues or a very mild learning difficulty, again she is due for a psychological assessment. We are still waiting for that because the service is very slow. We may not actually get that at all before the report is finalised, which would be unfortunate. (Interview with Brian, social worker, regarding Cooke family assessment)

> Jane described problems they were having with the adult psychiatric services, she said that they had referrals of parents with psychotic illnesses, some associated with drug use and some were not taking their medication. However, adult psychiatric services will not get involved with children's services. One psychiatrist was asked if a [social work] assessment was appropriate for a parent undergoing a psychiatric assessment. The psychiatrist refused to comment. (Informal discussion with Jane, social work manager, fieldnotes, 11 June 1997)

Here, there were problems in waiting for reports or services from other agencies, and an example of a professional refusing to become involved. In the case of the first assessment, the psychological report, which contained important new evidence, arrived after the social worker had reported his assessment conclusion to the court. It has been noted more widely that the demand for psychiatric input in child protection assessments outstrips supply (Murphy, 1995). The expectation that assessments might be carried out with multi-disciplinary input assumes that there are systems of communication and an element of trust between agencies. In some areas of the UK there are difficulties in liaison, particularly between health and social services (Birchall and Hallett, 1995).

Co-working

A further way in which social workers might come into contact with other perspectives is by co-working, that is, having two practitioners to carry out an assessment. This might involve, for example, a social worker assessing alongside a community mental health nurse, psychologist or a health visitor. It could also involve a social worker from another specialism, such as a mental health or learning disabilities team. The advantages of co-working across disciplines are, first, that practitioners can share areas of expertise. Second, the process of engagement may be helped if, for example, a parent already has a good relationship with their mental health nurse or health visitor. In the Coastal Cities study, co-working was always carried out 'in house' with two social work team members co-working. In some cases more experienced managers are used to advise less experienced social workers. This method is in contrast to social workers' normal practice of working alone (Pithouse, 1998) as the sole worker with a case, and this difference may cause social workers to reflect on their practice. It also gives the potential to provide alternative views to an individual's perception of a family, again possibly challenging the idea that information gathering is a neutral activity. In the Coastal Cities study, Laura spoke at length about the difficulties she had experienced in conducting the Jones family assessment alongside a colleague:

> We were really getting very, very caught up with our own different views in how we saw the mother. We would have a meeting beforehand about how we were going to approach it, but it wouldn't happen like that in the room ... which was giving her fairly mixed messages and also meant that we couldn't, the assessment couldn't progress to actually knowing where the mother was on her own continuum of development and therefore potential harm to the child ... What was said [by line managers] was they are your difficulties and you are going to have to go away and resolve them but they were intransigent they wouldn't resolve. They couldn't resolve because we would shout abuse ... so he felt that I was like a dog with a bone, wanting her to address those issues. So this time I was saying to her, 'I can't believe that you allowed your baby, you would like to have your baby, with a broken arm', and really face her with what was happening and she would get very upset and he would go in and rescue. He would say, 'We don't want to talk about that now'. ... So perhaps a session will move in two different directions and perhaps that will trigger things for one or the other, so perhaps that can cause one person some contention then and it can set up differences between the co-workers, how they're seeing the information and how they're processing that. So that can be difficult. And then there's incompatible attitudes and values, what's good enough and what's not good enough – that raises points of subjective things about 'Is that good enough parenting, where is our baseline, where do we measure it from, have some of us got different baselines from others, is that fair to a service user?'. (Interview with Laura, social worker, regarding Jones family assessment)

Here, Laura raises a number of significant points relating to co-working. She reports how she and her colleague shared different views on the seriousness of the case and of how to conduct the assessment. They were unable to agree a common approach or reach a shared analysis of what was emerging from the assessment. Laura states that her colleague's empathy with Ms Jones leads him to 'rescue' her, preventing difficult issues from being discussed. They were not able to find resolution through two standard routes, discussion or supervision. They couldn't discuss it – 'we would shout abuse' – and their line managers told them to sort it out between themselves. Finally, the experience appears to have exposed for Laura the subjective nature of the assessment work. She saw how their different attitudes, backgrounds and values led to different views on how the assessment was progressing and whether or not what they saw was 'good enough parenting'. The assessment process here is not an objective process of information gathering, but an arena in which differing perceptions of a family situation battle for recognition. Laura questions the fairness of the process for the recipient of the assessment.

   This vividly recounted experience of co-working was the most negative example of co-working in the Coastal Cities assessments. Another problem reported by social workers included the experience that assessments took longer for two people to complete, due to the need to discuss the sessions together before and after they took place. However, on the whole, social workers cited the experience of co-working as positive due to the opportunity for regular consultation or sometimes leadership from a more senior practitioner. Jane described how she regularly co-works with another colleague:

> I wouldn't say that we are telepathic by any means but, um ... we were very clear in where we were coming from and we could deal with difference in that. We could almost, I could almost work out what she might say next. Or what avenue she would go and vice versa. I feel that it has really created a buzz for us in working together and training together so it has been productive. I think the families benefit from that. (General interview with Jane, social work manager)

Her experience is in stark contrast to Laura's, reported above. It is possible that where social workers share similar values and attitudes, perhaps facilitated by shared gender identity or generational experiences, co-working is experienced as productive by social workers. However, this style of working can expose for social workers how individualised an assessor's opinion can be. This has the potential to cast doubt on the way in which social workers may understand their task: to gather the facts and ascertain the truth about a family. Whilst Laura's experience of co-working appeared to feel more negative than Jane's experience, it is possible to argue that Laura and her colleague's 'match' as co-workers was 'better' than that of Jane and her colleague. It is possible that where two colleagues have developed very similar ways of approaching their work, through years of working together, then they may unconsciously reinforce narrow or preconceived views about a family situation by agreeing with each other. Where co-workers tend to approach their work with different styles, professional backgrounds or sets of values, then each will be forced to challenge and justify their approach and analysis. This may lead to a more thorough and fairer assessment for the family involved. What would not help the family, however, would be open warfare between co-workers, which would probably be experienced as disconcerting or confusing by families.

Methods of Assessment

Having discussed the potential participants in an assessment, I will now move on to potential methods of assessment. After suggesting a range of methods, I will discuss the potential for methods of assessment to be oppressive or empowering for the service user.

Interviewing

Interviewing has long been the bread and butter of social work practice, perhaps so much so that we may risk taking less care of the planning and preparation of interviews than when considering other methods. Issues to consider with interviewing include:

- Who should carry out the interviews?
- Who should be interviewed?
- Should interviewees be seen together or alone?
- Should questions be pre-set, or should general themes be explored?

In many assessments, one social worker carries out all of the interviewing and is responsible for the entire assessment. This has the advantage of the family having the chance to develop a trusting relationship with one social worker. It can be very difficult to talk about emotional and personal areas of life with a range of assessing professionals. On the other hand, it may be helpful for another practitioner to carry out some interviews, perhaps because they have particular expertise, for example, in communicating with disabled children, or because the assessment relationship appears to be faltering, or simply to bring a fresh perspective to the assessment. For example, in one assessment that I carried out as a practitioner with young parents with mild to moderate learning disabilities, there had been an allegation concerning the father's sexualised behaviour towards children. He let me know that he would feel more comfortable talking about this area with another man and I was able to bring in a male colleague to conduct a series of interviews on this topic with him. As was discussed in Chapter 5, it should not necessarily be seen as a failing on the part of the service user if they indicate that they find one practitioner difficult to talk to. They *may* be trying to avoid difficult subjects that need to be addressed, but they may simply find it easier to talk to someone else of a different sex, age or personality.

Decisions to interview people singly, in pairs or in family groups will have a number of facets. In many cases service users may be given the choice as to how they would feel most comfortable. Where children are looked after in foster or residential care, or in cases where there are concerns about the child's wellbeing, they must be seen separately from their main carers or an alleged abuser at some point (Department of Health, 1999). Interviewing alone or in the presence of others will probably bring about different sorts of information. Many participants in an assessment may feel happier talking with other family members present, to act as supporters in a setting that may feel unfamiliar or even potentially threatening. Interviewing people together can lead to them 'jogging' each other's memories and a chance to explore different memories or explanations of events. Events or behaviours may be described in more detail as family members expand on each other's statements. Bringing a whole family together to share problems and plan solutions can be a potentially empowering experience, as many users of Family Group Conferences will testify (Lupton and Nixon, 1999).

There are some potential drawbacks that should be borne in mind when the assessment interviews with two or more people are being planned. Some family members will be unwilling to talk about certain aspects of their lives in front of others. In particular, people are less likely to talk about behaviour or beliefs that do not conform to the group 'norm' in front of others (Bloor et al., 2001). Also, in groups the power dynamics present in most families may be replicated, with more powerful family members possibly influencing the contribution of others, either overtly or covertly. Within families power differences related to gender and age are the most common, but in some families power will be exerted relating to disability and step-relationships. An example of a group assessment interview where power dynamics were evident can be seen in one of the assessment reports in the Coastal Cities study. Paige, aged 6, had been removed from home following allegations of scapegoating and unexplained injuries. The other family members present were her birth mother, stepfather and three teenage stepbrothers.

> On [date] a session working with the whole family was completed. Present at this session were Ms Johns, Mr White, Tim White, David White, Jonathan White and Paige Johns. The aim of this session was to 'demystify' [the assessment] and allow the children to ask questions about their family's involvement. Unfortunately, Mr White was unable to tolerate this discussion and became angry. Paige was distressed and Mr White asked her if she wanted him to leave, Paige nodded her head and Mr White went to sit in his car. This had a very negative effect on the rest of the family, who were openly hostile towards Paige. Ms Johns turned her back on Paige and the boys were obviously distressed about their father's behaviour, demonstrating an extreme level of anxiety that he return to the session. David and Tim made statements such as 'She does it on purpose', and 'It's all her fault'. Mr White returned to the session at David, Tim, Jonathan and Ms John's request; however, the work had to be abandoned. (Extract from court report, John/White family assessment)

Here it appears that Paige, the youngest family member, was isolated and verbally attacked by the rest of the family. Whilst many families will not be presenting problems as severe as this family's, the assessor should remain aware of power dynamics within families when planning whole family or couple interviews.

Both the potential advantages and disadvantages are well known to social researchers who have to make decisions about the use of focus groups and individual interviews in research design (Bloor et al., 2001). Interviewing pairs or larger groups of family members can be a revealing method for discovering family beliefs and assumptions and for observing relationships within the family. It will usually be necessary to combine these interviews with individual interviews in an in-depth assessment.

Planning the interviews

Many contemporary assessments take place according to fairly set formats in terms of topics to be covered. For example, the Assessment Framework in England and Wales has a detailed set of questions to which written responses are required in the Core Assessment recording forms. It was not anticipated by the Assessment Framework's authors that assessment interviews would consist of using these questions exactly as set, but that the answers to these questions should be known at the end of the assessment. The information might be gained from a number of sources, including previous assessments. The practitioner is then left with a choice of how to obtain the information. In a series of interviews with practitioners implementing the Assessment Framework in its first year it could be seen that practitioners are using varied methods of eliciting the required information:

With the Core Assessment [form] I don't actually use it with the clients, or the family. Usually I expect them first time just to tell me anything they want to tell me, and the questions I ask I think of then, and then go back on a second visit really to try and fill the gaps. (Interview with Gaynor, City Social Services)

To be frank, you know you need to get x, y and z information so you know you do it instinctively, do you know what I mean? It is not necessarily by following the format to the nth degree because if you have done it for quite a while you are doing it quite naturally. It is surprising how much information you can actually pick up in a very short period of time if you are experienced. (Interview with Lillian, City Social Services)

It is very clear because you are actually taking the assessment forms with you and saying that they need to complete these and I need to work with it. And they get to see the information that you are writing about, which I think is really good and it does involve people a lot more. (Interview with Caitlin, City Social Services)

The first two social workers do not use the set format on the guidance; Lillian states that this is because of her experience, Gaynor because of her wish to let families talk freely. Caitlin, on the other hand, finds that by overtly using a set format she is being transparent in her approach.

Some families will have a central issue that requires more exploration than other areas. This might include disability, experiences of bullying or harassment, mental health or substance misuse. Whilst the general principle of planning the assessment questions to suit individual circumstances holds, there are some areas where particular sets of additional questions might be used for specific circumstances. For example, the following checklist summarises Read and Clements' (2001: 44–5) suggestions of questions to be borne in mind during an assessment of a disabled child and their family:

- Has the service users' eligibility for both general income maintenance and disability related benefits (including health benefits) been checked?
- Do they need housing adaptations or assistance towards moving?
- Do they need aids and other equipment?
- Would parents and children benefit from short-term breaks, such as assistance within the home, a holiday or respite care services?
- Does the family require and wish help with care or domestic assistance on a longer-term basis?
- Does the disabled child have a reliable means of communication?
- What are the needs of other children in the family?
- Does the main carer need or wish to return to work, and what might facilitate this?

The answers to such questions may be found using a range of methods in addition to interviewing (including diary keeping, observation and ecomaps) and by involving all family members. Similarly, Murphy and Harbin (2001: 5) list additional areas to be explored by social workers using the Assessment Framework to assess families affected by substance misuse.

The wording of questions

Attention should be paid to the *wording* of questions, as well as to the subject matter. Better quality information will result where the practitioner has taken care with the questions. Whilst closed questions are efficient ways to elicit brief factual information, open questions will allow the participant more freedom to answer in a way that they wish. A skilful questioner will notice the actual words and phrases used by a family member and use these words themselves in follow-up questions. This demonstrates to the participant that they are being listened to and may allow them to feel freer to talk further about a particular topic.

Therapists and counsellors are able to provide a strong lead in listening and the use of questions. In systemic family therapy, the 'Milan School' developed the 'circular interview' as a means of gathering information about a family's problems and how the family understood them (Selvini Palazzoli et al., 1980). Whilst it is not suggested that any practitioner should attempt an interview of this kind without training, assessors may find that some of the *language* used in circular questions may be usefully employed in an assessment interview. The theory of circularity may be briefly described as the view that individuals should be understood within their context of inter-relationships and that interactions within families often occur as cyclical sequences that are connected with family beliefs (Nelson et al., 1986). Family members are usually asked to specify behaviours, they are asked about how the behaviour has changed over time and how it might change in the future, and they may be asked to compare and rank actions and beliefs. The intervention as a whole is intended to help break entrenched negative patterns, but for the purposes of assessment we may wish to borrow one aspect, the circular question, and use it to help stimulate new thinking about a situation alongside a family. Examples of questions might include:

- What is the main concern of the family now?
- How is this different from before you became ill?
- What will happen if things continue as they do now?
- Who is most concerned about this problem?
- Who next?
- What does your husband do when you and your son are arguing? (Nelson et al., 1986: 120–25).

Parton and O'Byrne draw on solution-focused therapy and the work of De Shazer to suggest the use of the 'miracle question' to enable service users to articulate goals and look to the future:

> Suppose that when you leave here, you go out and do what you are having to do, you get home have something to eat and later go to bed; and while you are asleep something miraculous/ magical happens and the problems that brought you here vanish, in the click of a finger; but because you were asleep you don't know this has happened. When you wake up in the morning what will be the first thing you will notice that will tell you this has happened? (Parton and O'Byrne, 2000: 103)

Practitioners may, then, wish to draw on the experience and knowledge base of various therapies and schools of counselling to help improve the quality of their assessment interviews, although it must be emphasised that this is only likely to be useful if some understanding is reached of the theoretical roots of such 'borrowings'.

Beyond interviewing

Many assessments will benefit from the use of other methods in addition to verbal interviewing, and some of these methods may take place within the context of an interview. Although *play and drawing* are generally recommended as assessment tools for children, many adults may find it useful to break in the midst of a discussion and explain their perspective or describe an event through making a sketch, positioning some model figures (or abstract objects that could represent people) or even re-enacting a scenario using a doll's house. Whilst I have used such techniques successfully with adults with learning disabilities, there is no reason why adults with a range of abilities may not find this helpful. I often explain to others that I personally find it difficult to explain or understand directions verbally and much prefer to see or draw a map.

There is a vast array of other methods for assessment that do not rely on verbal methods alone or that can be used as a spur to conversation. There are some *commercially available tools*, such as the 'Needs Game' produced by the Bridge Child Care Development Service in England, that asks family members to rank cards with pictures and words of children's needs. Practitioners could produce their own statement or picture cards to fit a particular assessment. For example, family members might be asked to discuss or rank a series of statement cards about family life. Discussions between family members whilst such an exercise is carried out might reveal patterns of power relations or conflict resolution and individuals may find out more about each other's views at the same time.

Well-known methods of exploring support systems and family networks are *the genogram and the ecomap*. Drawing up a family tree or genogram with someone who may come from a very disrupted and painful family background should not be undertaken lightly or without preparation. It may be helpful to give someone advanced warning that you hope to draw up a genogram in the next meeting and give them the option of doing this themselves in private. If someone is reluctant to do this exercise, then it is important to be clear whether the information is actually needed and, if it is, then explain why. Despite these potential difficulties, many individuals find the exercise revealing, perhaps noting for the first time family patterns of early parenthood or loss. Ecomaps (the drawing of a diagram showing sources of support, or stress to the individual) can also provide useful information for the assessment. It should not just suggest a passivity or weakness on the part of the service user – the ways in which he or she provides support to others can also be explored. I have found that some people do not respond well to this diagrammatic way of working and have, at times, used a questionnaire exploring similar areas. Questions might include:

- Who could you turn to if you needed to borrow a fiver in a hurry?
- What about if you needed £50?
- Who babysits for you?
- Who would give advice if you were worried about your baby?

Another method that can be used within an interview is the use of *vignettes*. Instead of being asked direct questions about their own situation, parents or children could be asked about what may or should happen next in a scenario read out to them (or shown on video or picture cards). Some people find it easier to talk about a subject matter if it is slightly removed in this way. They themselves may then draw parallels with their own situation, or the assessor could carefully do this. Vignettes have been used in social research with adults and children (Barter and Renold, 2001).

The final alternative to simple question-and-answer within the interview to be discussed here is the use of *scales and questionnaires*. Until recently, such instruments have not been in common usage within social work practice in the UK, particularly in fieldwork settings. With the Assessment Framework has come a set of standardised scales for use as part of assessments. These include scales for measuring home conditions, adult wellbeing and alcohol use. Accompanying these is some balanced advice for their use that emphasises that the use of such scales is unlikely to be successful if there is not a sustainable and positive relationship between assessor and assessed. Results from such scales can never take the place of other assessment methods, but may be useful to help validate evidence from other sources or to raise new issues that have not yet been aired within the assessment.

Some practitioners feel anxious about using scales or are suspicious of their usefulness. In research into the implementation stage of the Assessment Framework, only a minority of social workers reported that they had used the scales when conducting a core assessment (Thomas and Cleaver, 2002). A possible reluctance to use the scales is understandable, as most social work practitioners in the UK are untrained in using such methods. Whilst most of the questionnaires in the Assessment Framework have been academically validated, some of them have been changed and adapted to suit a child welfare context, and these adaptations have yet to be fully validated. If used in a clumsy or unplanned fashion, family members may find them worrying or threatening. However, when used thoughtfully and purposefully, there are clear benefits in including the use of such methods as one aspect of a family assessment. First, many people enjoy filling in such questionnaires and may find the process self-revealing. The method is transparent and understandable and may be seen to give some control over the process to participants who are able to complete questionnaires themselves. Scales therefore may be a useful way of engaging people into the assessment process and in working alongside families to identify problems and potential solutions. Second, questionnaires or scales may be used to set baselines and to monitor change. I once worked with a family about whom there were concerns about safety in the home. A detailed survey of their home using a home safety checklist revealed a number of potential dangers to small children and an action plan for change was produced. By the end of the assessment, a repeat use of the questionnaire revealed some concrete changes to the home, providing evidence not only that the home was safer, but also that the family were prepared to work to change their environment. Third, just as individual interviews may produce different information from group interviews, so may questionnaires produce different information from verbal discussions. Some people may be prepared to be more honest on aspects such as alcohol use when responding to a specific written questionnaire than when being asked general verbal questions. Parton and O'Byrne note that various potential responses to each question (for example, 'not at all', 'just a little', 'pretty much', 'very much') 'empower people to tell a story that may otherwise be difficult to tell because it has several shades of grey' (2000: 141).

Observation

Observation is a vital part of any assessment. It will take place on an informal basis throughout the assessment, for example, before, during and after interviews. Observation sessions may also be arranged on a more formal basis, such as arranging to observe a family at mealtime, if perhaps this has been identified as a stressful period, or to observe a child in school. It is another way in which we can access different information about a family situation and provides a chance to validate, or modify, information and understandings obtained through other means. Observing may give us some access to the informal aspects of family lives and relationships. As with group interviews, it may give us some insight into some of the shared understandings and unofficial family rules and boundaries that exist in all families. Altheide and Johnson, in discussing the role of observation in social research, describe these shared understandings as 'tacit knowledge' which:

> ... exists in that time when action is taken that is not understood, when understanding is offered without articulation, and when conclusions are apprehended without an argument. (1994: 492)

It is important to bear in mind three key principles: context, purpose and consent. In terms of context, no observed behaviour should be divorced from its environment. For example, many observations of family relationships in child welfare settings take place in family contact sessions. This is where parents who are living separately from their children spend pre-arranged time with their children, and where there are welfare concerns then this contact may be supervised. Any observations of the parent–child relationship should include in its analysis the understanding that such contact sessions can feel artificial to many family members and that their behaviour may be modified or constrained because of this. When parents only have one or two meetings with their child each week, they may feel enormous pressure for such times to be happy and special. Their behaviour may well be different when caring for their children on a full-time basis. To achieve a balanced view it is necessary, where possible, to see families in a number of different settings and at different times of day.

The wider social context is also of central concern to understanding observed behaviour. The gendered nature of our society that emphasises the mother's duties to parent often leads to a focus on the mother and neglect of the father's role, and this may impact on how parent–child interactions are observed (Tanner and Turney, 2000). Additionally, factors such as cultural differences, relating to ethnicity, nationality, religion and class, will also impact on the observer, the observed and the dynamics of their interactions.

The purpose of observation may range from a general aim of trying to understand family relationships and the effect of their environment on their everyday lives, to a more specific aim such as observing specific behaviours identified as a problem or as a contribution to the assessment of a child's development. The purpose will lead the way in planning the context and method of observation. For example, as a practitioner I was once assessing a single mother and her three very young children. She made the point that the children's behaviour and responses to her were very different when she was on her own with them from when there were other adults present. We agreed that I would observe her playing with them in a room in a family centre. My observation would take place through a one-way mirrored window to minimise the impact of my involvement in the interactions. Although all family members knew that I was there, they soon forgot and played as normal. I was able to make detailed notes of the children's behaviour and the mother's responses that we later shared and used as a basis for understanding and action.

Observations of children are vital parts of an assessment in child welfare, particularly at the level of in-depth assessment. It is through observing a child at play, perhaps eating, attending nursery and on a trip to the park with foster carers, that we can begin to build up a holistic view of the child. Whilst family contact sessions provide a good opportunity for observation, it must be remembered that these sessions have a specific and rather artificial context. Children's behaviour within these sessions cannot be understood unless their personal style and interactions with others are also observed in a range of other settings.

Like all other assessment activities, observation is not a neutral or objective method. The assessor must retain a reflexive awareness of the impact of their own presence and of their beliefs, experience, professional status and knowledge on the interaction. Ethical issues concerning consent and transparency of the method should also be explored with the family being assessed (Ellis et al., 1998). Tanner and Turney (2000) suggest that, whilst overt observations of family life may be experienced as oppressive by families, the quality of information gained will aid the production of a fairer assessment for families. It might be suggested that frank discussions with families about the potential advantages and disadvantages of this method could form the basis of negotiating the use of this method.

Documents

Most assessments will also involve the examination by the assessor of written records from a variety of sources. These may include weighty case files from within the social services department if the family has been involved with social workers for some time. In an in-depth assessment there are also likely to be the findings of previous and initial assessments, reports of health visitors, paediatricians, psychologists and schools, and possibly also police reports and court documents. Some families may themselves also produce written documents, such as diaries, self-assessment reports and commentary on the assessment process.

There are two key points that I wish to make in relation to written documentation. First, it should be treated with systematic care. In too many inquiries after children's deaths it has emerged that written records of events experienced by a child have not been systematically compiled and their cumulative meaning explored (Reder et al., 1993). Second, we need to maintain an understanding that the document is not a neutral exposition of the facts of a matter, but that any record will have been written by its author with a particular audience in mind. For example, professionals may write in a different style when they know that the subject of their report (for example, a parent) will be reading the report, than when they do not expect this. They may pay attention to making their language more accessible and they may also attempt to couch criticisms in slightly ambiguous language in order to avoid causing pain to the reader. As will be discussed in Chapter 9, professionals may also be writing documents in order to justify their decision-making to a future review or inquiry. Similarly, family members who provide written contributions to an assessment will have written these as an attempt to explain, advocate or reinforce their position to the professional audience. This attention to the intention of the writer is not intended to belittle written documents as valuable sources for assessments. Instead the suggestion here is that assessors should remain acutely aware of the social construction of documents, whatever their source, and that in their analysis practitioners should maintain a critical and reflexive stance towards them.

Assessment Methods and Power

Farmer and Owen (1995) suggest that in child protection social work the balance of power between social worker and client is subject to shifts according to the stage of the process. For example, during initial investigations, early assessments and case conferences, the social worker is in a very powerful position and able to make demands in areas such as frequency of visiting, access to family members and access to information. However, Farmer and Owen suggest that following an initial case conference, the power balance often shifts, with social workers required to negotiate entry to clients' homes and terms of agreement for future work. The in-depth assessment in child welfare may be seen as another phase during which most of the power is with the assessing social worker. This power can potentially be maintained or reinforced through the use of the assessment methods.

Some examples from the Coastal Cities study may serve as examples here. While many of the assessments in this study were conducted with a great deal of attention to issues of fairness and care, social workers could be seen to maintain power in a number of ways that were at times intentional and at others probably unintentional. Social workers laid out the conditions for the assessment, including the timetable, who should attend, what questions should be asked and where the assessment should take place. On occasion parents were refused permission to bring a companion with them, to be interviewed together rather than singly or to see questions in advance. Social workers used video cameras to record verbal assessment sessions and, at times, contact sessions. Some assessments were conducted with a manager or colleague watching the assessment sessions through a mirror (this was never covert). Both video recording and observation from a distance might have the disempowering effect for a client of feeling that their every movement is being monitored. Workers commonly wrote clients' answers to questions on a flip chart. Whilst this appeared to be done in an attempt to give immediate feedback and clarity to parents of how the session was progressing, the effect for clients might be one of a classroom setting where they themselves were the pupils.

A written contract, agreement or plan was presented to the clients near the beginning of most of the assessments. Whilst clients, in theory, were invited to contribute to the making of the contract or agreement, the sameness of the contracts suggests that the social work agencies were the main driving force behind the content and form of the agreements. Some agreements (used in child protection cases only) issued clear demands of the behaviour of parents, stating that they must attend the assessment whenever and wherever required and that they must co-operate in the assessment. Although such plans also contained the requirement that social work agencies should provide services, the clear message of such agreements is that the power remains with the social services department.

The social workers understandably wished to retain control over a process for which they may well be professionally answerable in court. They have a need to ensure that the assessment is thorough and covers all necessary areas. The increasingly legalistic basis of child protection work means that the potential scrutiny of the courts is always present, even when a case is not currently being heard in court (Parton et al., 1997). It is also possible that retaining control over the assessment is one of the ways in which social workers maintain their 'face' as professionals (Goffman, 1959) in a potentially difficult professional encounter. The in-depth assessment in child welfare introduces potential conflicts for the social worker in terms of the appropriate level of relationship to strike up with the client. There is a need to build up trust and openness in order to gain the level of information that an assessment of this depth requires. However, the social worker cannot afford to become too close. They are, in the main, assessing parents about whom serious allegations of child maltreatment have been made. They may well have to produce a report in which they make a recommendation that the parents are permanently separated from their children. There is a need to retain an element of authority and control which, as was seen above, is maintained through the assessment methods.

Despite the probable need to retain some authority and control in the small minority of cases where there are serious allegations of child maltreatment or neglect, most practitioners will wish families to experience assessments in a way that is as encouraging (and even potentially empowering) as possible. Some methods have the potential to be more encouraging than others. It may well be appropriate to ask participants in an assessment how they would like to be assessed: What would be the best ways of learning about them as a family? This question, if asked, should also, of course, be asked of the family members with less voice, such as children, who may be very perceptive in such matters. As has already been suggested, scales and questionnaires have the advantage of transparency and can be self-completed. Other methods to shift the power balance might include some elements of self-assessment, as is increasingly used in the assessment of foster carers and adopters. It is also essential that workers attend to practical methods of accessibility, including ensuring that people have the option of being assessed through their preferred language (including British Sign Language), even if they are fluent in English, and checking out whether people are literate before giving written information.

Conclusion

In this chapter parallels have been drawn between research design and the preparation needed before an in-depth assessment begins. Several commentators have commentated on the lessons that social work assessment may draw from *analysis* in qualitative research. Attention to *design* of an assessment will lay the foundations for thorough analysis and decision-making. For example, accessing a range of explanations for the family situation from participants (professional and family) will help the assessor avoid narrow or pre-emptive conclusions. Similarly, attempting to find out more about the family situation though a range of means (for example, interviews/discussions, observations and reading documents) may give more depth and validity to assessment conclusions.

The most important early task is to establish with the family and others what are the key questions for the assessment. Although these may change as the assessment continues, they will enable the assessment to become an individually designed one that fits the family's needs and preferences. In child welfare work we are often working with some of the most marginalised members of our society and it is important that the assessment design does not further oppress the family members by using methods that appear to reinforce power differences, or even to be coercive or punishing. In many cases assessment can be a creative intervention that will hopefully prove revealing and helpful to the family members as well as to the assessing professionals.

Suggestions for practice

The assessment questions

Broad areas may be set by family self-referral, a court direction or case conference recommendation.

More detailed questions will emerge in consultation with family members, other professionals and as the assessment progresses.

The assessment questions will aid decision-making about:

- *Participation*: which family members and associates to involve, co-working the assessment with another worker, involving other agencies. The principle is to try to gain a number of viewpoints.

- *Setting*: assessing in a range of settings is advised, especially for in-depth assessments. This may include a specialist centre, home, school and possibly the home of an extended family member, such as a grandparent. It is also worth trying to meet people at different times of day, if possible.
- *Time*: some assessments are time-constrained, for example, by the Assessment Framework (7 days for an initial assessment, 35 days for a core assessment) or by a court direction. A balance must be struck between reaching conclusions quickly so that plans can be put into place, and allowing enough time to see how a family responds to an intervention or changes through the current crisis.
- *Method*: using a range of methods gives more opportunity for family members to show their perspectives, experiences, abilities and needs and may make conclusions more firmly based.

Assessors should also pay attention at this stage to:

- *Access and partnership*: it was noted in this chapter that some assessment methods may be experienced as encouraging, even empowering, whilst others may be controlling, or even oppressive. It is important to pay attention to issues of access, including language choice and literacy.
- *Analysis*: the foundations for analysis should be laid at the stage of assessment design. Practitioners may wish to conduct a cultural review and begin to consider what may be some possible explanations for the family's difficulties. This is discussed in detail in Chapter 9.

9   Analysing and Reporting

Chapter summary

This chapter outlines a systematic form of practice for analysing assessment information. This involves working against our natural human tendency to search for information that will confirm our initial hypotheses. It is suggested that we should act reflectively and, wherever possible, alongside the family members being assessed, to develop an understanding of how the family difficulties are currently being experienced and maintained and how they may move positively forward. It is suggested that we must actively look for information that may throw doubt upon the prevailing explanation. We may draw upon our own practice knowledge, theory and research evidence, as well as the family's own theories, in order to develop conclusions that will be workable and promote the child's wellbeing.

This chapter also examines some key issues regarding the writing of assessment reports. The potential impact of standardised assessment forms on the production of assessment information is discussed, and consideration is given to the effects of audiences as diverse as court professionals and the families who are the subjects of the assessments. It is suggested that report contents should aim for balance: avoiding too brief discussions of individual children's lives whilst writing reams about their parents, covering environmental and social factors as well as individual ones, and positive as well as negative factors. It is also suggested that reports should include a brief account of the decision-making process and include the subjects of the assessment's views. The chapter ends by alerting professionals to the potential impact of subtle forms of language usage.

This chapter is about the process of analysis in assessment. It was noted in Chapter 8, in the discussion of assessment design, that analysis is a process that pervades an assessment from its very beginning, and in this chapter the stages of analysis are explained in detail. In Chapter 8, the parallels between research design and assessment design were drawn. Here it will be seen that the theory and practice of analysis in qualitative social research can provide us with a solid foundation for analysing the information that we gain during an assessment. In Chapter 3 it was seen that social workers often find it very difficult to articulate how they have reached a conclusion. It is hoped that social workers following the processes described here will be able to explain clearly to themselves and others (particularly families and courts) how they have built an understanding of the family situation and a set of recommendations for action. This chapter is also concerned with how we represent our assessments on paper, and consideration is given to fair and effective report writing.

Analysis in Assessment and in Social Research

In the debate about the relationship between social science knowledge and social work practice, it is often the case that it is solely the *products* of social scientific knowledge (for example, empirical research findings and theories) that social workers are urged to apply to practice. However, several authors suggest that in assessment practice, social science *processes* are in fact equally useful to the practitioner. In particular, processes of analysis in qualitative social research have particular relevance to social work assessment (Scott, 1989; Sheppard, 1995a, 1995b, 1998; Clifford and Cropper, 1997; White, 1997; Milner and O'Byrne, 1998).

Social work practitioners tend to be skilled communicators and are often good at eliciting and gathering information about people and their circumstances. However, for many social workers, difficulties arise when attempting to manage, make sense of and reach conclusions from this bulk of information. Early research on the workings of the Assessment Framework in England and Wales suggests that there continue to be problems in producing good quality analysis in assessment (Cleaver, 2002; Thomas and Cleaver, 2002).

A key difficulty arises from our natural human tendency to be 'verificationists' (Sheldon, 1987; Scott, 1998). This means that we tend to form an explanation for a family or individual's circumstances early on in our contact with them. Milner and O'Byrne (1998) suggest that the initial assessment of a case often shapes or determines any subsequent assessments and intervention strategies. Farmer and Owen (1995) found that assessments of risk formed at initial child protection case conferences tended to be repeated or reinforced at review conferences, even on occasions when new and possibly contradictory evidence had arisen. Parton (1998) speculates that this determining of a dominant explanation may come at the referral stage. The process of assessment often acts to confirm original explanations. We can do this by looking for information that is likely to be confirming, and also by ignoring information and sources that might throw doubt on the explanation. Many social workers aim to work against this tendency by aiming to be objective and neutral in their assessment work. However, it has already been argued in this book that objectivity is an impossible goal in human interactions. Additionally, our tendency to work with our original hypothesis is so strong that we need to do more than aim to be neutral: we need to use processes that actively force us to consider a range of possible ways of understanding a particular set of family circumstances.

Social work writers have therefore suggested that we should adopt some of the processes used to analyse data in qualitative research. There are several different ways of analysing qualitative research, of which one of the best known is analytic induction. Analytic induction involves a close examination of the research data. Hypotheses, explanations or rules are developed. These are examined in relation to all of the data available. If any data do not fit with the developing theory (these are called 'deviant cases'), then that theory is abandoned or modified. Further data collection takes place, with hypotheses being continually discarded or refined, until the process appears to be complete: all new data are confirming the developed hypothesis or explanation (Bloor, 1978a). Alternatively, *de*ductive approaches *begin* with concepts or hypotheses and examine data in the light of these. Sheppard (1995a: 274) points out that any division between the two methods of analysis is a false one because 'Concepts are neither developed out of observation, nor are they imposed *a priori*. They are interdependent.'

Sheppard (1995a) borrows Bulmer's term 'retroduction' to describe the fusion of two types of analysis: that which is drawn from data, and that which tests data against existing concepts. In social work assessments, the parallel is that we look for information which will test potential ways of understanding and helping the family situation *and* be open to developing new forms of understanding that are rooted in the information that is emerging. Whilst many social workers would always aim to be open to new ways of understanding and helping a family, there is a further aspect to the inductive approach to analysis in social research. This is that we should always look for data, or information, that might disprove, or at least throw doubt on, our understanding. The reason for such an orientation is that it actively works against our human tendency to distort what we see in order to fit with our fixed explanations. Further explanation of this process is given below.

So far in this chapter it has been seen that several writers have pointed to the potential usefulness in using social research techniques for analysis in assessment work. In particular, it has been suggested that social workers root their understanding of a family situation firmly in the information that arises during the assessment. In order to avoid simply confirming our original ideas through selective assessment work, we should also actively look for information that throws doubt on our thinking. The chapter continues with a detailed look at each stage of analysis, beginning with reflexivity.

Reflexivity in Analysis

> Neither observer nor observed come to a scene untouched by the world. Researchers and subjects hold worldviews, possess stocks of knowledge, and pursue purposes that influence their respective views and actions in the presence of the other. Nevertheless, researchers alone are obligated to be reflexive about what they see and how they see it. (Charmaz and Mitchell, 2001: 162)

The notion of reflective practice (and its similar but more complex cousin, reflexivity) has been mentioned as a vital stance at several points in this book so far, such as in relation to maintaining an awareness of our impact on the assessment relationship and when observing family situations. In Chapter 5, reflexivity was described as a process where we are critically aware of the impact of ourselves and our belief systems on the assessment, and of the service-user's response to this. This will include 'categories' associated with ourselves, such as gender, 'race' and professional status. It will also include our agency culture and dominant theories, practices and assumptions within our occupation (White, 1997). The analytical stages of an assessment are times where it is particularly important that we retain a position of being reflexive. Shaw (1997) has recommended to practitioners that a method for critical reflection suggested by McCracken (1988), in his text on interviewing in research, be applied to social work practice. In social research, McCracken suggests that at an early stage we carry out a 'cultural review'. This means that we systematically look at all of our cultural categories in relation to the subject at hand. To transfer this concept to assessment, and to take the example of assessing a four-year-old child from a travelling family about whom there were welfare concerns, we may wish to consider:

- What do I know about travelling families and communities?
- Where does my knowledge come from?
- What prejudices may I hold (positive or negative)?
- What do I know/expect about four-year-olds, their lives and needs?
- What might surprise me about this family, and why would this be a surprise?
- How might I be perceived by this family: the parents, the child, siblings, community?
- How might the assessment and my agency be perceived?
- What impact might the assessment have on this family's life and on their perceptions of their lives?
- What agency norms and practices do I take with me on an assessment? (For example, awareness of risk, thresholds of good enough parenting, resource restrictions.)

In setting ourselves such questions, and by reviewing our answers regularly, we give ourselves an opportunity for self-awareness about where our understandings of family situations come from. In McCracken's (1988: 33) words, the process will lead to 'familiarization and defamiliarization': we will be using our existing knowledge and creating a critical distance from that knowledge, simultaneously.

A further important element to the reflective approach to understanding family situations is to constantly check out our explanations with others. A key way of doing this in social work is through supervision, and the supervisor is in a position to enable the practitioner critically to examine the origins and strength of their hypotheses about an assessment (Munro, 1995; Sheppard, 1995a). It was seen in Chapter 8 that co-working an assessment enabled one of the Coastal Cities social workers to critically reflect on her approach to an assessment. Regular consultations with professionals from other agencies will also aid reflection. (Milner and O'Byrne, 1998, suggest that this is not done in group situations, where professionals tend to develop 'group think' and reinforce each other's views, rather than critically examine the evidence.) Finally, by sharing emerging thinking with those being assessed, you are likely to receive critical feedback that may allow you to develop your explanations in more depth and in a way that may fit with the service user's approach to life.

Building Hypotheses

The cornerstone of analysis in assessment work might be seen as the process of building hypotheses for understanding a family situation and developing these until they include a plan for the way forward. Here, the process of developing hypotheses and exploring these throughout the assessment is discussed. There is exploration of where hypotheses might come from, including social science theories, research evidence and practice wisdom. Finally, research evidence of how social workers appear to use explanations in assessment practice is examined.

First, I wish to discuss the use of the terms 'theory' and 'hypothesis'. Silverman (2000: 3) defines *theory* as arranging sets of concepts to define and explain phenomenon. A theory can never be proved or disproved, only found more or less useful. A *hypothesis*, on the other hand, is a *testable* proposition. Whilst, in an in-depth assessment, a hypothesis may never or rarely be proved to be true, by using analytic techniques we may throw doubt on some hypotheses and find others to be more soundly based on the assessment findings. A hypothesis may draw on theory as well as other sources (as discussed below) and apply this to the specific situation to hand. I therefore find the term 'hypothesis' useful in this context. 'Hypothesis' may come across as an overly 'scientific' and perhaps off-putting word in this very human context. I see hypothesis within an assessment as being a way of understanding the family situation and the best way to move forward, and therefore I also use the phrase 'way of understanding' and, sometimes, 'explanation'. 'Explanation' is not meant to necessarily imply that we need to reach an understanding of the underlying *cause* of the family difficulties – that is usually beyond our reach. Instead I suggest we aim for understanding, alongside the family members and other participants, of how the difficulties are being experienced (particularly by the child) and how they may be alleviated. In some cases it may be agreed by all that it would also be helpful to look at the antecedents to the problems, especially for therapeutic purposes.

The process

It should be remembered that, when developing our understanding of a child's situation, we are constantly trying to avoid our tendency to work with only one, early, hypothesis about the family, ignoring evidence that might contradict this theory. Sheppard outlines two processes of examining our hypotheses. We might examine each hypothesis one-by-one; he calls this 'progressive hypothesis development' (1995a: 275). We should then abandon any hypothesis that the emerging evidence does not appear to confirm and develop new ways of thinking about the family. Alternatively, we can develop several potential ways of understanding the family situation and explore all of these at the same time. Sheppard calls this 'comparative hypothesis development' (1995a: 275). As the assessment progresses, some hypotheses will appear to be more strongly supported by the evidence than others. There are three further elements to exploring our understandings of the family situation: attention to assessment methods, actively seeking evidence that might throw doubt on an explanation, and managing the assessment information. These are explored next.

An important aspect of exploring a range of explanations is to pay attention to methods. We should avoid using solely one assessment method that is likely to support just one hypothesis. As was suggested in Chapter 8, using a variety of methods (such as interviewing, observation, using questionnaires and observing whether supportive intervention is making any difference) is likely to produce a fair and broad-based assessment. This is because evidence from a range of sources will allow for a more meaningful exploration of potential hypotheses. A hypothesis that appears to be reinforced during an assessment interview with a parent may need to be adapted, given more depth or even abandoned after observing the parent and child together in their home setting and spending time gaining the perceptions of the child.

The second important element when developing our understanding of the family situation is to *actively* seek evidence that might disconfirm or at least challenge each hypothesis. This is because, in the inexact world of human interactions, it is relatively easy to find evidence to support our opinions if we are looking for it, and if we ignore the broader picture. We need to counter this tendency so that we can satisfy ourselves, those being assessed and, where relevant, the court, that we have thoroughly explored every angle. A key example might be child abuse. In many social work agencies cases categorised as child abuse are understandably a dominant concern. If this is the case, we might wish to ensure that we are additionally open to hearing other aspects of this family's experiences and concerns. This is not to suggest that we should not thoroughly investigate concerns about a child's wellbeing. The emphasis is on being open to alternative explanations and to the child's wider lived experience. Parton and O'Byrne write:

> ... exceptional behaviours that contradict the dominant story are unnoticed if we listen only to the dominant story. Without a belief in exceptions and a search for exceptions, data will be misleading. For this search to be successful, a human engagement is required where the worker comes from 'not knowing' and is able to listen, having engaged in 'problem-free' talk and asked exception-finding questions. (2000: 141)

A third aspect of the process of analysis is that we need to discover ways in which to manage our data so that all of the available information is available to us and retrievable when necessary. With the availability of computers and photocopiers it is possible to make multiple copies of assessment information. This means that notes can be made in margins highlighting information that supports or challenges key themes. This is similar to the process of coding in social research, which aids the organisation and retrieval of data. A close re-reading of the information will also allow new explanations and themes to emerge. It is worth remembering that the written information under analysis might include interview records, case files, observation notes, supervision notes, formal reports from other agencies and diaries or self-reports written by family members. On a computer, key words can be searched for and information copied and pasted under various headings. Data displays can be produced, including chronologies and genograms. It is also useful to compile tables displaying, for example, sources of information, methods of assessment, emerging themes and assessment work remaining.

Sources of hypotheses

Analysis of how a family is currently operating and how problems may be alleviated does not simply happen at the end of the information-gathering stage of an assessment. There are hypotheses (or, often, just one hypothesis) surrounding families from the moment of referral. Practitioners can identify these hypotheses, and generate a range of alternatives, early on in the process. Hypotheses come from a range of sources and it is important, as reflexive practitioners, that we are aware of these. We should also be aware about the values that we put upon these sources. Whilst professionals' hypotheses may be presented in a more sophisticated manner than those from service users, their relatives and neighbours, they do not intrinsically possess more value.

Service users' explanations

There will be differences in lived experiences between any worker and service user, often accentuated by poverty and educational background. Where there are additional differences such as age, ethnicity, gender and disability, then the gap is likely to be wider. If we acknowledge family members' expertise on their own lives, then we may be building an assessment where we are open to exploring a range of ways of understanding the situation. We should aim, where possible, to shift our position from one as 'expert' to one as 'not knowing' (Parton and O'Byrne, 2000). Family members' understandings of their own experiences should be listened to carefully and taken seriously, even if they clash with professional explanations. It is only by starting from this position that we may build a successful assessment relationship and develop the potential to move forward with a family. Family members themselves may have ideas about how their assessments of their own situation may be explored, and perhaps how change might be sought during the assessment. Children can be particularly insightful about such matters, if consulted. White suggests that we might try to help families 'find better stories' (1997: 751). Where possible, the emphasis should be on this being a collaborative process, rather than an imposition of our own explanation on a family. There will be some families with whom we work where the dominant family explanation is entirely unacceptable, because it actively supports some form of abusive behaviour. There will also be family members who deliberately try to conceal information that will cast them in a poor light.

Maintaining a willingness to listen to a range of viewpoints should not drift into gullibility. However, even in cases of denial of abuse, it can be possible to work with some families on how they might need to shift their behaviour in order to accommodate the concerns of others (Lusk, 1996).

Practitioners' explanations: practice wisdom

Practitioners who have conducted a 'cultural review' at the beginning of an assessment should have begun to generate some possible hypotheses about a family situation and to possess some self-awareness about where their under-standings come from. It has been noted that writers about social work have often imposed a clear division between practice wisdom and knowledge that has a clear theoretical or empirical base (Sheppard, 1998; Webb, 2001). Webb (2001) has noted that practice wisdom has a much lower official status than formal knowledge derived from research findings. However, Sheppard (1998) suggests that the notion of the reflective practitioner allows that knowledge might not simply be produced *for* social work, but *as a result of* social work. In an earlier work, Sheppard (1995a) argues that where practice wisdom has been developed through the analytic processes described above (searching for confirming and disconfirming evidence and critical reflection), then that wisdom is likely to be valuable. Such knowledge, if produced within a context of clear supervision and critically informed team discussions, may well produce knowledge that is practice *wisdom* rather than practice *prejudice*.

Therefore it is likely that, in addition to the careful attention to be paid to various family members' viewpoints, a second source of hypotheses will come from practitioners' carefully considered practice experiences. These will be likely to have a surer footing if they draw on our third and fourth sources of hypotheses: research evidence and theory.

Evidence-based practice

There is a wealth of research evidence relating to almost all aspects of the social care field. Our analysis of assessment information is likely to be stronger if we draw upon the accumulated wealth of knowledge from international social research. Two major questions are faced by practitioners who attempt to build their understandings of a family situation drawing from this evidence base:

- *Which* research evidence is relevant?
- *How* can it be applied to this particular assessment?

It is, of course, unwise for a practitioner to look at one small research study and assume that the findings are valid for all similar situations. There may well be contradictory conclusions from another study. We therefore need to search for a range of research findings on a topic and critically evaluate their worth. Fortunately, for many topics, this work is done for us by researchers who have conducted

Table 9.1   Examples of websites that provide access to research evidence

Electronic library of social care: http://www.elsc.org.uk
Making research count: http://www.uea.ac.uk/swk/research/mrc/welcome.htm
Research in practice: http://www.rip.org.uk/
Centre for evidence-based social services: http://www.ex.ac.uk/cebss/
The Campbell Collaboration: http://www.campbellcollaboration.org/
The Cochrane Developmental, Psychosocial and Learning Problems Group:
    http://www.bris.ac.uk/Depts/CochraneBehav/index.html

critical appraisals, research reviews, systematic reviews or meta-analyses of the field in question. These reviews are done to varying degrees of rigour and their findings may be more or less accessible to the lay reader. However, there are some reviews of research that have been designed to be accessible to practitioners (see, for example, Jackson and Thomas, 1999 and MacDonald, 1999). There are also several organisations that produce research summaries, often linked to universities or voluntary sector organisations, listed in Table 9.1.

One of the criticisms of evidence-based practice is that its proponents are seen to value only particular forms of knowledge, such as large quantitative studies (Webb, 2001). It is important to note that different research methods will provide different forms of knowledge. Randomised Control Trials aim to provide clear information about the outcomes of particular interventions. User evaluations may provide information on satisfaction levels and perceptions of the service. Close observations of practitioners at work (such as the Coastal Cities study) may provide insight into detailed processes of practice and an opportunity for practitioners to recognise and reflect on their own practice (Bloor, 1997). Much research work in the social care field originates from North America and findings do not automatically translate across the legal, cultural and institutional differences of other national contexts.

Webb (2001) argues that the advocates of evidence-based practice assume that evidence can straightforwardly be applied to practice situations. This ignores, he argues, the complexity of decision-making in the context of interagency arenas, resource constraints and outcome measurements. It also ignores our human tendency to attend to only some aspects of evidence (a tendency mentioned throughout this chapter), especially if the contradictory evidence might lead to a conclusion that will feel uncomfortable. Sheldon counters these arguments by stating that we cannot be fatalistic about these human tendencies: 'When the answer matters in the long-term it cannot be given up on' (2001: 805).

Using theory

Many practitioners are anxious about using formal theories, and some gratefully abandon thinking formally about them on leaving college. This does not mean, however, that any practitioner is operating within a theory-free zone. Many of our explanations about how people are functioning, and about how best to help them, are drawn from our knowledge of theories, but often we do not self-consciously link our explanations to a formal or named theory. Coffey and Atkinson (1996: 140) helpfully suggest that we think of using theory as simply 'having and using ideas'. They suggest that these ideas might be drawn from our own thoughts about what is going on, from the perspectives of those being researched/assessed (these form our first two sources of explanations above), or 'can be influenced by your understanding, sympathy, curiosity, or antagonism in relation to particular "schools" of ideas' (1996: 140). When we are having ideas about one particular case we will be engaging in informal theorising, but when we start to relate this particular situation to other cases and to wider society, then we are likely to be linking with more formal theories. In the academic field of social work a wide range of theories originating from several social science disciplines are commonly drawn upon, including cognitive-behaviourism, attachment theory, psycho-dynamic theory, solution-focused approaches, feminism, narrative approaches and broad-based ecological understandings. Formal theories help us to organise our thoughts and understanding of the world in a systematic way, and to explain our understandings to others, including service users. Theories should also help guide further action.

In the same way that it is not always possible to simply apply empirical research findings directly and straightforwardly to a practice situation, it is not always possible to find a neat 'fit' between one formal theory and a particular context. In particular, single theories will not provide a full understanding of all aspects of a family's social world, although some will be more useful than others in a particular situation. As reflective practitioners we can constantly adjust our understanding of theories according to the particular practice situation we are engaging with. We can also use a critical engagement with theory in order to challenge our understanding of a family situation. Payne (1998: 132) suggests that we might use a 'critical contrastive approach'. We can reflect on the ade-quacy of our current theoretical understanding of an issue by thinking about how other theoretical approaches might criticise our understandings. For exam-ple, by focusing on difficulties in family relationships, drawing perhaps on attachment theory, are we ignoring the impact of institutional and environ-mental factors such as racism and poverty on family members? Here we are sys-tematically analysing our assessment information by exploring a range of hypotheses, drawing on formal theories. Finally, we may find that although several formal theories might help us to develop a deeper understanding of a family situation, one emerges as the most useful. The theory's usefulness might be that it merges well with the family's own understandings of their lives and that it provides the most helpful basis for action.

Reaching Conclusions

I always feel that they're not finished. Core assessments are finished when it's the case con-ference tomorrow! And initial assessments are finished when you've contacted everyone, or at least when you've phoned the GP four times, they've never replied and you have to move on to another one. (Interview with Gaynor, social worker, City Social Services)

Gaynor reflects some of the real world practical difficulties faced by social workers attempting to conduct thorough and fair assessments. In both social research and in social work, we are working within a context of resource constraints and deadlines. In social research, projects sometimes finish because the funding has run out, rather than because the research team feels that they have comprehensively researched the topic at hand. In social work, the timetables of court and case conference often dictate the pace of an assessment, with social workers sometimes being forced to reach some form of conclusion despite feeling that not every relevant avenue has been thoroughly explored.

In an ideal practice scenario we might borrow a phrase from research and continue assessing until we reach 'saturation point'. This means that our information gathering is no longer throwing up new or surprising information, but is continuing to support and build upon the strongest themes and explanations. Although this point might be difficult to achieve with a family that appears to be in a constant state of change, we may still be able to conclude that certain factors are contributing to the instability and to agree a series of goals that aim to achieve stability.

If an assessor has followed the process described above, they will have been carrying out a constant process of reviewing the significance of the assessment information throughout the assessment. As hypotheses are built (and others discarded), these can be shared with others in order to gain critical feedback. Emerging understandings and conclusions can be shared with the supervisor, the family being assessed and other professionals. Edna, a social worker from the voluntary sector family centre in the Coastal Cities study, tells of how the Assessment Framework has encouraged her to work in this way:

> I think the new framework is asking you to evaluate all the time, which is much more helpful. Obviously [this helps] when it comes to drawing everything together and writing up a report but it is also helpful when you are liaising with other professionals. Because you are doing that, your evaluation, and you are not waiting for the end to come to these grand conclusions, it is there, and you can test that out with other professionals as well. (Edna, Hillside Family Centre)

The model here, therefore, is one of constant critical and reflective enquiry, where emerging conclusions are opened up to scrutiny and amendment by ourselves and others. To return to the assessment discourses described in Chapter 3, this is closer to the 'reflective evaluation' discourse than the 'scientific observation' discourse.

What should conclusions look like?

First, conclusions are never going to be indisputable. There is debate around the extent to which we should be certain about our conclusions. Parton (1998) and Taylor and White (2000) write that we should not be afraid of uncertainty because it would be untrue to suggest that we can reach a *correct* conclusion in such an inexact arena as that of human relationships. White (1997: 750) suggests that practitioners embrace a situation of multiple explanations, 'for along with uncertainty comes hope for change'. She also suggests that we aim for a 'fit' with family explanations, except where those explanations are leading to hurt or abuse. Sheppard et al. (2001) assert that if practitioners follow a rigorous method of analysis they should be able to arrive at an explanation *'that is the least likely to be wrong'* (2001: 881). This is, in fact, similar to the argument proposed by Taylor and White (2000). They draw on Latour's work to refute the notion that a relativist position which rejects certainty must mean a 'moral abyss' where explanations that, for example, justify abuse are equally valid to other explanations. Instead, 'science can claim to be *relatively* sure *at this moment* about things it describes' (2000: 30). In social work assessment with children and their families we are sometimes asked to reach conclusions about life-changing matters, such as the removal of a child for adoption. It is difficult, but it seems necessary, for professionals and society more generally to accept that such decisions are made on the basis of an analysis that is never going to be certain. However, in order to achieve the 'least wrong' conclusion we need a rigorous and reflexive approach to analysing the multiple accounts that we are presented with during an assessment.

Second, the most useful conclusions may be those that look forward rather than look back. Parton and O'Byrne (2000) suggest that knowing the cause of problems is not always needed in order to build solutions. Causes can be pathologising and may well 'come from the worker's head rather than from the data' (2000: 141). On the other hand, for some family members, being enabled to reach an explanation for how their problems came about – for example, through childhood trauma, social learning, social exclusion or domestic abuse – may help them to agree to forward-looking solutions with the assessor. However, even if the conclusion incorporates a causal explanation of the family difficulties, it can also incorporate an analysis of how the family's current difficulties are being perpetuated and of how the situation may move forward. A helpful conclusion might therefore be *solution focused* and where possible those solutions should fit with family members' desires and preferred ways of working. Milner and O'Byrne (1998) also suggest that the solutions should be *testable*. Conclusions may therefore state how they will be tested or evaluated. For example, if there are thought to be risks to the child if he or she were to be returned home, what would need to change in order for those risks to be reduced to an acceptable level, and how will it be known that this has happened?

Third, as was discussed in Chapter 4, conclusions need to be *flexible* enough to be able to accommodate changing circumstances. Sheppard et al. (2001) remind us that conclusions will always be provisional, with the knowledge that human situations can change rapidly or new evidence may emerge. It was noted in Chapter 4 that when decisions about permanent placement for adoption are being made, then a final conclusion on the placement choice will have to be reached, although such cases do not form the majority of child welfare cases. Even decisions about permanent placement away from home may need to build some flexibility into aspects, such as contact arrangements, to allow for the changes in the child's and their birth and adoptive families' needs and desires. Flexibility should not, of course, be pursued at the expense of a child's need for stability and security.

Finally, conclusions may be *complex*, in that they reflect the complicated lives of the families being assessed. A hypothesis may have been adapted to incorporate exceptions in the evidence. For example, a conclusion might be that the capacity of both parents to meet the basic care needs of their toddler is poor, perhaps due to depression, learning disability, lack of suitable accommodation or substance misuse (or perhaps all of these). This conclusion may also incorporate exceptions to this generalisation, the pockets of parenting strengths. These strengths may form the basis for building a solution-focused conclusion (which should not be confused with an over-optimistic conclusion). The acknowledgement of exceptions and contradictions within a conclusion avoids the temptation to argue an overwhelming case to a court or case conference. In the UK and the US, a generally adversarial approach to child welfare legal proceedings might be seen to encourage the suppression of contradictory evidence. However, in England and Wales, government guidelines dictate that, 'where the welfare of children is the paramount consideration, there is a duty on all parties to make full and frank disclosure of all matters relevant to welfare whether these are favourable or adverse to their own particular case' (quoted in Brayne et al., 2001).

Building Hypotheses and Reaching Conclusions: a Summary

The understandings or hypotheses that are to be worked with during an assessment may draw on all of the four sources outlined above: the self-assessments of various family members, our own understandings derived from practice and personal experience, the findings of empirical research and, finally, hypotheses drawing on formal theories. It has been suggested that our self-awareness about the origins of our hypotheses will be enhanced if we conduct a cultural review early on in the process. We may then continue to reflect on the impact on our developing hypotheses of ourselves, the other participants, and the assessment process itself, throughout the assessment. By using a range of assessment methods and by actively searching for evidence which might contradict our dominant explanation(s), we are more likely to produce understandings and ways forward that are well founded.

How do Social Workers Analyse in Practice?

In Chapter 3 it was seen that in the Coastal Cities study practitioners found it difficult to name or describe their processes of analysis when conducting assessments. Several other research studies have aimed to examine how social workers in child and family social work analyse and reach decisions in assessment work. Three research studies will be discussed here, each of which used different research methods. Scott's (1998) study used a semi-longitudinal approach (including observation and repeated in-depth interviewing) to examine the assessment methods of statutory child protection social workers and hospital social workers. Munro (1999) conducted a content analysis of all 45 child abuse inquiry reports published in the UK between 1973 and 1994. Sheppard and colleagues (2001) used case vignettes to examine the processes of hypothesising and hypothesis testing amongst 21 experienced British social workers.

Both Scott's and Munro's studies found that many practitioners tend to stick with their original risk assessments and to see new evidence in the light of this. Munro (1999) found that risk assessments were usually only revised where there was professional observation of a severe injury to a child (moderate injury and injuries reported by family and neighbours were less likely to trigger revisions). Both authors found that assessors tended to draw their evidence from a narrow arena, linked to the initial hypothesis. Data sources that were found to be regularly ignored included children's accounts (especially where they contradicted the hypothesis), written records (in Munro's study) and the home environment (by hospital social workers in Scott's study).

In both Scott's and Sheppard et al.'s studies, a tendency was seen of social workers failing to develop a range of potential hypotheses, or of using assessment methods that might explore more than one hypothesis. Sheppard and colleagues noted that the depth of hypotheses varied, with some that might be described as 'partial hypotheses' (2001: 871) relating to only some aspects of the case. They also note that ' ... practically a quarter of social workers were not considering more than one alternative as a means of explaining or defining the cases with which they were presented' (2001: 874).

All three studies were able to find examples of practitioners who were able to explore more than one hypothesis through a range of data sources and be open to revising their initial assessment. Inevitably, standards of analysis were mixed, with examples of both wide-ranging and narrow assessment practices. The question arising from these findings appears to be: Is it possible to train practitioners to use a rigorous method for analysis such as analytic induction, or is our human tendency to seek evidence to fit our initial single hypothesis and to avoid the complexity of working with multiple explanations too strong? (Scott, 1998).

Reporting the Assessment

Written documents

Long periods of time are spent by practitioners in writing the reports of their assessment work. Records can be seen as an important means of self-defence for front-line workers (Garfinkel, 1967; Dingwall et al., 1995). White (1998c: 3) has suggested that they may be part of a process of 'prospective exoneration' in anticipation of any future inquiry into the author's decision-making. Taylor and White (2000: 143) suggest that an analysis of an organisation's written records and reports can reveal elements of professional and institutional priorities, interpretations of what constitutes reality and 'background expectancies' of an organisation.

Increasingly, welfare departments provide standard forms for assessment reports. This follows from an understandable urge to ensure consistency of service, thoroughness of assessment work and ease of completion for busy practitioners.

It should be noted, however, that the recording of assessment work on standard forms constitutes an intervention in the assessment process that is not neutral. Taylor and White (2000) note that many assessment forms require a simplification of the complex picture of many family situations. The structure of the form pares down some elements, whilst amplifying others. The assessment process is not recorded, only the results. Forms with 'yes/no' sections (even where there is room for a few additional comments) may imply a more clear and certain picture of family life than the assessment process can actually produce. The information is often recorded after much deliberation and compromise. Even if the current assessor is aware of all the contextual information that provides 'ifs ... ' and 'buts ... ', the recording of fixed responses on a form gives the information a solidity for other readers. The information is often then compiled into local and national statistics and may provide a basis for resource distribution and policy-making. Thus, whilst forms that have been thoughtfully produced have many advantages for practitioners, we should remain aware that their use is not an entirely neutral activity.

Audience

There is a range of possible audiences for written documents (Garfinkel, 1967; Bull and Shaw, 1992; Atkinson and Coffey, 1997). Audiences for assessment reports include adults and older children being assessed, babies and younger children when grown up, the guardian *ad litem*, the court, the supervisor, other professionals, future social workers and researchers. This wide range of audiences form a great challenge for social workers to write to a high standard, and yet be accessible to different levels of understanding and register. It was noted in Chapter 3 that social workers may tend to present their court reports in scientific objective language. Whilst it is important for professional credibility that court reports are written in scrupulously good English (or whatever is the language of the court), the nature of the assessment should not be changed. Therefore, if much of the information is uncertain, if the assessment was conducted with close engagement with the family and a careful listening to a range of accounts, then, it can be argued, this is what should be in the report. It is tempting to try to repackage a primarily qualitative activity into one of measurements and precision.

The service user, or subject of the report, is a vital audience member. We discuss below the issue of incorporating the accounts of those being assessed into the report. The final report should be read by, or to, the service user. This should preferably take place before the report is seen by anyone else (except perhaps a supervisor) so that any factual inaccuracies may be altered. Family members may also wish to challenge interpretations of information and to have the chance to add their challenges or clarifications to the report (this process is institutionalised in the Assessment Framework recording forms). Accessibility of a report is improved by avoidance of jargon, the use of 'plain English' (see Hopkins, 1998, for an accessible guide), the translation of the report into the family members' preferred languages and the provision of the report on audiotape for those unable to read. A simplified version may be produced for children.

Contents of the report

Due to the proliferation of standardised recording forms for assessment and for court and other official reports, the overall ordering and content of our assessment reports are often fairly prescribed. This does not mean, however, that we cannot include some of the following three aspects in our assessment reports. The first aspect is balance, the second is the need to incorporate service users' accounts and the third is to provide an account of the process of decision-making.

First, the word 'balance' here is used to suggest that a report should be rounded in its coverage. In Chapter 6 it was noted that in the Coastal Cities study some reports appeared unbalanced, in that several pages of reporting were devoted to profiles of the parents, whilst children were sometimes described in just a few sentences. It was difficult to gain a sense of the children's individuality through the reports. Additionally, only certain aspects of the children's lives were reported, usually their developmental attainments and their relationship with their parents as seen in contact sessions. A balanced report of a child's needs will provide information on broader aspects of the child's life. Further aspects of balance include the need to report strengths as well as problems and to give weight to environmental and societal factors in addition to individual issues. It is a human tendency to over-attribute causes for people's difficulties according to personal factors (for example, lack of self-control) and to underestimate the effects of environmental factors such as poverty and poor housing (Kagle, 1988; Gambrill and Shlonsky, 2000). This attributional tendency is also evident in the law, at least in England and Wales. King and Piper (1995) suggest that, in the way that the law 'thinks', parents are seen as direct or indirect causes of harm to children, and environmental and social factors are not considered.

Second, it is suggested here that a report should incorporate the views and understandings of the subjects of the assessments, including those whose voices are not always reported, such as children and parents living out of the family home. As Parton and O'Byrne suggest:

> There is a need, therefore, to move from trying to 'reproduce' lives on paper to writing more collaborative accounts that draw on the meanings of service users. (2000: 143)

It has been suggested above that our conclusions should aim to draw on the accounts of those being assessed. It was seen in Chapter 5 that the assessments in the Coastal Cities study, where the parents and the social workers agreed on the origins of their problems and the way forward, were also those where the children and their parents were reunited. Whilst it was suggested in Chapter 5 that this could be problematic where it favours the more articulate and those who simply agree with the professionals, it is also possible that those were the assessments where more collaborative assessment relationships were established, with careful listening by both the assessor and assessed. It is also possible to report service users' accounts directly, through quoting or leaving space for them to make their own contributions.

The final point to be made here about the content of reports is that it may be both helpful and fair to include a brief account of the decision-making process. This might include an account of the range of understandings and ways forward considered, and the way in which the final conclusions were reached. This may have included the process described above of searching for both supporting evidence and evidence that would appear to throw doubt upon a way of understanding the situation. It may also have included the testing and refining of hypotheses through consultation with supervisors, other professionals and family members. A brief statement about the process will help the report's audience assess its validity.

Language use

The final area of consideration in this discussion about writing assessment reports is the issue of language. Here the focus is on some of the more detailed aspects of writing, including ordering, choice of words and the tone of writing. Some of the basic elements of professional writing should form the foundation for a consideration of the language of reports. Reports should be well written and checked by a colleague or supervisor. It is difficult to see even glaring errors in our own work when we have been staring at the page for some time. A further basic point is to avoid words that have sexist or racist undertones, such as the use of 'he' for 'he or she' or associating the word 'black' with negativity. We should also avoid words that can be pathologising and imprecise, such as 'manipulative'.

Whilst most social workers will understand the need for professionally written reports, some may remain unaware of the potential effects of more subtle forms of language use. For example, the legitimacy of certain accounts of the family situation can be subtly altered by the use of terms such as 'claims', 'reports', 'alleges' and 'states'. In the Coastal Cities study, family members' accounts of historic events from their own childhood were usually reported unproblematically as factual. However, their versions of current or recent events were more likely to be treated as problematic, especially where they conflicted with the accounts of professionals. For example, a parent's account of their own difficult childhood would be reported as fact, whereas their account of recent events would be couched in terms such as 'alleged' and 'claims'. Milner and O'Byrne (1998) suggest that reports may contain a 'pitch' and cast doubt on statements by using terms such as 'unfortunately' and 'however'. They also note the rise of euphemistic, rather than openly condemnatory, language as a result of client access to records. An example from the Coastal Cities study is of a mother having 'many male visitors to the home' (Smith family assessment report). There are many male callers to my home – relatives and friends paying visits – but this is surely not what is meant in relation to Ms Smith.

Two further subtle effects can be caused by the structure of reports: by ordering and listing. The order in which items are mentioned might imply a prioritisation. The beginning and end of most reports are the most important parts, and here is where the vital information (for example, risk assessment and summary) should lie. Whilst ordering can imply prioritisation, listing can have the opposite effect of conflating information and implying that all items on the list are of equal value.

To return to the Smith family assessment referred to in the paragraph above, 15 risks or concerns are listed together in the first section of the report. These encompass a wide range of behaviours and events, including serious injuries experienced by the children: burns, other physical injuries and possible sexual assault. The list also includes issues of the children's poor behaviour not being controlled by their mother, the poor health of the mother, the dirtiness of the house and the aforementioned neighbour's report of male callers to the home. The reader is left in no doubt that the two boys have suffered harm and that the family faces multiple problems. However, the list structure appears to lead to a conflating of a wide range of behaviours so that they all appear to be *equally* 'risky' or potentially harmful to the child. Some of the items listed are not discussed again in the report, but their listing invokes a general climate of risk. In this case the lack of distinction between confirmed episodes of harm and more speculative allegations almost appears to diminish the serious injuries experienced by the children.

We cannot escape language, therefore we need to choose some words instead of others and we need to prioritise information. However, all of us should take time to be critical of our own writing and to maintain an awareness of the possible subtle effects of our choice of words. It is surely more ethical and effective to straightforwardly state which information appears to be trustworthy or of most importance, and where risks lie, than to use euphemisms or other tactics to hint at what we mean.

Conclusion

During this chapter Scott's (1998) question was noted: Is it possible to train practitioners to use a rigorous method for analysis such as analytic induction or is our human tendency to seek evidence to fit our initial single hypothesis and to avoid the complexity of working with multiple explanations too strong? It seems that the ability of practitioners to work against lay interpretations and human tendencies is what distinguishes us as professionals. The complexity of analysis demonstrates that assessment is much more than simply a technical and procedural task. Hopefully, with the right training, support and resources, practitioners may be enabled to develop their analytic skills in order to produce assessment reports that are thorough, fair and produce recommendations that will provide a positive way forward for children and their families.

Suggestions for practice

- As professionals we need to take active steps to work against our human tendency to seek only the information that we wish to find.
- By undertaking a 'cultural review' at the start of the assessment we may be enabled to practice reflexively.
- We need to be critically aware of the value we put on information from different sources.

- Sharing our emerging thoughts with others – family members, supervisors, other professionals, co-workers – can aid critical reflection on the assessment work.
- Practitioners may wish to incorporate in their conclusions elements that are solution focused, testable, flexible and not overly simplistic.

10 Conclusion

Even after we learn all about our client, from him and his acquaintances ... we fail to know him at all. (Trout, 1939, quoted in Mailick, 1991: 5)

Perhaps the dilemma is that however thorough the observation or assessment, the professional will only have a brief snapshot of what makes up the relationship between the adult and the child. (Schofield, 1996: 45)

We have our technical information, but no one knows the intricacies of that parent–child relationship as they themselves do – the nuances, that shared look. It's very difficult to get access to that. (Interview with Brian, social worker, Coastal Cities study)

These three extracts set the theme for this concluding chapter. There are many challenges associated with in-depth assessment in social work. Whilst the aim of such an assessment might be to gain a thorough understanding of an individual or family, the practitioner is always left with the knowledge that they will have gained only a partial glimpse into another's life. In this book an attempt has been made to problematise assessment and to move away from the notion that the facts about a family may be straightforwardly assembled and a correct conclusion reached. There is unlikely to ever be one, correct assessment conclusion. Using an analysis influenced by social constructionism, it has been suggested that, rather than pursuing an unattainable goal of the absolute truth, we should pay more attention to individuals' explanations and understandings of their situation. In other words, what is true to family members, rather than an absolute truth. In doing this we need to acknowledge that there may be several sets of understanding or explanation within a family. It also does not mean that we should naïvely accept all that is said to us. It is human nature to wish to accentuate our positives to others and to minimise our involvement in that which we know our listener will disapprove of, especially if the listener has power over us.

However, it may be argued that, by working alongside family members wherever possible, an *acceptable* understanding of the family's situation and the best plan for moving forward should be reached. An acceptable plan would be one that met the child's needs for safety and wellbeing as the highest priority. But it will have most chance of success if it is acceptable to the key players in the assessment – the child and their main carers (with the acknowledgement that child and adult members of one family are unlikely to have uniform needs and opinions). It also needs to be acceptable to the courts and to meet the requirements of laws and formal guidance. Additionally, it will have more chance of success if it is an acceptable conclusion for key professionals involved. The ordering of acceptability should be noted. It is too tempting for professionals to decide the solutions in advance and then to try to persuade the family members to follow these. Assessment practice that begins with careful listening to family members' understandings and solutions, and works from there, is more likely to be both equitable and workable. It should be acknowledged, however, that in some cases painful decisions regarding the removal of a child from home will have to be reached that some or all family members do not agree with. The practitioner will wish to ensure that she or he has followed a fair and thorough process before making such a decision.

Having reiterated some of the main overall principles of assessment practice from the book, I will next draw together some of the more detailed assessment themes that emerge from the preceding chapters. I then discuss some aspects of evaluating assessment work before summarising suggested principles that together might lead to fair and thorough assessment practice.

Key Themes in Child and Family Assessment

This book has focused on three main areas:

- Discussion about the nature of assessment.
- Issues of practice particularly pertinent to the assessment of children and families: the assessment relationship between adult carers and assessors, involving children and assessing parenting and parental lifestyles.
- Discussion of the overall processes of an assessment, particularly in relation to assessment design and analysis. Here a comparison has been made between assessment and qualitative social science research methods.

I will discuss these three areas in turn, highlighting the main points raised in previous chapters.

The nature of assessment

Whilst it may seem difficult for busy practitioners to spend time pondering the nature of assessment, rather than seeking practice solutions to immediate problems, consideration of this issue is vital because it affects every assessment action. There are a number of different ways of viewing assessment, and the adoption (either conscious or unconscious) of one of these approaches over another is likely to alter policies or individual practices. We have seen, in Chapter 2, that assessment policy over the last half-century can be viewed as having taken a range of approaches: diagnostic, predictive, broad social and bureaucratic. There is considerable overlap between these, and some sets of assessment guidance may be seen to incorporate more than one approach. It has been seen that in England and Wales there have been attempts to move from a narrow concentration on risk in child welfare to an approach that also incorporates a broad assessment of need.

The approach that individual teams and practitioners will take when using such guidance will also be affected by their stance when assessing families. In

Chapter 3 it was seen that individual social workers often struggle with competing discourses. Many feel that taking an objective, scientific approach, requiring the maintaining of a distance from the family members and a position as expert, is the dominant expectation of courts and indeed is the more 'correct' way to proceed. Some also report that they have found that the best way to proceed in their own assessment practice is to get alongside those being assessed and try to reach a deep, shared and reflective understanding of the situation. These ways of understanding assessment practice also relate to two of the models of assessment practice outlined by Smale et al. (1993): the questioning model and the exchange model.

A further aspect relating to the nature of assessment was raised in Chapter 4. Here it was seen that, in addition to practical considerations, issues of time and change can affect how we understand assessment. It was seen that, whilst assessment conclusions are generally seen as temporary and open to revision, there are a few cases where more fixed and permanent decisions must be made, particularly in cases of adoption. Often practitioners need to make decisions about whether they are seeking change during an assessment, or hope to assess the likelihood of future changes. They also have to try to write assessment conclusions that are dynamic enough to adapt to the rapid changes that families in crisis often experience. Thus practitioners must decide whether they understand assessment as producing a snapshot of a family at one point in time, or are able to encompass past, present and future elements.

Different understandings of assessment and different assessment policies are not absolute and none is clearly right or wrong. In some severe child abuse cases, particularly where a main carer appears to present a continuing danger to the child and there is a need to provide clear evidence for the court, it may well be appropriate to adopt an expert, objective approach. Whilst it has been seen that a predictive approach has clear limitations when applied to individual families, it is likely to be useful when assessing the needs of a population in order to plan service provision. In general, however, it will be clear to the reader that I favour a reflective approach to assessment, adopting a stance similar to Smale and colleagues' (1993) exchange model.

Assessment with children and families

The first theme of the book summarised above – the nature of assessment – is relevant to all assessment work in the field of social welfare. The second major theme of the book has addressed issues that are particularly relevant to assessment in the child welfare arena: the assessment relationship with the main carers, involving children and assessing parenting.

Whilst the relationship between the assessed and the assessor is important in all assessment work, it holds particular relevance in the field of child welfare. Many families do come forward to social work agencies and ask for help, but some are reluctantly complying with the suggestion that they be referred for assessment, whilst others are downright hostile and only participate in the face of court action or in an attempt to reunite with their children. Forming a working relationship with parents, extended family members and children in a family therefore poses particular challenges for the assessing practitioner. In Chapter 5 it was noted that in the Coastal Cities study this developing relationship appeared to be crucial to the outcome of the assessment. Positive recommendations to reunite children and their parents or to maintain children at home occurred, in this small sample, where the assessor and the main carer(s) were able to agree how the family had got into crisis and how they might move forward. It therefore seems important that careful attention is paid to the processes of engaging families in an assessment.

There appears to be a tendency in child and family social work, noted in the Coastal Cities study and in other research findings, to place an emphasis on the level of parents' co-operation with the assessment process when reaching assessment conclusions. It is vital, in order to ensure a just process, that the assessment is made accessible to those who find it difficult to engage. The assessment relationship appears to be established and maintained through talk, especially in the intensive assessment interviews. This has the potential to exclude the less articulate, but may be alleviated by the use of a broad range of assessment methods. Attention to accessibility includes establishing a right to assessment through the language most comfortable for those being assessed, paying attention to the gender and other cultural attributes of the assessor, making written information understandable and, if necessary, encouraging the use of an independent advocate. Some individuals will still not wish to co-operate with an assessment and may indeed be dangerous and aggressive people to be around, but at least a fair opportunity will have been offered.

Social work in the field of child welfare has often been a process largely undertaken between women social workers and mothers (Scourfield, 2003). Others have been excluded or excluded themselves. The gendered nature of the work is, at times, stark. Women social workers are often anxious about their own safety when working with violent men, but also may be expecting mothers to sort out, or eject, the violent men in their lives. Where fathers and other extended family members can be included in an assessment, the assessment is likely to be better informed and a message is given that the welfare of children in a family may be the responsibility of all family members. It is acknowledged, however, that there are no easy solutions to engaging men in child welfare assessments, especially where there are concerns about men's violence to women or children in the family.

Children have also often been excluded from assessments, despite being the focus of the concerns. In Chapter 6 it was noted how children's voices may be at times silenced through a number of means (Hall et al., 1997), such as not reporting their views or suggesting that a child's views are unreliable. Descriptions of young children are often brief or impersonal. It is sometimes suggested that there is a tension between listening to the views of children and making decisions that are in their best interests. There was some limited evidence in the Coastal Cities study of children's voices being reported and valued where their views coincided with those of the professionals around them. In Chapter 6 it was also noted that children themselves may take a balanced view of this issue, often reporting that they wish to be listened to but that adults also need to make decisions concerned with their welfare and protection.

A final topic pertinent to the assessment of children and families is the assessment of parenting. Here, social constructionism is particularly relevant to our understanding of parenting. Acceptable parenting standards are not absolute and norms have varied enormously over time and across cultures. Social workers in the Coastal Cities study were keen to emphasise that they were not looking for perfect parenting. Indeed, as long as minimum standards of care were reached, practical parenting standards did not appear to be as important indicators of assessment outcomes as aspects of the assessment relationship such as parental co-operation or willingness to change their lifestyle. In terms of assessing parenting, the Assessment Framework approach in England and Wales suggests individually assessing the needs of each child (which will vary according to age and ability) and the capacity of the child's main carers to meet those needs. This appears to be a more sensible way to proceed than comparing all parents to one standard set of norms or checklist, although it lacks the attractive simplicity of the latter.

The process of assessment: comparisons with social research

In 1996 I ceased being a practising social worker who specialised in carrying out in-depth child welfare assessments and began researching how others carried out these assessments. It immediately struck me how closely the two worlds interconnected. For, indeed, an in-depth assessment of a child and their family is essentially a piece of qualitative research. Just as there are a number of different stances, approaches and ways of understanding assessment, so there are in qualitative research, but there are some overall principles and methods that can usefully be shared between the two disciplines. These parallels have been noted by a number of authors, including Clifford and Cropper (1997), Sheppard (1995a, 1995b) and White (1997). Social workers have long experience of carrying out in-depth interviews, and it was noted in Chapter 6 that many researchers with children have used methods from practice in order to enable children to talk about their experiences. This area of research has developed in recent years, and there are now some methods developed in research with children that practitioners may find helpful.

It is, however, in the major areas of assessment design and analysis that I would advocate a close attention to social science methodology. In Chapters 8 and 9 it was suggested that principles relating to research design and analysis might usefully be transferred to assessment practice. Some transferable ideas in terms of research design include the notion of triangulation and the establishment of research or assessment questions. Whilst triangulation, or using a range of assessment methods, does not guarantee the validity of the conclusions, it is likely to make the assessment more broadly based and thorough. It should help to critically explore ideas with a family about their situation by exploring their strengths and difficulties from a variety of angles. It may also make assessments more accessible and interesting for family members. Establishing the key questions for the assessment will help enormously with the planning and design of an assessment, just as the setting of research questions is a central element of research design. These questions may be formed alongside family members and other informants, such as extended family, other professionals and referring bodies, such as courts. The questions will often change as the assessment progresses.

Many social workers and other assessing practitioners find analysis of voluminous, qualitative information to be the most difficult part of an assessment. Many practitioners, through experience, and because personable types are often drawn in to social welfare work, are good at engaging and forming relationships with families and are able to gather a lot of information about the family through skilful and empathetic interviewing. However, some experience difficulties in making sense of this information and forming useful conclusions that are grounded in the assessment evidence. This has been noted in early research into the use of the Assessment Framework in England and Wales (Cleaver, 2002; Thomas and Cleaver, 2002). Drawing on the work of Sheppard (1995a, 1998) and White (1997) among others, I suggest in Chapter 9 that social workers could tackle their analysis of assessment information using analytic techniques developed in social research. Principles such as rooting explanations in the evidence, searching for disconfirming evidence (that which might challenge the dominant explanation(s)) and being reflective and critical of our own role in the assessment should produce analysis that is thorough and fair. We can never be sure that we have reached the 'right' conclusion, but hopefully through such methods we can reach one that is soundly based and justifiable.

A Model of the Assessment Process

It has therefore been suggested that a large number of factors affect the assessment process, making it a more complicated process than simply gathering information and reaching a conclusion. Berg (1992) offers an analysis of decision-making in medicine, which suggests that decisions are mediated by a large number of factors. The process of child and family assessments might be presented in a similar manner, as seen in Figure 10.1.

This figure summarises just some of the elements that come into play during the process of assessment. Whilst these observations arise from the Coastal Cities study assessments, it is possible that similar factors affect child and family assessment processes more generally. All have the potential to inter-relate and affect each other. Even the original referred problem may become redefined during this process (Berg, 1992). In-depth assessments in social work are complex and mediated by a large number of factors. Yet it is tempting for social workers to present them as neat, logical series of decisions, based entirely on the facts of the individual cases. The reporting requirements of courts and other institutions encourage this trend.

I have argued in this book that in-depth assessments in child welfare can never be neat, entirely logical or objective pieces of work. However, I do believe that critical, reflective practitioners can carry out assessments that are thorough

Figure 10.1   The process of assessment: mediating elements

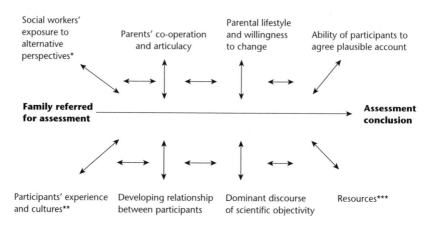

Notes
* including child's, other disciplines, colleagues etc.
** including age, ethnicity, sex, locality, occupational culture.
***including time, guidance, staff experience and availability, case-loads, etc.
Source: Adapted from Berg, 1992: 168.

and fair. A framework of suggested ways of achieving this is included at the end of this chapter. Practitioners may also wish to consider ways in which they may evaluate whether they have achieved thorough and fair assessment practice, and this is considered in the next section.

Evaluating Assessment Practice

Evaluation with a capital 'E' tends to be associated by practitioners as something formal, time-consuming, concerned with measurement and performance indicators and relating to service level concerns rather than direct practice concerns (Shaw, 1996). It is seen as something that is essentially outside of their immediate practice concerns, an 'add-on' that involves a separate set of procedures from practice. However, Shaw argues that it is also possible for practitioners to evaluate *in* practice. Indeed, he argues that this is an essential need for social work:

> ... social work and those who receive the services provided by social workers, need the kind of practitioners that a commitment to evaluating will foster – practitioners who are able to make imaginative, lateral 'translations', who are empirically informed, who work as both outsiders and insiders within social work, who are reflexive practitioners, committed to falsifying their favourite practice, and above all are engaged to evaluate both for and with those who use their services'. (Shaw, 1996: 8)

Most of those hopes for practitioners' attitudes and skills listed by Shaw are very similar to the attitudes and skills for assessment discussed throughout this book.

In particular, the need to be reflexive and to be able to 'falsify' or look for that which might throw doubt on our dominant explanations have been discussed as key elements of thorough analysis in assessment work. Looking more broadly, the literature on evaluating in social work is extensive and interested practitioners will find useful further reading elsewhere (for example, Broad, 1999; Shaw and Lishman, 1999). However, I will briefly suggest some ways in which practitioners may wish to evaluate their own assessment practice. I will discuss four aspects: the evaluation of self, of user views, of outcomes and of accessibility and inclusion.

It can be argued that the critical, reflective practitioner is engaged in constant self-evaluation through 'reflecting-in-action' (Schön, 1991, see Chapter 3). It is suggested in Chapter 9 that assessors conduct a 'cultural review' of their own categories, constructions or understandings of an assessment situation before beginning an assessment. This may be returned to during and after the assessment, to reflect on how the experience of the assessment has affected our constructions of the particular situation, our understanding of the task of assessment and perhaps our understanding of self. Thus one aspect of evaluation will be to evaluate what the assessment has meant for ourselves, professionally and personally.

The second aspect is to evaluate how the assessment has been experienced by the family members being assessed. There can be difficulties in enquiring about service users' satisfaction with a service. Consumers generally tend to over-report satisfaction, for a host of different reasons (Shaw, 1996). One key difficulty in child welfare is the powerless position many families feel themselves to be in, due to sanctions available to statutory agencies and the courts. Nonetheless, it is of course important that families are asked about their experiences of the assessment and this may be done, for example, by anonymous questionnaire, in-depth or semi-structured interview or a focus group. Social service agencies may develop a standard method of eliciting their clients' views, so that results may be compared in a large-scale and systematic manner. If family members are consulted about their experiences throughout an assessment, then it may be possible to adjust assessment methods and approaches that are felt to be uncomfortable, oppressive or otherwise counterproductive. Reviewing with a family member at each meeting how they are experiencing the process of assessment can become an integral part of assessment practice. Asking family members, including children, how they wish to evaluate the service they have received is probably the most sensible way to proceed. It should be remembered that a question about the experience of an intervention, such as an assessment, is very different from the question, 'What difference has it made to your everyday life?'. This leads us to the third aspect of evaluation, the issue of measuring outcomes.

Evaluating outcomes is a very broad subject, which there is only space here to discuss briefly. Useful discussions about measuring outcomes in social work can be found in Stevens (1999) and MacDonald (1999). Sellick and Thoburn (1996) note the complexity of evaluating outcomes for looked after children, where a vast range of inter-relating factors may affect outcomes, including the characteristics and experiences of the child, the quality of support to placement, the parenting provided within the placement, extraneous factors, including peer group and education, and chance. Important questions that must be asked when examining outcomes are:

- Who defines desirable outcomes?
- In whose interests do they serve?
- Are only immediate outcomes of interest, or is it possible to measure intermediate and long-term outcomes? (Stevens, 1999).

The setting of outcomes to be measured, in other words, has political, ethical and practical dimensions. Lupton and Nixon (1999: 159) note that there has not been enough involvement by children and their families in defining what may be desirable outcomes. They provide an example of how outcomes may be identified for measuring the success of family group conferences. In their example, immediate outcomes include whether an adequate and sustainable plan was produced, intermediate outcomes include whether the child was retained within/returned to the family network, and ultimate results include whether the child was protected from abuse or neglect. In setting outcomes to be measured in assessment practice, an agency may have outcomes that will be measured for each assessment (such as the production of a plan and access issues discussed below) and outcomes that may be agreed on a case-by-case basis with family members and other involved agencies.

Last, I wish to suggest that it is helpful to evaluate the levels of inclusion and participation achieved during the assessment. This should apply as much to a court-ordered assessment relating to child abuse, where the family is reluctant to attend, as to where the assessment involves a self-referral for support. Basic aspects of accessibility and inclusion may be asked of each assessment:

- Was each family member given the opportunity to work through the medium of the language of their choice?
- Were all written records made readily available and translated, audiotaped or summarised where necessary?
- Are all buildings and facilities physically accessible to all family members?
- Was the sex of the assessing staff discussed with family members, particularly where this may be affected by culture, religion or histories of abuse?
- Was thought given to offering an advocate to family members, particularly children and those with mental health problems or learning disabilities?
- Was the timing and location of sessions negotiated with family members?

Attention to many of these issues is a legal requirement in some countries. It also fits with the basic approach to assessment in this book where there has been an emphasis on building a supportive and listening relationship with family members from the start of an assessment, wherever possible.

Levels of participation may be monitored by measuring the assessment practice against one of the scales or benchmarks of participation developed in relation

Figure 10.2 The 'climbing wall' of participation

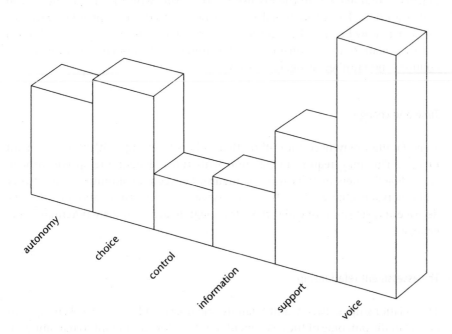

to discussions of partnership practice (such as Pugh et al., 1987; Marsh and Fisher, 1992). One example is the model of a 'climbing wall' of participation, developed by Thomas (2000) in which factors associated with facilitating children's participation are listed (see Figure 10.2). Unlike other models that adopt a hierarchy of levels of participation, Thomas argues that some aspects may be more important than others according to particular circumstances. For example, a child who chooses not to attend a meeting or assessment session may feel that they have exercised both choice and autonomy, but their voice will not have been heard. Other children may have been given much opportunity to express their views, but feel that they have had little control over how their views are used in decision-making.

Towards Thorough and Fair Assessment Practice

It was stated in the introduction of this book that it was not intended to simply criticise current assessment practice using the evidence from the Coastal Cities study and other research referred to in the course of the discussion. Nor is the book intended to suggest in a prescriptive way that there is any one correct way to proceed with assessment work. Instead, the hope is that the discussion in the book will aid practitioners and students in critically reflecting on their own approaches to assessment. However, it was also noted in the introduction that many readers find it helpful to read summaries that detail the implications for practice contained within the discussion. Therefore, whilst risking reductionism and distortion, I have included practice points at the end of most chapters. These may now be brought together to form a statement of both principles and practical matters to be considered when undertaking in-depth assessments of children and families, as detailed below.

Time and change

Some families may need more time than others to engage with the assessment process. This may require negotiation with those demanding speedy conclusions. Practitioners may wish to distinguish between a commitment to change and observable changes in behaviour. Assessment conclusions should aim to be decisive and yet (in most cases) flexible enough to accommodate potential future change.

The assessment relationship

The relationship between adult family members and social workers appears crucial in the outcome of the assessment. It is therefore important to maximise the chance of a positive engagement in the assessment. This might include paying equal attention to the impact of the practitioner and the family member on the relationship, involving advocates or trusted professionals from other agencies and not over-relying on verbal interviewing where levels of articulacy might prejudice the outcome. Essentially, children's experiences of family life are more important than their parents' attitudes to professionals.

Children in assessments

Three main areas require our attention: the information given to children, how we listen to children, and how we represent children's lives and their views. Attractively produced materials such as information packs, videos or websites can provide basic information about assessments. Children will also need specific information about their own assessment and can be consulted on the best method for finding out about their lives and opinions. Research suggests that children are particularly concerned about confidentiality and honesty. Ways in which we might listen to children are summarised in Chapter 6. When representing children's lives we will produce a more rounded picture if we consider all aspects of the child's everyday life and if we avoid trying to simply 'check-off' the child's skills against developmental milestones. When representing their wishes we should recognise that these may change, as the child's experiences change, and that it may help fears about confidentiality if we agree with them in advance how their views will be reported.

Assessing parenting and family life

As with all aspects of assessment, it is important to listen carefully to both parents' and children's experiences of family life. It is important to avoid determinist and universalising explanations for particular groups, whether they are from a particular cultural or religious group or facing specific problems such as domestic violence or substance misuse. It may well be necessary to consult an expert opinion and research findings about a particular family difficulty. Parenting is multiply determined, and strengths in one area may partly compensate for difficulties elsewhere. Above all, it seems necessary to assess whether the specific parenting needs of a child in their context are being met, rather than attempting to apply a universal yardstick of good enough parenting.

Assessment design

Negotiating and setting the main assessment questions will aid decision-making about setting, timescale and methods. The general principle is to aim for using multiple methods, in a range of settings, over time. It is helpful to expose oneself to a range of perspectives, including family members and other professionals. Involving family members in the assessment design may aid accessibility and engagement.

Analysing and reporting

As professionals we need to take active steps to work against our human tendency to seek only the information that we wish to find. We should critically reflect on the value we place on information and it is often helpful to share our emerging analysis with other professionals and family members. Chapter 9 contains suggestions for the contents of a balanced assessment report that pays attention to the subtleties of language choices.

Core Principles

The core principles identified and promoted within this book are therefore as follows:

- Consulting family members (including children) about the assessment aims, methods of assessment and how to evaluate the assessment work.
- Working with an openness to others' perspectives, especially professionals from other disciplines and family members.
- Working with a stance of consulting and listening, rather than measuring from an expert distance.
- Maintaining the safety and welfare of the child as top priorities (whilst being aware that these are not always clearly definable).

- Ensuring access to the assessment process through careful attention to aspects such as assessment methods, language choice, gender, cultural norms and literacy and articulacy levels.
- Being constantly critical and reflexive about dominant explanations for a particular family situation and aiming not for the correct conclusion, but the one that is most useful and least likely to be wrong.

In Chapter 1, I noted an awareness that many practitioners currently feel under siege due to rising referral rates and high staff turnover. In such a climate it can be difficult to find the space to reflect on our practice. Key aims become meeting targets for completing assessments and conducting review meetings. However, it can be seen that most of the practice points and principles outlined above are not particularly demanding in terms of physical or time resources (although material and time resources aid the task tremendously). Instead, the principles rely on practitioners reaching a particular understanding of assessment, adopting a stance and approaching their work in a certain frame of mind. I hope that this will be within the reach of all.

APPENDIX: Assessment Exercises

Here are seven exercises designed for both students and practitioners. The aim of these exercises is to facilitate reflection on the themes of the book. The exercises can be carried out in informal or formal learning settings. Exercises 1, 2, 3, 6 and 7 can be carried out individually. Exercises 4 and 5 are designed for group settings.

Exercise 1: Approaches to Assessment

Johnny is the father and lone carer of two teenage children. He was widowed six years ago and remains single. Johnny has recently contacted your social work team asking for help in caring for his children. He finds their behaviour difficult to manage, often feels depressed and fears that he may harm one of the children through frustration. Simon, the allocated social worker, believes that it is important to explore Johnny's childhood experiences, his marriage and bereavement in order to understand what is causing his current difficulties. Gita, his manager, believes that assessments should be future-orientated and not dwell on the past. She believes that Simon should be helping Johnny work out how his life could be changed for the better.

- Write a list of points that would support each argument.
- What theories are Simon and Gita drawing on?
- Who do you agree with?

Exercise 2: The Assessment Relationship

Samantha is the 19-year-old mother of two children (Kai 3 and Megan 18 months). She recently separated from the children's father, Lee (21), who has moved back in with his mother. Both children have been accommodated in local authority care on several occasions due to concerns of neglect due to the couple's chaotic drug use. There is suspected domestic violence, but Samantha has refused to discuss this. Lee was educated in a specialist unit for children with mild learning difficulties. The family is white and English speaking. The local authority is considering taking care proceedings and you have been asked to conduct an assessment of the family.

- What will you be bringing to the assessment relationship with this family?
- What is the potential contribution of your age, gender, ethnicity, education, professional status and class background?
- How might the various family members view you?
- What knowledge and values relating to the family situation do you hold?
- What aspects of your employing agency's organisational priorities are relevant here?
- How will you approach the assessment in order to maximise your chances of building a successful assessment relationship with the family?

Exercise 3: Children's Views

You are to conduct an assessment with a family of three children: Sean 13, Stacey 6 and Ben 3. They are thought to be in need of support due to the mental health difficulties experienced by their lone mother. Sean is of dual heritage (Nigerian and white Scottish), whilst Stacy and Ben are both white Scottish. Stacy attends a special school for children with moderate learning difficulties.

- How might you go about learning about these children's everyday life experiences and their wishes and feelings?

Exercise 4: Assessing Parenting

Work within a small group. As a group write a list of positive parenting behaviours. This might include items such as: provide nutritious meals, praise good behaviour, ensure that necessary medication is taken, read books together. Try to include at least 30 items. Now, each individual should write each item under one of three headings: essential parenting, good parenting, ideal parenting. Compare the lists and explain to the other group members how you came to categorise each behaviour. Analyse how differences of opinion might arise and what this might mean for assessment practice.

Exercise 5: Assessment Methods (1)

- Pair up with a friend or colleague. Take turns telling each other a story about something that happened in your family (childhood or current family). This should be an important event but not a traumatic one.
- Tell the story again. This time use objects as props whilst you are telling the story. Perhaps use some small plastic figures, dolls or puppets to represent the characters, or draw the scene.
- Review together the differences and similarities in the experiences of telling the stories using both styles.
- Now discuss what this might mean for assessment practice using talking and other ways of communicating.

Exercise 6: Assessment Methods (2)

Select one of the scales from the Assessment Framework (Department of Health, 2000d: available from http://www.doh.gov.uk/pdfs/qpallquestions.pdf). Fill it in, applying the questions to yourself and (if applicable) your family. Imagine that you will be asked to share your responses with your tutor, practice teacher or line manager. Consider the following:

- Did you learn anything new about yourself or change your understanding in any way?
- How helpful would your responses be in helping someone else understand your situation?
- How has this experience affected the way in which you might use the scale with a service user?

Exercise 7: Language Use in Report Writing

Consider the following statements:

- It is the consultant paediatrician's view...
- Ms Jackson alleges ...
- Ms Jackson reports ...
- The Health Visitor reports ...
- Ms Jackson has informed me ...
- Discussion with the Probation Officer revealed that ...
- The parents hold the belief that ...
- Mr Blythe has acknowledged that ...
- Mr Blythe states ...
- Mr Blythe suggested ...

All are taken from one (generally well-written) report from the Coastal Cities study. Consider what impact the phrases used might have on the 'truth claims' of statements that would follow.

References

Abney, V.D. (2002) 'Cultural competency in the field of child maltreatment', in J.E.B. Myers, L. Berliner, J. Briere, C.T. Hendrix, C. Jenny and T.A. Reid (eds), *The APSAC Handbook on Child Maltreatment* (2nd edn). Thousand Oaks, CA: Sage. pp. 477–86.

Abrahams, C. (1994) *The Hidden Victims – Children and Domestic Violence.* London: NCH Action for Children.

Adam, B. (1995) *Timewatch: The Social Analysis of Time.* Cambridge: Polity.

Adams, R. (1996) *Social Work and Empowerment.* Basingstoke: Macmillan.

Ainsworth, M., Blehar, M., Waters, E. and Wall, S. (1978) *Patterns of Attachment.* Hillsdale, NJ: Erlbaum.

Alanen, L. (1994) 'Gender and generation: feminism and the "child question"', in J. Qvortrup, M. Bardy, G. Sgritta and H. Wintersberger (eds), *Childhood Matters.* Aldershot: Avebury. pp. 27–42.

Alaszewski, A. (1997) 'Critical commentaries (organisation and administration)', *British Journal of Social Work*, 27 (3): 443–49.

Alderson, P. (2000) *Young Children's Rights: Exploring Beliefs, Principles and Practice.* London: Jessica Kingsley.

Allison, G. (1971) *Essence of Decision: Explaining the Cuban Missile Crisis.* Boston, MA: Little, Brown.

Altheide, D. and Johnson, J. (1994) 'Criteria for assessing interpretative validity in qualitative research', in N.K. Denzin and Y.S. Lincoln (eds), *Handbook of Qualitative Research.* Newbury Park, Sage, pp. 485–499.

Anderson, T. (1990) *The Reflecting Team: Dialogues and Metadialogues.* Broadstairs: Borgmann.

Aries, P. (1962) *Centuries of Childhood.* London: Jonathan Cape.

Atkinson, L. and Butler, S. (1996) 'Court-ordered assessment: impact of maternal noncompliance in child maltreatment cases', *Child Abuse and Neglect*, 20 (3): 185–90.

Atkinson, P. and Coffey, A. (1997) 'Analysing documentary realities', in D. Silverman (ed.), *Qualitative Research: Theory, Method and Practice.* London: Sage. pp. 45–62.

Ayoub, C., Jacewitz, M.M., Gold, R.G. and Milner, J.S. (1983) 'Assessment of a program's effectiveness in selecting individuals "at risk" for problems in parenting', *Journal of Clinical Psychology*, 39 (3): 334–9.

Backe-Hansen, E. (1992) 'Permanency planning in a Norwegian context', *Adoption and Fostering*, 16 (2): 35–9.

Banach, M. (1998) 'The best interests of the child: decision-making factors', *Families in Society*, 79 (3): 331–40.

Barber, J.G. and Delfabbro, P (2000) 'The assessment of parenting in child protection cases', *Research on Social Work Practice*, 10 (2): 243–56.

Barter, C. and Renold, E. (2001) ' "I wanna tell you a story": exploring the application of vignettes in qualitative research with children and young people', *International Journal of Social Research Methodology*, 3 (4): 307–23.

Barth, R.P. (1997) 'Permanent placements for young children placed in foster care: a proposal for a child welfare services performance standard', *Children and Youth Services Review*, 19 (8): 615–31.

Beck, U. (1992) 'From industrial society to the risk society: questions of survival, social structure and ecological enlightenment', *Theory, Culture and Society*, 9 (1): 99–123.

Belsky, J. and Vondra, J. (1989) 'Lessons from child abuse: the determinants of parenting', in D. Cicchetti and V. Carlson (eds), *Child Maltreatment: Theory and Research on the Causes and Consequences of Child Abuse and Neglect*. Cambridge: Cambridge University Press. pp. 153–202.

Berg, M. (1992) 'The construction of medical disposals: medical sociology and medical problem solving in clinical practice', *Sociology*, 14 (2): 151–80.

Berk, L.E. (2002) *Infants, Children and Adolescents* (4th edn). Boston, MA: Allyn and Bacon.

Berlin, S. (1982) 'Cognitive behavioural interventions for social work practice', *Social Work*, 27 (3): 218–26.

Birchall, E. and Hallett, C. (1995) *Working Together in Child Protection*. London: HMSO.

Bloor, M. (1978a) 'On the analysis of observational data: a discussion of the worth and uses of inductive techniques and respondent validation', *Sociology*, 12 (3): 545–52.

Bloor, M. (1978b) 'On the routinised nature of work in people-processing agencies: the case of adeno-tonsillectomy assessments in ENT out-patients clinics', in A. Davies (ed.), *Relationships Between Doctors and Patients*. Farnborough: Saxon House. pp. 29–47.

Bloor, M. (1997) 'Addressing social problems through qualitative research', in D. Silverman (ed.), *Qualitative Research: Theory, Method and Practice*. London: Sage. pp. 221–38.

Bloor, M., Frankland, J., Thomas, M. and Robson, K. (2001) *Focus Groups in Social Research*. London: Sage.

Brandon, M., Schofield, G. and Trinder, L. (1998) *Social Work With Children*. London: Macmillan.

Brayne, H., Martin, G. and Carr, H. (2001) *Law for Social Workers* (7th edn). Oxford: Oxford University Press.

Broad, B. (ed.) (1999) *The Politics of Social Work Research and Evaluation*. Birmingham: Venture Press.

Bronfenbrenner, U. (1979) *The Ecology of Human Development*. Cambridge, MA: Harvard University Press.

Brooks, D. and Webster, D. (1999) 'Child welfare in the United States: policy, practice and innovations in service delivery', *International Journal of Social Welfare*, 8 (4): 297–307.

Browne, K. and Saqi, S. (1988) 'Approaches to screening for child abuse and neglect', in K. Browne, C. Davies and P. Stratton (eds), *Early Prediction and Prevention of Child Abuse*. Chichester: Wiley. pp. 57–85.

Buckley, H. (2000) 'Beyond the rhetoric: a "working" version of child protection practice', *European Journal of Social Work*, 3 (1): 13–24.

Bull, R. and Shaw, I. (1992) 'Constructing causal accounts in social work', *Sociology*, 26 (4): 635–49.

Burman, E. (1994) *Deconstructing Developmental Psychology*. London: Routledge.

Butler, I. and Williamson, H. (1994) *Children Speak: Children, Trauma and Social Work*. Harlow: Longman.

California Health and Social Services (2001) Analysis of the 2001–02 Budget Bill: *Child Welfare Services*, http://www.loa.ca.gov/analysis_2001/health_ss/hss_20_CWS.htm Accessed 10 August 2001.

Campbell, D., Draper, R. and Huffington, C. (1992) *Second Thoughts on the Theory and Practice of the Milan Approach to Family Therapy*. London: Karnac.

Campion, M. (1995) *Who's Fit To Be A Parent?*. London: Routledge.

Cash, S.J. (2001) 'Risk assessment in child welfare: the art and science', *Children and Youth Services Review*, 23 (11): 811–30.

Charmaz, K. and Mitchell, R.G. (2001) 'Grounded theory in ethnography', in P. Atkinson, A. Coffey, S. Delamont, J. Lofland and L. Lofland, *Handbook of Ethnography*. London: Sage.

Clark, A. and Moss, P. (2001) *Listening to Young Children: The Mosaic Approach*. London: NCB.

Cleaver, H. (2002) 'Research findings informing the Integrated Children's System: the assessment framework'. Paper presented at the DIPSW and Child Care Programmes Conference, 20 March 2002, London.

Cleaver, H. and Freeman, P. (1995) *Parental Perspectives in Cases of Suspected Child Abuse*. London: HMSO.

Cleaver, H., Unell, I. and Aldgate, J. (1999) *Children's Needs – Parental Capacity: The impact of parental mental illness, problem alcohol and drug use and domestic violence on children's development*. London: HMSO.

Clifford, D. (1998) *Social Assessment Theory and Practice*. Aldershot: Ashgate.

Clifford, D. and Cropper, A. (1997) 'Parallel processes in researching and assessing potential carers', *Child and Family Social Work*, 2 (4): 235–46.

Coady, N. (1993) 'The worker–client relationship revisited', *Families in Society*, 74 (5): 291–8.

Cochrane Collaboration (2002) http://www.cochrane.org/ Accessed 20 July 2002.

Coffey, A. (1993) 'Double entry: the professional and organisational socialisation of graduate accountants'. PhD dissertation, Cardiff University.

Coffey, A. and Atkinson, P. (1996) *Making Sense of Qualitative Data*. London: Sage.

Coleman (1997) 'The parenting of adolescents in Britain today', *Children and Society*, 11 (1): 44–52.

Collinson, D.L. (1988) '"Engineering humour": masculinity, joking and conflict in shop-floor relations', *Organization Studies*, 9 (2): 181–99.

Colton, M., Drury, C. and Williams, M. (1995) *Staying Together*. Aldershot: Arena.

Colton, M., Sanders, R. and Williams, M. (2001) *An Introduction to Working With Children*. Basingstoke: Macmillan.

Coohey, C. (1996) 'Child maltreatment: Testing the social isolation hypothesis', *Child Abuse and Neglect*, 20 (3): 241–54.

Connell, R.W. (1995) *Masculinities*. Cambridge: Polity.

Corby, B. (1993) *Child Abuse: Towards a Knowledge Base*. Buckingham: Open University Press.

Corby, B. (1996) 'Risk assessment in child protection work', in H. Kemshall, and J. Pritchard (eds), *Good Practice in Risk Assessment and Risk Management*. London: Jessica Kingsley. pp. 13–30.

Corby, B. and Millar, M. (1997) 'A parents' view of partnership', in J. Bates, R. Pugh and N. Thompson (eds), *Protecting Children: Challenges and Changes*. Aldershot: Arena. pp. 75–86.

Corsaro, W.A. (1997) *The Sociology of Childhood*. Thousand Oaks, CA: Pine Forge.

Coulton, C.J., Korbin, J.E. and Su, M. (1999) 'Neighborhoods and child maltreatment: a multi-level study', *Child Abuse and Neglect*, 23 (11): 1019–40.

Cox, A. and Walker, S. (2002) *The HOME Inventory: A Training Approach for the UK*. Brighton: Pavilion.

Craft, J. and Bettin, C. (1991) 'Case factor selection in physical child abuse investigations', *Journal of Social Service Research*, 14 (3–4): 107–123.

Cuzzi, L.F., Holden, G., Grob, G.G. and Bazer, C. (1993) 'Decision making in social work: a review', *Social Work in Health Care*, 18 (2): 1–22.

Dalgleish, L.I. and Drew, E.C. (1989) 'The relationship of child abuse indicators to the assessment of perceived risk and the court's decision to separate', *Child Abuse and Neglect*, 13 (4): 491–506.

Daniel, B. (1999) 'Beliefs in child care: social work consensus and lack of consensus on issues of parenting and decision-making', *Children and Society*, 13 (3): 179–91.

Daniel, B. (2000) 'Judgements about parenting: what do social workers think they are doing?', *Child Abuse Review*, 9 (2): 91–107.

Daniel B., Wassell, S. and Gilligan, R. (1999) *Child Development for Child Care and Protection Workers*. London: Jessica Kingsley.

Daro, D. and Donnelly, A.C. (2002) 'Child abuse prevention', in J.E.B. Myers, L. Berliner, J. Briere, C.T. Hendrix, C. Jenny and T.A. Reid (eds), *The APSAC Handbook on Child Maltreatment* (2nd edn). Thousand Oaks, CA: Sage. pp. 431–48.

Davies, L. and Krane, J. (1996) 'Shaking the legacy of mother blaming: no easy task for child welfare', *Journal of Progressive Human Services*, 7 (2): 3–22.

Denzin, N.K. (1970) *The Research Act in Sociology*. London: Butterworths.

DePanfilis, D. (1996) 'Implementing child mistreatment risk assessment systems: lessons from theory', *Administration in Social Work*, 20 (2): 41–59.

DePanfilis, D. and Scannapieco, M. (1994) 'Assessing the safety of children at risk of maltreatment: decision-making models', *Child Welfare*, 73 (3): 229–45.

Department of Health (1988) *Protecting Children: A Guide for Social Workers Undertaking a Comprehensive Assessment.* London: HMSO.

Department of Health (1991) *Looking after Children.* London: HMSO.

Department of Health (1995a) *Child Protection: Messages from Research.* London: HMSO.

Department of Health (1995b) *The Challenge of Partnership in Child Protection: Practice Guide.* London: HMSO.

Department of Health (1999) *Working Together to Safeguard Children.* London: The Stationery Office.

Department of Health (2000a) *Framework for the Assessment of Children in Need and their Families.* London: Department of Health.

Department of Health (2000b) *Assessing Children in Need and Their Families: Practice Guidance.* London: The Stationery Office.

Department of Health (2000c) *Framework for the Assessment of Children in Need and their Families: Guidance Notes and Glossary for Records.* London: Department of Health.

Department of Health (2000d) *Framework for the Assessment of Children in Need and their Families: The Family Pack of Questionnaires and Scales.* London: Department of Health.

Department of Health (2001) *National Adoption Standards for England.* London: Department of Health.

Department of Health (2002) *Health and Personal Service Statistics,* http://www.doh.gov.uk/public/states1.htm Accessed 1 July 2002.

Department of Health and Social Security (1985) *Social Work Decisions in Child Care.* London: HMSO.

Department of Health and Social Security (1988) *Report of the Inquiry into Child Abuse in Cleveland.* London: DHSS.

Dingwall, R. (1989) 'Some problems about predicting child abuse and neglect', in O. Stevenson (ed.), *Child Abuse: Professional Practice and Public Policy.* Hemel Hempstead: Harvester Wheatsheaf. pp. 28–53.

Dingwall, R., Eekelaar, J. and Murray, T. (1995) *The Protection of Children* (2nd edn). Aldershot: Avebury.

Dobash, R.E. and Dobash, R.P. (1979) *Violence Against Wives.* New York: Free Press.

Dobash, R.P., Dobash, R.E., Wilson, M. and Daly, M. (1992) 'The myth of sexual symmetry in marital violence', *Social Problems,* 39 (1): 71–91.

Dosnajh, J.S. and Ghuman, P.A.S. (1998) 'Child-rearing practices of two generations of Punjabi parents: development of personality and independence', *Children and Society,* 12 (1): 25–37.

Doueck, H.J., Bronson, D.E. and Levine, M. (1992) 'Evaluating risk assessment implementation in child protection: issues for consideration', *Child Abuse and Neglect,* 16 (Sept/Oct): 637–46.

Douglas, M. (1992) *Risk and Blame: Essays in Cultural Theory.* London: Routledge.

Drake, B. (1994) 'Relationship competencies in child welfare services', *Social Work,* 39 (5): 595–602.

Duncan, G. and Worrall, J. (2000) 'Social policy and social work in New Zealand', *European Journal of Social Work,* 3 (3): 283–95.

Dwyer, J. (1997) 'Setting standards for parenting – by what right?', *Child Psychiatry and Human Development,* 27 (3): 165–77.

Edwards, J. (1995) '"Parenting skills": views of community health and social service providers about the needs of their "clients"', *Journal of Social Policy,* 24 (2): 237–59.

Egelund, T. (1996) 'Bureaucracy or professionalism? The work tools of child protection services', *Scandinavian Journal of Social Welfare,* 5: 165–74.

Ellis, L., Lasson, I. and Solomon, R. (1998) *Keeping Children in Mind: A Model of Child Observation Practice.* London: CCETSW.

English, D.J. and Pecora, P.J. (1994) 'Risk assessment as a practice method in child protective services', *Child Welfare,* 73 (5): 451–73.

Erickson, M.F. and Egeland, B. (2002) 'Child neglect', in J.E.B. Myers, L. Berliner, J. Briere, C.T. Hendrix, C. Jenny and T.A. Reid (eds), *The APSAC Handbook on Child Maltreatment* (2nd edn). Thousand Oaks, CA: Sage. pp. 3–20.

Family Rights Group (1991) *The Children Act 1989: Working in Partnership with Families.* London: HMSO.

Family Rights Group (2001) *Taking Care of the Children: Video for Family Members*. London: FRG.

Farmer, E. and Owen, M. (1995) *Child Protection Practice: Private Risks and Public Remedies*. London: HMSO.

Featherstone, B. (2001) 'Putting fathers on the child welfare agenda', *Child and Family Social Work*, 6 (2): 179–86.

Featherstone, B. and Trinder, L. (1997) 'Familiar subjects? Domestic violence and child welfare', *Child and Family Social Work*, 2 (3): 147–59.

Ferguson, H. (1997) 'Protecting children in new times: child protection and the risk society', *Child and Family Social Work*, 2 (3): 221–34.

Fernandez, E. (1996) *Significant Harm: Unravelling Child Protection Decisions and Substitute Care Careers of Children*. Aldershot: Avebury.

Fokini, V. (1999) 'Country notes: Russia', *European Journal of Social Work*, 2 (2): 209–24.

Forrester, D. (2000) 'Parental substance misuse and child protection in a British sample', *Child Abuse Review*, 9 (4): 235–46.

Franklin, B. (1995) 'The case for children's rights: a progress report', in B. Franklin (ed.), *The Handbook of Children's Rights*. London: Routledge. pp. 3–22.

Franklin, C. and Jordan, C. (1995) 'Qualitative assessment: a methodological review', *Families in Society*, 76 (5): 281–95.

Gambrill, E. and Shlonsky, A. (2000) 'Risk assessment in context', *Children and Youth Services Review*, 22 (11–12): 813–37.

Garfinkel, H. (1967) *Studies in Ethnomethodology*. Englewood Cliffs, NJ: Prentice Hall.

Garrett, P.M. (2003) 'Swimming with dolphins: the new assessment framework, New Labour and new tools for social work with children and families', *British Journal of Social Work*, 33 (4): 441–64.

Gaston, L. (1990) 'The concept of the alliance and its role in psychotherapy', *Psychotherapy*, 27 (2): 143–53.

Gelles, R. and Loseke, D. (1993) *Current Controversies on Family Violence*. Newbury Park, CA: Sage.

Ghate, D. and Hazel, N. (2002) *Parenting in Poor Environments*. London: Jessica Kingsley.

Ghate, D., Shaw, C., Hazel, N. (2000) *Fathers and Family Centres: Engaging Fathers in Preventative Services*. York: York Publishing Services.

Gibbons, J., Conroy, S. and Bell, C. (1995) *Operating the Child Protection System*. London: HMSO.

Giddens, A. (1990) *The Consequences of Modernity*. Cambridge: Polity.

Giddens, A. (1991) *Modernity and Self-Identity*. Cambridge: Polity.

Gilgun, J. (1988) 'Decision-making in interdisciplinary treatment teams', *Child Abuse and Neglect*, 12 (2): 231–9.

Gilligan, R. (1998) 'The importance of schools and teachers in child welfare', *Child and Family Social Work*, 3 (1): 13–25.

Gilligan, R. (1999) 'Working with social networks: key resources in helping children at risk', in M. Hill (ed.), *Effective Ways of Working With children and their Families*. London: Jessica Kingsley. pp. 70–91.

Goffman, E. (1959) *The Presentation of Self in Everyday Life*. Welwyn Garden City: Doubleday.

Golding, K. (2000) 'Parent management training as an intervention to promote adequate parenting', *Clinical Child Psychology and Psychiatry*, 5 (3): 357–71.

Gordon, L. (1988) *Heroes of Their Own Lives*. New York, NY: Viking Penguin.

Gough, D. (1993) *Child Abuse Interventions: A Review of the Research Literature*. London: HMSO.

Gould, N. (1999) 'Developing a qualitative approach to the audit of inter-disciplinary child protection practice', *Child Abuse Review*, 8 (3): (193–9).

Gracia, E. and Musitu, G. (2003) 'Social isolation from communities and child maltreatment: a cross-cultural comparison', *Child Abuse and Neglect*, 27 (2): 153–68.

Green, R. (2000) 'Applying a community needs profiling approach to tackling service user poverty', *British Journal of Social Work*, 30 (3): 287–303.

Griffiths, D.L. and Moynihan, F.J. (1963) 'Multiple epiphyseal injuries in babies ("Battered Baby Syndrome")', *British Medical Journal*, 11 (5372): 1558–61.

Hague, G. and Malos, E. (1998) 'Inter-agency approaches to domestic violence and the role of social services', *British Journal of Social Work*, 28 (3): 369–86.

Hall, C., Sarangi, S. and Slembrouk, S. (1997) 'Silent and silenced voices: interactional construction of audience in social work talk', in A. Jaworski (ed.), *Silence: Interdisciplinary Perspectives*. Berlin: Mouon de Gruyter. pp. 181–211.

Hall, P. (1982) 'Approaching the problem', in McGrew, A. and Wilson, M. (eds), *Decision Making: Approaches and Analysis*. Manchester: Manchester University Press. pp. 41–7.

Hallett, C. (1989a) 'Child abuse inquiries and public policy', in O. Stevenson (ed.), *Child Abuse: Professional Practice and Public Policy*. Hemel Hempstead: Harvester Wheatsheaf. pp. 110–144.

Hallett, C. (1989b) 'The gendered world of the social services department', in C. Hallett (ed.), *Women and Social Services Departments*. Hemel Hempstead: Harvester Wheatsheaf.

Handelman, D. (1983) 'Shaping phenomenal reality: dialectic and disjunction in the bureaucratic synthesis of child abuse in urban Newfoundland', *Social Analysis*, 13 (1): 3–36.

Hendrick, H. (1994) *Child Welfare: England 1872–1989*. London: Routledge.

Hester, M., Pearson, C. and Harwin, N. (2000) *Making an Impact – Children and Domestic Violence*. London: Jessica Kingsley.

Hetherington, R., Cooper, A., Smith, P. and Wilford, G. (1997) *Protecting Children: Messages From Europe*. Lyme Regis: Russell House.

Hill, M. (1997) 'Research review: participatory research with children', *Child and Family Social Work*, 2 (3): 171–83.

Hill, M., Lambert, L., Triseliotis, J. and Buist, M. (1992) 'Making judgements about parenting: the example of freeing for adoption', *British Journal of Social Work*, 22 (Aug.): 373–89.

Hobbs, S. (2002) 'New sociology and old psychology', in B. Goldson, M. Lavalette and J. McKechnie (eds), *Children, Welfare and the State*. London: Sage. pp. 29–41.

Holland, S. (1999) 'The comprehensive assessment in child protection social work'. PhD dissertation, Cardiff University.

Hollis, F. (1964) *Casework: A Psychosocial Therapy* (2nd edn). New York, NY: Random House.

Hopkins, G. (1998) *Plain English for Social Services: A Guide to Better Communication*. Lyme Regis: Russell House.

Horvath, A. and Symonds, B. (1991) 'Relation between working alliance and outcome in psychotherapy: a meta-analysis', *Journal of Counseling Psychology*, 38 (April): 139–49.

Howarth, J. (2000) *The Child's World: Assessing Children in Need – A Reader*. London: NSPCC/Department of Health/University of Sheffield.

Howe, D. (1992) 'Child abuse and the bureaucratisation of social work', *Sociological Review*, 40 (3): 491–508.

Howe, D. (1993) *On Being a Client*. London: Sage.

Howe, D. (1994) 'Modernity, postmodernity and social work', *British Journal of Social Work*, 24 (5): 513–32.

Howe, D. (1996a) 'Surface and depth in social work practice', in N. Parton (ed.), *Social Theory, Social Change and Social Work*. London: Routledge. pp. 77–97.

Howe, D. (1996b) 'Attachment theory in child and family social work', in D. Howe (ed.), *Attachment and Loss in Child and Family Social Work*. Aldershot: Ashgate. pp. 7–17.

Howe, D. (1998) 'Relationship-based thinking and practice in social work', *Journal of Social Work Practice*, 12 (1): 45–56.

Howe, D., Brandon, M., Hinings, D. and Schofield, G. (1999) *Attachment Theory, Child Maltreatment and Family Support*. Basingstoke: Macmillan.

Howitt, D. (1992) *Child Abuse Errors: When Good Intentions Go Wrong*. London: Harvester Wheatsheaf.

Hudson, B.L. and Macdonald, G.M. (1986) *Behavioural Social Work: An Introduction*. Basingstoke: Macmillan.

Humphries, C. (1999) 'Avoidance and confrontation: social work practice in relation to domestic violence and child abuse', *Child and Family Social Work*, 4 (4): 77–87.

Jack, G. (2000) 'Ecological influences on parenting and child development', *British Journal of Social Work*, 30 (6): 703–720.

Jackson, S. and Thomas, N. (1999) *What works in creating stability for looked after children?*. Ilford: Barnardo's.

James, A., Jenks, C. and Prout, A. (1998) *Theorising Childhood*. Cambridge: Polity.

Jellinek, M., Murphy, M., Poitrast, F., Quinn, D., Bishop, S. and Goshko, M. (1992) 'Serious child mistreatment in Massachusetts: the course of 206 children through the courts', *Child Abuse and Neglect*, 16 (2): 171–85.

Jones, C. (2002) 'Children, class and the threatening state', in B. Goldson, M. Lavalette and J. McKechnie (eds), *Children, Welfare and the State*. London: Sage. pp. 102–19.

Jones, H. (2002) Speech by Helen Jones, Department of Health, at the DIPSW and Child Care Programmes Conference, 20 March 2002, London.

Jones, L. (1993) 'Decision making in child welfare: a critical review of the literature', *Child and Adolescent Social Work Journal*, 10 (3): 241–62.

Kagle, J. (1988) 'Overcoming "person-al" errors in assessment', *Arete*, 13 (2): 35–40.

Kähkönen, P. (1999) 'The assessment of parenting in the child welfare practice', *Children and Youth Services Review*, 21 (7): 581–603.

Katz, I. (1997) *Current Issues in Comprehensive Assessment*. London: NSPCC.

Katz, L. (1996) 'Permanency action through concurrent planning', *Adoption and Fostering*, 20 (2): 8–13.

Kelley, S. (2002) 'Child Maltreatment in the context of substance abuse', in J.E.B. Myers, L. Berliner, J. Briere, C.T. Hendrix, C. Jenny and T.A. Reid (eds), *The APSAC Handbook on Child Maltreatment* (2nd edn). Thousand Oaks, CA: Sage. pp. 105–17.

Kempe, C.H., Silverman, F.N., Steel, B.F., Droegemueller, W. and Silver, H.K. (1962) 'The battered child syndrome', *Journal of the American Medical Association*, 18 (1): 17–24.

King, M. and Piper, C. (1995) *How the Law Thinks About Children* (2nd edn). Aldershot: Arena.

Korbin, J.E. (2003) 'Neighborhood and community connectedness in child maltreatment research', *Child Abuse and Neglect*, 27 (2): 137–40.

Koren-Karie, N. and Sagi, A. (1992) 'Professional decisions made by social workers regarding infant–mother attachment', *Children and Youth Services Review*, 14 (5): 439–59.

Krane, J. and Davies, L. (2000) 'Mothering and child protection practice: rethinking risk assessment', *Child and Family Social Work*, 5 (1): 35–45.

LAC (2000) *Prime Minister's Review of Adoption: Report from the Performance and Innovation Unit*, Local Authority Circular 16. London: Department of Health.

Lafolette, H. (1980) 'Licensing Parents', *Philosophy and Public Affairs*, 9 (2).

Langan, M. (1998) 'Radical social work', in R. Adams, L. Dominelli and M. Payne (eds), *Social Work: Themes, Issues and Critical Debates*. Basingstoke: Macmillan. pp. 207–17.

Lee, T. and Piachaud, D. (1992) 'The time-consequences of social services', *Time and Society*, 1 (1): 65–80.

Lindsey, D. (1994) *The Welfare of Children*. Oxford: Oxford University Press.

Little, M. (1997) 'The re-focussing of children's services', in N. Parton (ed.), *Child Protection and Family Support*. London: Routledge. pp. 25–38.

Lloyd, E. (ed.) (1999) *Parenting Matters: What Works in Parenting Education?* Ilford: Barnardo's.

Lloyd, M. and Taylor, C. (1995) 'From Hollis to the Orange Book: developing a holistic model of social work assessment in the 1990s', *British Journal of Social Work*, 25 (6): 691–710.

London Borough of Brent (1985) *A Child in Trust: the Report of the Panel of Inquiry into the Circumstances Surrounding the Death of Jasmine Beckford*. London: London Borough of Brent.

London Borough of Lambeth (1987) *Whose Child? The Report of the Public Inquiry Into the Death of Tyra Henry*. London: London Borough of Lambeth.

Lupton, C. and Nixon, P. (1999) *Empowering Practice? A Critical Appraisal of the Family Group Conference Approach*. Bristol: Policy.

Lusk, A. (1996) 'Rehabilitation without acknowledgement', *Family Law*, 26 (December): 742–5.

Lyon, C. and Parton, N. (1995) 'Children's rights and the Children Act 1989', in B. Franklin (ed.), *The Handbook of Children's Rights*. London: Routledge. pp. 40–55.

Macdonald, G. (1999) *What Works in Child Protection?* Ilford: Barnardo's.

MacDonald, K. and MacDonald, G. (1999) 'Perceptions of risk', in P. Parsloe (ed.), *Risk Assessment in Social Care and Social Work*. London: Jessica Kingsley. pp. 17–52.

Mailick, M. (1991) 'Re-assessing assessment in clinical social work practice', *Smith College Studies in Social Work*, 62 (1): 3–19.

Malloch, M. and Webb, S. (1993) 'Intervening with male batterers: a study of social workers' perceptions of domestic violence', *Social Work and Social Sciences Review*, 4 (2): 119–47.

Marsh, P. and Fisher, M. (1992) *Good Intentions: Developing Partnership in Social Services*. York: Community Care/Joseph Rowntree Foundation.

Martinez-Brawley, E.E. and Mendez-Bonito Zorita, P. (1998) 'At the edge of the frame: beyond science and art in social work', *British Journal of Social Work*, 28 (2): 197–212.

Mayer, J.E. and Timms, N. (1970) *The Client Speaks*. London: Routledge and Kegan Paul.

McBeath, G. and Webb, S.A. (1990) 'Child protection language as professional ideology in social work', *Social Work and Social Sciences Review*, 2 (2): 122–45.

McCracken, D.G. (1988) *The Long Interview*. Beverly Hills, CA: Sage.

McCurdy, K. (1995) 'Risk assessment in child abuse prevention programs', *Social Work Research*, 19 (2): 77–87.

McGee, C. (1997) 'Children's experiences of domestic violence', *Child and Family Social Work*, 2 (1): 13–23.

McGrew, A. and Wilson, M. (eds) (1982) *Decision-making: Approaches and Analysis*. Manchester: Manchester University Press.

Meyer, C. (1993) *Assessment in Social Work Practice*. New York, NY: Columbia University Press.

Mills, L.G. and Yoshihama, M. (2002) 'Training children's services workers in domestic violence assessment and intervention: research findings and implications for practice', *Children and Youth Services Review*, 24 (8): 561–81.

Milner, J. and O'Byrne, P. (1998) *Assessment in Social Work*. Basingstoke: Macmillan.

Minty, B. and Pattinson, G. (1994) 'The nature of child neglect', *British Journal of Social Work*, 24 (6): 733–47.

Morrison, T. (1996) 'Partnership and collaboration: rhetoric and reality', *Child Abuse and Neglect*, 20 (2): 127–40.

Mullender, A. (1996) *Rethinking Domestic Violence: The Social Work and Probation Response*. London: Routledge.

Mullender, A. (1997) 'Domestic violence and social work: the challenge to change', *Critical Social Policy*, 17 (1): 53–78.

Mullender, A., Hague, G., Kelly, L., Malos, E. and Iman, U.F. (2000) 'Children's Needs, Coping Strategies and Understanding of Woman Abuse'. Research Report, ESRC 5–16 programme, University of Hull.

Mullender, A. and Morley, R. (eds) (1994) *Children Living with Domestic Violence*. London: Whiting and Birch.

Munro, E. (1995) 'The power of first impressions', *Practice*, 7 (3): 59–65.

Munro, E. (1999) 'Common errors of reasoning in child protection work', *Child Abuse and Neglect*, 23 (8): 745–58.

Murphy, M. (1995) *Working Together in Child Protection: An Exploration of the Multi-disciplinary Task and System*. Aldershot: Arena.

Murphy, M. and F. Harbin (2001) 'Background and current context of substance misuse and child care', in F. Harbin and M. Murphy (eds), *Substance Misuse and Child Care*. Lyme Regis: Russell House. pp. 1–8.

Murphy-Berman, V. (1994) 'A conceptual framework for thinking about risk assessment and case management in child protective services', *Child Abuse and Neglect*, 18 (2): 193–201.

Myers, J.E.B. (2002) 'Risk management for professionals working with maltreated children and adult survivors', in J.E.B. Myers, L. Berliner, J. Briere, C.T. Hendrix, C. Jenny and T.A. Reid (eds), *The APSAC Handbook on Child Maltreatment* (2nd edn). Thousand Oaks, CA: Sage. pp. 403–428.

Nazroo, J. (1995) 'Uncovering gender differences in the use of marital violence: the effect of methodology', *Sociology*, 29 (3): 475–94.

Neale, B. (2001) 'Welfare and citizenship for children after separation and divorce: children's perspectives'. Paper presented at the Young Voices Conference, 26 September 2001, London.

Nelson, T., Fleuridas, C. and Rosenthal, D.M. (1986) 'The evolution of circular questions: training family therapists', *Journal of Marital and Family Therapy*, 12 (2): 113–27.

Newson, J. and Newson, E. (1989) *The Extent of Parental Physical Punishment in the UK*. London: Approach. Cited in Nobes and Smith (1997).

Nobes, G. and Smith, M. (1997) 'Physical punishment of children in two-parent families', *Clinical Child Psychology and Psychiatry*, 2 (2): 271–81.

NSPCC (2000) *The Child's World: Assessing Children in Need, Training Pack*. London: NSPCC/University of Sheffield/Department of Health.

NSPCC (2001) *Power Pack*. London: NSPCC.

OED (2002) *Oxford English Dictionary Online*, http://dictionary.oed.com/ Accessed 23 April 2002.

O'Hagan, K. and Dillenburger, K. (1995) *The Abuse of Women within Childcare Work*. Buckingham: Open University Press.

O'Quigley, A. (2000) *Listening to Children's Views: The Findings and Recommendations of Recent Research*. York: Joseph Rowntree Foundation.

Otway, O. (1996) 'Social work with children and families: from child welfare to child protection', in N. Parton (ed.), *Social Theory, Social Change and Social Work*. London: Routledge. pp. 152–71.

Packman, J. and Randall, J. (1989) 'Decision-making at the gateway to care', in O. Stevenson (ed.), *Child Abuse: Professional Practice and Public Policy*. Hemel Hempstead: Harvester Wheatsheaf. pp. 88–109.

Pardeck, J., Murphy, J. and Chung, W. (1994a) 'Social work and postmodernism', *Social Work and Social Sciences Review*, 5 (2): 113–23.

Pardeck, J., Murphy, J. and Chung, W. (1994b) 'Postmodernism and social work: a response to Professor Parton', *Social Work and Social Sciences Review*, 5 (2): 127–9.

Parker, R. (1999) *Adoption Now: Messages from Research*. Chichester: Wiley.

Parton, N. (1985) *The Politics of Child Abuse*. Basingstoke: MacMillan.

Parton, N. (1991) *Governing the Family: Child Care, Child Protection and the State*. London, MacMillan.

Parton, N. (1994a) 'The nature of social work under conditions of (post)modernity', *Social Work and Social Sciences Review*, 5 (2): 93–112.

Parton, N. (1994b) '(Post) social work: a response to Pardeck, Murphy and Chung', *Social Work and Social Sciences Review*, 5 (2): 124–6.

Parton, N. (1996a) 'Child protection, family support and social work: a critical appraisal of the Department of Health research studies in child protection', *Child and Family Social Work*, 1 (1): 3–11.

Parton, N. (1996b) 'Social work, risk and "the blaming system"', in N. Parton (ed.), *Social Theory, Social Change and Social Work*. London: Routledge. pp. 98–114.

Parton, N. (1998) 'Risk, advanced liberalism and child welfare: the need to rediscover uncertainty and ambiguity', *British Journal of Social Work*, 28 (1): 5–27.

Parton, N. and O'Byrne, P. (2000) *Constructive Social Work*. Basingstoke: Macmillan.

Parton, N., Thorpe, D. and Wattam, C. (1997) *Child Protection, Risk and the Moral Order*. Basingstoke: Macmillan.

Payne, M. (1996) *What is Professional Social Work?* Birmingham: Venture.

Payne, M. (1998) 'Social work theories and reflective practice', in R. Adams, L. Dominelli and M. Payne (eds), *Social Work: Themes, Issues and Critical Debates*. Basingstoke: Macmillan. pp. 117–37.

Payne, M. (1999) 'Social construction in social work and social action', in A. Jokinen, K. Juhila and T. Poso (eds), *Constructing Social Work Practices*. Aldershot: Ashgate.

Perlman, H.H. (1957) *Social Casework: A Problem-solving Process*. Chicago, IL: University of Chicago Press.

Petr, C. (1988) 'The worker–client relationship: a general systems perspective', *Social Casework*, 69 (10): 620–26.

Pithouse, A. (1998) *Social Work: The Social Organisation of an Invisible Trade* (2nd edn). Aldershot: Avebury.

Polansky, N.A., Chalmers, M.A., Buttenwieser, E. and Williams, D.P. (1981) *Damaged Parents: An Anatomy of Child Neglect*. Chicago, IL: University of Chicago Press.

Pollock, L.A. (1983) *Forgotten Children: Parent–Child Relations from 1500 to 1900*. Cambridge: Cambridge University Press.

Pozatek, E. (1994) 'The problem of certainty: clinical social work in the postmodern era', *Social Work*, 39 (4): 396–403.

Pringle, K. (1998) *Children and Social Welfare in Europe*. Buckingham: Open University Press.

Proctor, E.K. (1982) 'Defining the worker–client relationship', *Social Work*, 27 (5): 430–35.

Pugh, G., Aplin, G., DeAth, E. and Moxon, M. (1987) *Partnership in Action: Working with Parents in Pre-School Centres*. London: NCB.

Rashid, S.P. (1996) 'Attachment reviewed through a cultural lens', in D. Howe, (ed.), *Attachment and Loss in Child and Family Social Work*. Aldershot, Ashgate: pp. 59–77.

Read, J. and Clements, L. (2001) *Disabled Children and the Law*. London: Jessica Kingsley.

Reder, P., Duncan, S. and Gray, M. (1993) *Beyond Blame: Child Abuse Tragedies Revisited*. London: Routledge.

Richardson, J. and C. Joughin (2002). *Parent Training Programmes for the Management of Young Children with Conduct Disorders*. Trowbridge: The Royal College of Psychiatrists/Cromwell.

Richmond, M. (1917) *Social Diagnosis*. New York, NY: Russell Sage Foundation.

Roberts, K. and Lawton, D. (2001) 'Acknowledging the extra care parents give their disabled children', *Child: Care, Health and Development*, 27 (4): 307–319.

Robinson, L. (1998) 'Social Work Through the Life Course', in R. Adams, L. Dominelli and M. Payne (eds), *Social Work: Themes, Issues and Critical Debates*. Basingstoke: Macmillan. pp. 78–88.

Rosen, A., Proctor, E., Morrow-Howell, N. and Staudt, M. (1995) 'Rationales for practice decisions: variations in knowledge use by decision task and social work service', *Research on Social Work Practice*, 5 (4): 501–523.

Rosen, H. (1981) 'How workers use cues to determine child abuse', *Social Work Research and Abstracts*, 17/18 (Winter): 27–34.

Rowe, J. and Lambert, L. (1973) *Children Who Wait*. London: Association of British Adoption Agencies.

Russell, P. (1998) *Having a Say! Disabled Children and Effective Partnership in Decision Making*. London: Council for Disabled Children/NCB.

Ryburn, M. (1991) 'The myth of assessment', *Adoption and Fostering*, 15 (1): 20–27.

Scannapieco, M. (1999) 'Kinship care in the public child welfare system: a systematic review of the research', in R.L. Hegar and M.Scannapieco (eds), *Kinship Foster Care: Policy, Practice and Research*. Oxford: Oxford University Press. 141–54.

Schofield, G. (1996) 'Attachment theory, neglect and the concept of parenting skills training: the needs of parents with learning disabilities and their children', in D. Howe (ed.), *Attachment and Loss in Child and Family Social Work*. Aldershot: Ashgate. pp. 36–58.

Schofield, G. and Thoburn, J. (1996) *Child Protection: The Voice of the Child in Decision-making*. London: Institute for Public Policy Research.

Schön, D. (1991) *The Reflective Practitioner*. Aldershot: Arena.

Scott, D. (1989) 'Meaning construction and social work practice', *Social Service Review*, 63 (1): 39–51.

Scott, D. (1998) 'A qualitative study of social work assessment in cases of alleged child abuse', *British Journal of Social Work*, 28 (1): 73–88.

Scott, S., Jackson, S. and Backett-Milburn, K. (1998) 'Swings and roundabouts: risk anxiety and the everyday worlds of children', *Sociology*, 32 (4): 689–705.

Scourfield, J. (2003) *Gender and Child Protection*. Basingstoke: Palgrave Macmillan.

Secretary of State for Social Services (1974) *Report of the Inquiry into the Care and Supervision Provided in Relation to Maria Colwell*. London: HMSO.

Sellick, C. and Thoburn, J. (1996) *What Works in Family Placement?* Ilford: Barnardo's.

Selvini Palazzoli, M., Boscolo, L., Cecchin, G. and Prata, G. (1980) 'Hypothesizing – circularity-neutrality: Three guidelines for the conductor of the session', *Family Process*, 19 (1): 3–12.

Sharland, E., Jones, D., Aldgate, J., Seal, H. and Croucher, M. (1995) *Professional Interventions in Child Sexual Abuse*. London: HMSO.

Shaw, I. (1996) *Evaluating in Practice*. Aldershot: Arena.

Shaw, I. (1997) *Be Your Own Evaluator*. Wrexham: Prospects.

Shaw, I. and Lishman, J. (1999) *Evaluation and Social Work Practice*. London: Sage.

Sheldon, B. (1987) 'The psychology of incompetence', in Blom-Cooper, L. (ed.), *After Beckford: Essays on Themes Connected with the Case of Jasmine Beckford*. London: Royal Holloway and Bedford New College. pp. 17–31.

Sheldon, B. (2001) 'The validity of evidence-based practice in social work: a reply to Stephen Webb', *British Journal of Social Work*, 31 (5): 801–809.

Sheppard, M. (1990) 'Social work and community psychiatric nursing', in P. Abbott and C. Wallace (eds), *The Sociology of the Caring Professions*. London: Falmer. pp. 67–89.

Sheppard, M. (1995a) 'Social work, social science and practice wisdom', *British Journal of Social Work*, 25 (3): 265–93.

Sheppard, M. (1995b) *Care Management and the New Social Work*. London: Whiting and Birch.

Sheppard, M. (1998) 'Practice validity, reflexivity and knowledge for social work', *British Journal of Social Work*, 28 (5): 763–81.

Sheppard M. (2002) 'Depressed mothers' experience of partnership in child and family care', *British Journal of Social Work*, 32 (1): 93–112.

Sheppard, M., Newstead, S., DiCaccavo, A. and Ryan, K. (2001) 'Comparative hypothesis assessment and quasi triangulation as process knowledge assessment strategies in social work practice', *British Journal of Social Work*, 31 (6): 863–85.

Sheridan, M. (1975) *Reports on Public Health and Medical Subjects* No. 102. London: HMSO.

Sidebottom, P. (2001) 'Culture, stress and the parent–child relationship: a qualitative study of parents' perceptions of parenting', *Child: Care, Health and Development*, 27 (6): 469–85.

Silverman, D. (2000) *Doing Qualitative Research*. London: Sage.

Simmonds, J. (1991) 'Making professional judgements of significant harm', in M. Adcock, R. White and A. Hollows (eds), *Significant Harm*. Croydon: Significant. pp. 137–55.

Sinclair, R. (1998) 'Research Review: involving children in planning their care', *Child and Family Social Work*, 3 (2): 137–42.

Singh, S. (1997) 'Assessing Asian families in Scotland: a discussion', *Adoption and Fostering*, 21 (3): 35–9.

Sloan, M. (1999) *Substance Misuse and Child Maltreatment*. Norwich: UEA Social Work Monographs.

Smale, G., Tuson, G., Biehal, N. and Marsh, P. (1993) *Empowerment, Assessment, Care Management and the Skilled Worker*. London: NISW.

Smith, C. (1999) 'Social work as rights talk: the eclipse and re-emergence of morality and values talk'. Paper presented at the BASW/University of Central Lancashire conference: 'Social Work: Making a Difference', March 1999, Southport.

Smith, C. and White, S. (1997) 'Parton, Howe and postmodernity: a critical comment on mistaken identity', *British Journal of Social Work*, 27 (2): 275–95.

Smith, M. (2001) 'Research into parenting: background'. Paper on the JRF children and young people website, http://www.irf.org.uk/funding/priorities/cypfc.asp Accessed 2 July 2001.

Smith, M. and Grocke, M. (1995) *Normal Family Sexuality and Sexual Knowledge in Children*. London: Royal College of Psychiatrists/Gorkiel Press.

Smith, S. (1995) 'Permanence revisited – some practice dilemmas', *Adoption and Fostering*, 19 (3): 11–16.

Social Services Inspectorate (1986) *Inspection of the Supervision of Social Workers in the Assessment and Monitoring of Cases of Child Abuse when Children, Subject to a Court Order, Have Been Returned Home*. London: Department of Health and Social Security.

Stainton Rogers, R. and Stainton Rogers, W. (1992) *Stories of Childhood: Shifting Agendas of Child Concern*. Hemel Hempstead: Harvester Wheatsheaf.

Stanley, N. (1997) 'Domestic violence and child abuse: developing social work practice', *Child and Family Social Work*, 2 (3):135–45.

Stevens, M. (1999) 'Assessing outcomes in child welfare', in C. Lupton and P. Nixon (eds), *Empowering Practice? A Critical Appraisal of the Family Group Conference Approach*. Bristol: Policy.

Stevenson, O. (1989) *Child Abuse: Professional Practice and Public Policy*. Hemel Hempstead: Harvester Wheatsheaf.

Swift, K. (1995) *Manufacturing 'Bad Mothers': A Critical Perspective on Child Neglect*. Toronto: University of Toronto Press.

Tallman, I. and Gray, L.N. (1990) 'Choices, decisions and problem-solving', *Annual Review of Sociology*, 16: 405–433.

Tanner, K. and Turney, D. (2000) 'The role of observation in the assessment of child neglect', *Child Abuse Review*, 9 (5): 337–48.

Taylor, C. and White, S. (2000) *Practising Reflexivity in Health and Welfare*. Buckingham: Open University Press.

Testa, M.F., Shook, K.L., Cohen, L.S. and Woods, M.G. (1996) 'Permanency planning options for children in formal kinship care', *Child Welfare*, 75 (5): 451–70.

Thoburn, J., Lewis, A. and Shemming, D. (1995) *Paternalism or Partnership? Family Involvement in the Child Protection Process*. London: HMSO.

Thomas, N. (2000) *Children, Family and the State: Decision-making and Child Participation*. London: Macmillan.

Thomas, N. and Cleaver, H. (2002) *Framework for the Assessment of Children in Need and their Families: Study of Implementation in Wales*. Final Report, January 2002, University of Wales, Swansea and Royal Holloway, University of London.

Thomas, N. and O'Kane, C. (1998) *Children and Decision-making: A Summary Report*. Swansea: International Centre for Childhood Studies, University of Wales.

Thomas, N. and O'Kane, C. (2000) 'Discovering what children think: connections between research and practice', *British Journal of Social Work*, 30 (6): 819–35.

Thomas, N., Philipson, J., O'Kane, C. and Davies, E. (1999) *Children and Decision Making: A Training and Resource Pack*. Swansea: International Centre for Childhood Studies, University of Wales.

Thompson, M.J.J., Raynor, A., Cornah, D., Stevenson, J. and Sonuga-Barke, E.J.S. (2002) 'Parenting behaviour described by mothers in a general population sample', *Child: Care, Health and Development*, 28 (2): 149–55.

Thorpe, D. (1994) *Evaluating Child Protection*. Milton Keynes: Open University Press.

Trout, B. (1939) 'How do we come to an understanding about clients?', in F. Lowry (ed.), *Readings in Social Casework: 1920–1938*. New York: Columbia University Press. pp. 243–48.

Veltman, M.W.M. and Browne, K.D. (2002) 'The assessment of drawings from children who have been maltreated: A systematic review',. *Child Abuse Review*,11 (1): 19–37.

Wald, M.S. and Woolverton, M. (1990) 'Risk assessment: the emperor's new clothes?', *Child Welfare*, 69 (6): 483–511.

Walkerdine, V. (1993) 'Beyond developmentalism?', *Theory and Psychology*, 3 (4): 451–69.

Waterhouse, L. and Carnie, J. (1992) 'Assessing child protection risk', *British Journal of Social Work*, 22 (1): 47–60.

Wattam, C. (1992) *Making a Case in Child Protection*. Harlow: NSPCC/Longman.

Wattam, C. (1996) 'Evaluating the evidence', in D. Platt and D. Shemmings (eds), *Making Enquiries into Alleged Child Abuse and Neglect: Partnership with Families*. Brighton: Pennant Professional/NSPCC. pp. 232–47.

Webb, S. (1994) ' "My client is subversive!" Partnership and patronage in social work', *Social Work and Social Sciences Review*, 5 (1): 5–23.

Webb, S. (2001) 'Some considerations on the validity of evidence-based practice in social work', *British Journal of Social Work*, 31 (1): 57–79.

Webster-Stratton, C. (1999) 'Researching the impact of parent training programmes on child conduct problems', in E. Lloyd (ed.), *Parenting Matters: What Works in Parenting Education?* Ilford: Barnardo's.

Weedon, C. (1997) *Feminist Practice and Poststructuralist Theory*. Oxford: Blackwell.

Westcott, H. and Cross, M. (1996) *This Far and No Further: Towards Ending the Abuse of Disabled Children*. Birmingham: Venture.

White, S. (1996) 'Regulating mental health and motherhood in contemporary welfare services: anxious attachments or attachment anxiety?', *Critical Social Policy*, 16 (1): 67–94.

White, S. (1997) 'Beyond retroduction? Hermeneutics, reflexivity and social work practice', *British Journal of Social Work*, 27 (5): 739–54.

White, S. (1998a) 'Interdiscursivity and child welfare: the ascent and durability of psycho-legalism', *The Sociological Review*, 46 (2): 265–92.

White, S. (1998b) 'Time, temporality and child welfare', *Time and Society*, 7 (1): 55–74.

White, S. (1998c) 'From realism to relativism and back (via the body) to pragmatism and common sense: an ethnographer's personal journey'. Paper presented at the British Sociological Association Conference, April 1998, University of Edinburgh.

Winnicott, D. (1965) *The Family and Individual Development*. London: Tavistock.

Wise, S. (1990) 'Becoming a feminist social worker', in L. Stanley (ed.), *Feminist Praxis: Research, Theory and Epistemology in Feminist Sociology*. London: Routledge. pp. 236–49.

Wise, S. (1995) 'Feminist ethics in practice', in R. Hugman and D. Smith (eds), *Ethical Issues in Social Work*. London: Routledge. pp. 104–119.

Woodcock, J. (2003) 'The social work assessment of parenting: An exploration', *British Journal of Social Work*, 33 (1): 87–106.

Yerbury, M. (1997) 'Issues in multidisciplinary teamwork for children with disabilities', *Child: Care, Health and Development*, 23 (1): 77–86.

Index